MegaSkills

MegaSkills®

How Families Can Help
Children Succeed in School
and Beyond

Dorothy Rich

Foreword by Senator Bill Bradley

Houghton Mifflin Company · Boston · 1988

To my parents,
who taught me the
most important things
I know about MegaSkills

For information about permission to reproduce selections from this book,
write to Permissions, Houghton Mifflin Company, 2 Park Street, Boston,
Massachusetts 02108.

Library of Congress Cataloging-in-Publication Data

Rich, Dorothy.
  MegaSkills : how families can help children succeed in school and beyond.
  Bibliography: p.
  Includes index.
    1. Children — United States — Life skills guides.
  2. Education — United States — Parent participation.
  3. Success — United States.   I. Title.
  HQ792.U5R53 1988   649'.1   88-12730
  ISBN 0-395-46848-5
  ISBN 0-395-46849-3 (pbk.)
  ISBN 0-395-49378-1 (special edition)

Printed in the United States of America

Q 10 9 8 7 6 5 4 3 2 1

Book design by Patricia Dunbar

MegaSkills® curriculum is a registered trademark of Dorothy Rich.

Contents

Section C
Strengthening the Three R's at Home

Section D
The MegaSkills Support Network: People Helping People

Foreword
by Senator Bill Bradley

America's educational system is under increasing scrutiny as we confront the possibility of a work force ill-prepared to face the twenty-first century. The link between education and economic vitality has been widely and loudly trumpeted. Yet I believe that the economic battles of tomorrow are being won and lost not only in our classrooms but also in our nation's living rooms, family rooms, bedrooms, and kitchens. It is in these settings that the family's influence on educational outcomes is exercised. It is here that the first seeds of a love of learning and a respect for education are sown. I am talking not simply about helping children with their homework but about instilling such values as responsibility, hard work, and commitment to school success. I believe that if children bring these values with them to school, the job of teachers becomes easier.

A 1966 landmark report by the sociologist James Coleman and his colleagues found that family environment was more strongly related to student achievement than any other factor, including school quality. Evidence of the importance of parent involvement in education continues to accumulate. It has been shown that parent involvement raises the academic achievement of students, improves children's attitudes and performance at school, helps parents understand the work of schools, enables parents and children to communicate better, and builds school-community relationships in an ongoing, problem-preventing way.

In recent years, we have seen tremendous changes in the structure of family life. More and more children are being raised in single-parent families, two-parent families where both parents work, and other variations on what we have thought of as the "traditional" family. What has not changed is that families, across all economic and racial lines, care about their children and their children's schooling. However, many families lack the help they need to turn their love into practical, school-supportive action at home.

MegaSkills® provides that help. In this book, Dorothy Rich shares hundreds of activities that parents and children can undertake together. These activities, which supplement and reinforce the work of the school, not only encourage parents to work with their children on basic skills such as math and English, but they also help parents think about new ways to teach their children motivation, responsibility, caring, and confidence.

Dr. Rich has had a long and laudatory career as an advocate for the involvement of parents as educators of their children. For over twenty years, Dr. Rich has worked to gain recognition for the "forgotten factor" in school success — the family. Her Home and School Institute is widely regarded as the source of much of the creative energy behind the development of innovative, effective parent-school partnership activities. *MegaSkills* captures that energy and creativity with activities that are simple in their implementation but far-reaching in their effects. Like most parents, I have a hectic schedule, but I have made these activities a top priority — they are both useful and great fun to do.

I firmly believe that trying to educate children without the involvement of families is like trying to play a basketball game without all of the players on the court. We will achieve the educational results our children deserve only if we involve their first teachers — the family.

Preface

This book on educational reform will directly affect the life of your child.

It tells what you can do now in your own home to help your child become more self-disciplined, more excited about learning, and more able to learn.

It explains what I call "MegaSkills" — the values, the attitudes, and the behaviors that determine success in and out of school. You know in your bones that they are important, but you may not know how to teach them.

This book shows you how.

For over twenty-five years I have been working in classrooms and living rooms across this nation, figuring out how to translate serious concerns about American education into practical action every family can take.

This is why I started the Home and School Institute.

Better schools are needed and changes are being made. But you don't have to wait for a restructuring of classrooms or for large-scale programs. They are worth working for, but they will take time. You can make educational change now, immediately, in your own home.

The activity "recipes" in this book may look too easy or like too much fun to do any good. Make no mistake. As a long-time curriculum designer, I have learned that the toughest assignment is to take a complex issue like "motivation" and design a seemingly simple way to work with it. In this book are hundreds of carefully designed and tested learning "recipes."

I have heard the doubts and questions. Will our children do them? Do we have the time? Will they do any good?

The answer is *yes*.

When I first started developing "recipes" and talking about how spoons and clocks and bikes and all the usual paraphernalia of the home can help teach children important skills, I mumbled the word "recipe" under my breath, almost apologizing for it. It sounded too homespun to be educationally significant, certainly compared to all the formal studies and treatises being written on the subject.

I apologize no longer. The parents and the children in our Institute programs opened my eyes.

They told me and my colleagues and anyone else who would listen that doing these "recipes" with their children helped to change their lives at home. Even I am surprised when I hear parents tell about their experiences in words like these: "I see my kids in a new way." "Now I can teach my children."

The children have a more poignant response. Over and over they say, "These recipes made my parents have time for me."

I hear these words from a growing number of children today. What our children really want from us is *time* — more than they are getting now.

The children's pleas, often scrawled in big, awkward print on student survey forms, make me sad. But they also make me happy.

I now realize that this program — which I thought was teaching MegaSkills, such as confidence, and basic skills, such as reading — was also teaching love ... the love expressed in spending time together.

WHAT CAN PARENTS DO?

In the last two decades, the message from educational research has been that families are important educators, that education is bigger than schooling alone.

But for years that message was heard by only a few experts.

At the same time, parents were told, "Hands off, you don't know what you are doing, leave it to the schools."

That message unfortunately has been heard by many parents.

Over twenty years ago, when I began to hear the mixed messages being sent to parents, I decided I had to find a way to help parents know what they could do and what they should do to help children learn. I analyzed the research studies; I did my own research; I started parenting and teacher training programs.

It got to the point where I was talking to myself, and I heard myself saying, "Figure out what every family can do. Come up with a system that works, and share it. Don't make it too hard or too big. Make it look so simple, so easy, everyone can do it.

"Make it practical. Make it enjoyable. Remember, it doesn't take a lot of time to do a lot of good."

I knew I had to come up with a system that is small enough to handle; one that's active, that gets people doing things together, experiencing success together.

I also knew that the system I wanted had to remind parents that they don't need to be perfect to be good, and that goes for their children, too.

My system had to provide children with alternate routes to success, so that what they do at home is different from what they do in school. Home and school are different places. They need to reinforce, not duplicate, one another.

I knew I had to tell parents that there is a new kind of involvement in education today, different from being involved in children's schooling alone, which has usually meant meetings and time spent at the school. That's because fewer and fewer parents, especially employed mothers, can participate that way anymore.

I wanted to tell parents not to feel guilty. What they need to care about is how they are involved in their children's education well beyond the school setting.

I knew I wanted to help parents convey to their children that learning matters, and that they matter. And I had to find ways to help parents encourage kids and to feel encouraged themselves, to help parents and teachers look at what's right instead of what's wrong.

Through all of these years, I have heard the very real concerns of both parents and teachers, while I lived in both worlds. Through it all I heard my own inner voice, and I determined to share what I have learned with every parent and teacher who would listen.

The Institute programs I founded and this book are the result.

INSIDE THIS BOOK

Let me tell you what is in this book and why it's here. Like pieces of a pie, each part fits into my vision of education — the beliefs, the skills, the people, and the resources that have to be brought together to help children learn.

Section A — MegaSkills: The Stuff Achievement Is Made Of — defines MegaSkills and how important they are and how important families are in their children's education.

Section B — Teaching MegaSkills at Home: What to Do and How to Do It — provides "home learning recipes" to help children practice MegaSkills and build these inner engines for learning.

Section C — Strengthening the Three R's at Home — supplies "recipes" that show how the three R's can be reinforced beyond the school walls.

Section D — The MegaSkills Support Network — examines the people-to-people links in the MegaSkills network and how they work together.

Section E — Creativity: The Spark and the Satisfaction — explains the role of the arts and imagination in children's learning.

Section F — MegaSkills: Powerful and Surprising — helps take stock of and shares MegaSkills secrets.

The Appendixes — Here you will find:

MegaSkills Measure — a quiz for parents highlighting daily activities that build MegaSkills.

The Children's MegaSkills Library — children's literature illustrating MegaSkills, chosen expressly for this book by the Association for Library Service to Children/American Library Association.

Organizations to Know About — national groups with information and materials for parents.

The Handwriting on the School Wall — research notes and brief description of Home and School Institute programs.

MegaSkills Recipes, Chapter by Chapter — cross-references by skill and age group for all "recipes" presented here.

The good part of bringing you a program after it's been tested for twenty years is that a lot has been learned along the way. The bad part is that some readers may say, "Why didn't I do this sooner?" My answer is, "Start now. Don't worry about what you did or did not do before."

The education in this book is serious, but it's not grim. It's play and pleasure and the delight in learning and in time spent together. I want to put in a plug for play, before and during the years that children go to school. In discussions about education, play can be ignored or treated like a pesky little sister. I was a little sister. And I had to learn how to be alone a lot because much of the time big brothers do not want to play with little sisters.

So I spent time with my paper dolls, dressing and undressing lovely ladies and handsome men. The dolls had wonderful conversations; they went on dates; and their brothers never left them behind.

I learned a lot from my paper dolls. They lived in a dollhouse where they ate, slept, talked to each other, and sometimes got angry. Through them, I heard myself think and tried to figure out how others think. Having this time to dream and to imagine is an important steppingstone to MegaSkills.

A NEW DAY, A NEW WAY

Opportunities to make a real difference in our children's lives, when they still want our company and still want to listen to and talk to us, rarely knock twice. Here, in this book, are ways to take advantage of these opportunities, to spend happy, important time with children. After reading this book, if you decide you want to learn about having MegaSkills workshops in your community, see Appendix D for more information.

Education is never finished. A good education opens doors and raises lots of questions. MegaSkills enable us to seek answers and keep us questioning and wanting to know and to understand more.

This book is essentially about building our children's love of learning, not in the abstract, but in the specific, the real, the practical. This love of learning is what makes it possible for teachers to teach successfully. Without exaggeration, it is also what America's future depends on.

Section A.
MegaSkills: The Stuff Achievement Is Made Of

Chapter 1.
MegaSkills and Our Children

It is generally agreed that children need certain basic skills (usually called the three R's) in order to succeed. But for children to learn and keep learning basic skills at school, they need to learn another important set of basics at home.

I call it "MegaSkills." They are our children's inner engines of learning. Though reinforced in the classroom, they get their power from the home.

I know it's fashionable to talk about mega-this and mega-that, and because of this, in some ways, I hesitate to use the word "MegaSkills." But when I think about what it really takes for children to learn and use the skills they learn, when I think about what it takes to resist the temptations of taking drugs or dropping out of school, I think about attitudes and abilities that are bigger than ordinary skills. I think about confidence and motivation, perseverance and problem solving. And the word "MegaSkill" to define these seems appropriate and right. A MegaSkill, like confidence, is a long-lasting, achievement-enhancing skill. It's what makes possible the use of the other skills that we learn. MegaSkills keep children reading long after they learn to decode the alphabet. A MegaSkill is like gas to make the car go.

A MegaSkill is a catalyst. It's like yeast making bread rise. It's like a megaphone — designed to send the voice farther than it can ordinarily reach. That's what MegaSkills do for the bits and pieces of learning that children acquire in school and out. MegaSkills make it possible for children not only to learn but to use that learning as part and parcel of everyday life.

This book explains how to help children develop the following MegaSkills:

Confidence: feeling able to do it

Motivation: wanting to do it

Effort: being willing to work hard

Responsibility: doing what's right

Initiative: moving into action

Perseverance: completing what you start

Caring: showing concern for others

Teamwork: working with others

Common Sense: using good judgment

Problem Solving: putting what you know and what you can do into action

These aren't the only MegaSkills, but these play a strong role in determining success in school and beyond. They don't drop from the sky and land on a lucky few. They can be taught at home by parents, even today. They are the values that undergird our work ethic, our national character, and our personal behavior.

TOMORROW IS NOT FAR AWAY

We don't know for sure whether our children are learning today what they will need tomorrow, but we do know that children will need the skill and ability to take what they know and put it together in new ways to solve new problems. The academic term for this is "transfer."

To be useful for the 1990s and beyond, education has got to transfer. Little is really known now about what technical skills will be needed for the twenty-first century. We don't know the specific situations our children will face or even the machines they will use. What we do know is that our children will have to be able to use and adapt what they learn today. They need knowledge-enhancing skills, good any year and any place. They need MegaSkills.

THE IMPORTANCE OF MEGASKILLS TODAY

There is justifiable concern about American education today and about whether our children are learning enough and working hard enough. The remarkable school success of recently arrived Asian immigrant children has prompted questions about what these children have that American youngsters don't have.

What American children must have are abilities that include reading, writing, and math — but that also go beyond them. We know that while it is an essential to be able to read, it is not enough.

The problem is not that our children don't learn how to read. They do. Educational research has indicated that most of our children do learn the basics of reading and math in the early grades. Many children, however, do not keep on reading and wanting to learn more.

There are books on how parents can help children learn to read and perform better on tests. *MegaSkills* is about how families can help children not only acquire basics but go beyond them to get on the road to being a learner for life. No school is an island. The job of the home is to help students use what they have been taught so that the school is surrounded by a community of learning, enthusiasm, and support.

Every parent and teacher wants children who are smart, motivated, responsible, cooperative, good listeners, contributors with self-confidence, self-discipline, and good judgment. This is no small order.

Coincidentally, these are the very qualities this nation needs in its citizens now and for the next century — learners who can and who want to keep on learning.

THE NEVER-ENDING REPORT CARD

MegaSkills are on every report card, often in the areas called "citizenship" or "level of effort." We're graded on them all through life. Look at these examples:

In-School Report Card
Displays self-confidence.
Is willing to take risks.

On-the-Job Report Card
Shows ability and willingness
to make decisions.

In-School Report Card	On-the-Job Report Card
Completes work independently. Understands and applies new concepts.	Demonstrates ability and willingness to solve problems.
Is responsive. Demonstrates self-control.	Delegates responsibility or authority as applicable.
Concentrates on work. Masters new materials and techniques.	Has integrity. Is results-oriented and employs innovative approaches.
Values quality of work.	Has knowledge and technical skills. Completes assignments.
Shows courtesy and consideration. Maintains a sense of fair play.	Shows ability to work with people. Maintains positive personal relationships.

The first page of each chapter in Section B, "Teaching Mega-Skills at Home," points to the connection between the in-school and on-the-job report card.

Children aren't born with MegaSkills. They learn them, and parents and teachers teach them, not all at once and not perfectly, but little by little, day by day.

LUCK AND EFFORT

When I talk about MegaSkills, especially with young professionals, I am sometimes greeted with disbelief — "How can I believe in such old-fashioned ideas as effort, initiative, and perseverance, when what really matters is luck, being in the right place at the right time, plus the all-important who-you-know?"

Of course I believe in luck — in the luck of not being hit by a speeding car, in the luck of being born basically healthy, in the luck of living in a caring home and in going to a good school. I even occasionally knock wood.

It takes luck, but it takes more. I believe that for most of us to be lucky, we first have to put in the effort, for example, to be in the right place at the right time. In the inimitable words of former baseball great Branch Rickey, the general manager of the Brooklyn Dodgers who brought the first black player, Jackie Robinson, to the major leagues, "Luck is the residue of effort."

Success isn't a lot of money or a lot of ready-made good luck. Those aren't bad, but most of us won't have them. What we do have is the capacity to try. I believe that success is in the trying, in our power to deal constructively with the breaks in life, good and bad, and to keep on going. Success is the ability to make some of our own good breaks and not wait for luck to strike. That's what MegaSkills enable us to do.

I CARE ABOUT YOU

Many children today feel they are not getting the time they need. And it's not because Mother is employed outside the home or because there are more single parents. I hear the cry for time coming from children of unemployed mothers and from children with two parents in the home.

Most parents are making all-out, caring efforts with children. Anyone picking up this book is a person who cares. But as busy adults, we can forget how much our children need us.

I've heard the excuses, and there aren't any good ones. "I'm just too busy" and "My kid doesn't want to do anything with me, anyway," are not acceptable, not now when our children need parents as much as they do.

What does this time together do? It says to a child, "I care about you. I want to spend special time with you. I want to hear what is on your mind and what you are feeling. You are important. You are needed."

When I talk about parent-child time together, I am not talking about trying to use absolutely every minute in the most productive way possible. We'd feel enormous pressure, and it wouldn't work. Children need time to relax and to think and to be on their own, and so do parents.

I am talking about special moments that adults who care for children can help to create. It doesn't take a lot of time to do a lot of good. Activities in this book usually take ten, fifteen, or twenty minutes. They focus on the critical make-or-break elementary school years. Here is when lifelong learning patterns are set into place. The goal is to help children become learners over the long haul, for a lifetime, not to be souped up for a short term.

MegaSkills is for all adults who care for children — parents, aunts, uncles, grandparents, baby sitters, foster parents. Fathers today are playing an increasingly important role in the care and education of their children. This is good for kids, but it's even better for dads. Every activity in this book works as well for fathers as it does for mothers.

OUR CHILDREN'S WORLD: A SCARY PLACE

The world is increasingly a frightening place, with temptations and pitfalls for children that just didn't seem to exist before. There are more reasons for us all to be worried.

When I went to school, no one offered me drugs. AIDS was unheard of. The music I listened to had sweet lyrics and melodies compared to today's torrid words and music. The movies (I went to almost all of them) showed waves crashing against the shore instead of explicit sex scenes. There was violence in films, but it seemed as if we knew what was real and what wasn't. I never thought dropping out was even a choice, and while I was told over and over to be "a good girl," my family really didn't have to worry about my getting pregnant because I automatically said *no*. There just wasn't any other answer. There seemed to be a communally shared sense of right and wrong and a greater sense of safety.

All this isn't meant to be a song of praise for the good old days, which by no means were all that good. It's to emphasize that children now face new and different pressures . . . for which they need to be prepared.

As a youngster, I didn't know a lot about grown-up things. Looking back, I don't think I needed to know everything all at once, all so soon. Looking around now, it seems that children are being told and shown more than they want to know or need to know. It's as if anything goes, and it is making real growing up harder. Parental guidance is more than suggested. It's essential.

Today many children, including those with advantages, are full of stress. Some feel suicidal. I hear many reasons, from the threat of nuclear war to the threat of their parents' divorce to fears about getting bad grades.

I can't say with absolute certainty that spending time on MegaSkills activities will keep children in school, off drugs, not pregnant, and free of AIDS. But if we believe — and there is evidence to believe — that having a sense of self-esteem along with increased academic skills will help keep kids out of trouble, then we have to feel that time spent with children developing these is the best possible vaccine that families can use.

HOPE: A VITAL INGREDIENT

There's a well-known story of two children put in a room that contains a big pile of manure. One child looks at the pile and falls into despair. The other starts searching the room, saying, "With all this manure, there must be a pony somewhere."

The child who hopes for the pony and starts searching for it has a better chance of finding good things all through life.

I believe that in everyday ways we can help children feel more hopeful and optimistic. Children need to be able to expect and to predict. They need a sense of schedule and of routine. That's why activities in this book for family calendars and homework systems are important.

Children need to be able to believe in themselves and in the people around them. Children need to feel that they matter. That's why these activities, which seem so easy, yet which help children gain a sense of competence and confidence, have results that are surprisingly complex.

What is in these modest activities that makes them so potent? What it boils down to, I think, is that the experience of doing the activities helps to change parents' ways of seeing themselves as teachers of their children and of seeing their children as learners. They help families work together.

That is the wonder and power of MegaSkills.

OUR GOLDEN AGE FOR LEARNING

I really do believe that this is a remarkable and wonderful time to be a parent. No, I am not crazy, and I am not a Pollyanna. This is a golden age of learning, but families have to know how to take advantage of it.

As an elementary grader, I went to a little library in that small Michigan town where I grew up. Most of the information I got for my reports came from ten-year-old encyclopedias. Today on television and through computers is a world of information I never knew. If anyone had told me as a kid that I would fly across the country in a few hours or use a word processor or sleep under an electric blanket, I would have had a hard time believing it.

Yet all this is so accepted today that it makes me wonder — hopeful and a little scared — about what we can't envision about tomorrow. All we can count on for sure is that we will have to keep on learning.

EDUCATIONAL CHANGE IN EVERY HOME

Institutional educational change, as in the education reform movement, is always long in coming, even when change is wanted as much as it is by parents and teachers today. Experts say school change can take thirty years. That is why it is so important not to wait for changes to happen "out there." Our children aren't waiting.

Educational change can start in every home today. I know this from experience with thousands of teachers and parents across the country. I don't pretend it's all that easy. It's always been hard to be a concerned parent. It may be even harder today. There is so much pressure on families, so much going on outside the home. Parents are busy and children don't "mind" automatically. But the education this book talks about is doable by everyone.

Chapter 2.
First Steps: The MegaSkills
Program and How It Works

It happens in every home. Children forget, they demand, they are uncaring, they are irresponsible — you love them and you hate them and you wish they would stop just growing and just grow up.

And as a parent who has just lost your temper for the fifteenth time that day, you say, *There has got to be a better way.*

That's what I said to myself twenty-five years ago. I set to the task of trying to figure out not just what to *say* but what to *do*, without hurting my child or myself when for the tenth time that day my darling child said:

"I forgot."

Or

"I can't find them anywhere."

Or

"I want to watch more TV."

Or

"I need some money."

Every parent has at least a dozen more to fill in.

We all want our children to remember, to be responsible, to be concerned. As a teacher I thought, "If I can figure out how to teach the parts of speech, I ought to be able to come up with some ways to help teach these important basics."

I think that's when I started the MegaSkills program.

Believe me, it didn't start out with headlines. It started in my kitchen when my older daughter, then five and now twenty-eight, said on the phone, calling from school, "I forgot my lunch." And I screamed back, "Well, you are supposed to remember."

I am not absolutely sure that was the exact moment of the inception of the program, but it's close, and I said to myself, "You're such a terrific teacher — OK, teach something really hard, like *personal responsibility.*"

Using what I knew from the classroom, I decided that my method would focus on what is to be taught and then break it into teachable bits — like the directions of a recipe.

That was the beginning of the *home learning recipe.* It is the heart of the program.

IT STARTS AT HOME

Over this quarter century, I have designed and tested hundreds, actually thousands, of "recipes" to enable parents to help their children learn. The goal then and now is to help parents set the framework for their children's learning, not just for tomorrow's test, but for the whole school year and the next and the next.

This program uses everyday things, like doing laundry or paying bills, and places, like supermarkets or gas stations, for teaching. It is easy. It is fun. It takes little time. Everyone can do it. It costs no money. The idea is to enable children to apply outside of school what they learn in school. It does not duplicate what children achieve in school, and it builds positive attitudes toward school and learning.

Even today the home can do a lot of things the school can't. A parent is with children at times and in places available only at home and in the neighborhood — at breakfast, while watching TV, during a bus ride. These are the moments that prepare children for school, reinforce the school, and extend its impact.

COMMON SENSE IS STILL IN FASHION

The MegaSkills in this book are old-fashioned. They are full of common sense and experience. And they're modern, too, because many parents today have forgotten or never learned what to do at home to pave the way for their children's school success. In recent years education became the job for the school and usually for the school alone. We now know education has to be a home-school team effort.

Today, in this country, we are thinking and doing more about self-help rather than waiting for big institutions or even government to do the job. We know from nationwide polls that parents are ready to help their children. The signs are good.

There is a coming together of ideas and understandings that were not around before. Today there is research showing that families are important educators of their children, teaching even when they don't know they are teaching. Today more and more teachers realize that to educate children they have to work with parents. As a parent, I was told, "Hands off, you don't know how to do it." Today, thanks to this research and to common sense, we know better. No matter how good they are, teachers cannot do the job alone.

This book uses a straightforward formula as the basis for all of the "recipes": *Why Do You Do It? What Do You Need? What Do You Do?* and *More Ideas.* The formula provides a habit-forming, continuing way to think about and use everyday moments for teaching and learning.

Children do not have to sit with paper and pencil quietly at desks in order to learn. For a lot of learning, this can be the wrong way to teach. Children, young ones especially, need physical activity and the opportunity to ask questions, to explore, and to experiment without competitive pressures. That's what these activities provide.

WHAT'S IN A HOME LEARNING RECIPE?

A home learning recipe has to meet certain standards to qualify for the program. I explain these ingredients for two reasons: (1) so that you can see how the "recipes" in this book were prepared, and (2) so that you can create home learning recipes on your own, long after you complete those in this book.

A home learning recipe has to:

Tie to Schoolwork but Not Be Schoolwork: Children need ways to succeed at home that are different from school but at the same time help them succeed in school. Parents need ways to help their children learn other than by nagging, "Did you do your homework?"

Be Serious and Be Fun at the Same Time: Every "recipe" in this book has a serious academic purpose. Not one says it will teach you how to have fun with your children. You know how to do that. The trick of these "recipes" is that you will be teaching an awesome subject such as responsibility and having fun at the same time.

Have a Teachable Focus: When you teach responsibility, for example, you start by teaching one part of it, like "following directions." And you look for a practical, concrete way to teach it. You don't send a very young child upstairs to "clean a room." You send a young child to do one thing: to make the bed or to vacuum the rug or to open the shades. It's even helpful to resist sending an older youngster to *"clean up that whole mess at once."* Good teaching is a step-by-step operation.

Be Easy to Do, Take Little Time, and Cost Little or No Money: Parents can teach and learn with their children joyously, without worry, without hassle. That won't happen with "recipes" that only a martyr parent could or would do.

You won't find activities in this book on how to weave baskets or design chessboards with children. I was never able to rush out for Popsicle sticks or other special arts and crafts items after a day at work. I needed activities that could be done alongside my household routines, using whatever I had at home. Today's busy parents need these easy-to-do "recipes" more than ever.

Not every parent is a born teacher. I try to provide a "handle" or a strategy for teaching so that you can jump right in with "recipes" that, for example, help children organize their belongings or know what to do when the TV is turned off. I want you to use these ideas to take off on your own, using your and your child's creativity to come up with additional "recipes."

A good home learning recipe gives everyone a chance to succeed. There is no one right way to do it. A recipe is a road map, not a set of rigid rules. The activity itself is designed to provide a feeling of accomplishment. It gives parents a chance to step back and children a chance to step forward. The idea is to help both parent and child feel good and get to know each other better in the bargain.

DIFFERENT "RECIPES" FOR DIFFERENT AGES

It makes sense that what works for preschoolers won't work for fifth graders. Parents have to be ready to change gears as children grow. The "recipes" in each chapter give activities for children of different ages.

You'll notice that the activities aim at increasingly more grown-up interests and understandings.

Around ages four through six, many of the "recipes" have to do with getting ready for school and using primary school subjects like counting, sorting, and early reading at home.

Around ages seven through nine, many of the "recipes" focus on helping children get organized, build study skills, and develop solid work habits.

Around ages ten through twelve, "recipes" work toward helping children understand themselves, their friends, and their family. Activities aim at developing greater self-reliance, building career awareness, and establishing healthy habits and self-esteem that can help prevent destructive habits, such as drug abuse.

These are not hard and fast age and grade distinctions. Many four-year-olds will enjoy a "seven-year-old" activity, and vice versa. Use all and any of the activities that appeal to you and your child. I indicate ages only to provide some guidance for selecting activities. I hope that all of the activities in whole or in part will be useful to everyone.

Providing activities that span the age ranges is a challenge. Some activities for the ages-four-to-six group may call for some reading skills that are more appropriate for six-year-olds than for four-year-olds. For children who do not yet read, I recommend that parents read all directions aloud, that children dictate their ideas for parents to write, and that symbols be used alongside words as needed. In labeling a dresser drawer, draw a sock next to the word "socks." In marking off danger points at home, use a sign next to the word "danger." In making lists of what to do in the morning, draw pictures to show toothbrushing and so forth. Don't worry if your children are not reading early, but provide the clues that will gradually ease them into reading.

The "recipes" are designed to be used at any time, summer and vacation days as well as school days. What parents do with children over the summer can make a great deal of difference in their school success.

THE MAKING OF A LEARNER

One "recipe" will not result in overnight, cataclysmically positive change. If it does, I want you to be sure to get in touch with me immediately.

In our school-to-home programs, we use a series of eight "recipes" over a period of eight weeks, one a week. This is designed to get parents and youngsters tuned in to the idea of using "recipes."

If you ask my advice, I'd suggest reading through the entire book and its collection of "recipes" first, starring or checking the ones that appeal to you. Use Appendix E, which lists "recipes" by skill and age group. Then ask your child to help you select the ones you both like.

Work out your own schedule — but guard against overkill. Once a week is really fine. You can build a whole year of activities as you go along. Remember that abilities in academics are not so different from abilities in sports. Just as in sports, it takes practice to gain confidence, to acquire motivation, and to achieve.

You might ask, "How am I going to know when my kids are learning?"

My answer: You will. You will hear your children say, "Let me try it." You will almost hear a click that says, "Now I understand." You will hear, "Let me show you! Let me! Let me!" And you had better get out of the way, and let them.

STAYING WITH THE PROGRAM

Sometimes a book like this will get you and the children going. But it can be tough to keep on going after the novelty and first flush of enthusiasm wear off. Like a good diet, one of the secrets of this program is that it has to become a habit. In a diet you eat good foods most of the time, not just once a month. That's true with these MegaSkill-building activities. Use them on a regular basis. If you've used one part of an activity, go back to it to find the extra idea you haven't tried. Think of ways you can build on what you have done. Improvise, be creative; you can't do anything wrong.

Section B.
Teaching MegaSkills at Home: What to Do and How to Do It

REPORT CARD	
Now — In School	**Later — On the Job**
Gordon enjoys tackling new projects and making new friends.	Mr. Smith does not shy away from hard jobs. He meets challenges head on and has excellent interpersonal skills.

Chapter 3.
MegaSkill One: Confidence

We know what we're hearing when children say:

"I just can't do that."

"The other kids are better than I am."

"I'm scared."

"I won't try it."

We're hearing a child's cry for more confidence. It cuts to the heart. Somehow when our children don't feel confident, it does something to our own confidence as well.

This chapter involves children in positive experiences right around the home. They don't cost money or take a lot of time. But they increase children's sense of control, build children's courage, build their sense of family, and reduce their fears of the new and unexpected. They work to give children an "I Can Handle That" attitude.

Our goal is to help children develop a sense of self-respect and respect for others, which is the base of real confidence. It's this foundation they add to all through life.

"I remember the potholder I made in third grade, made out of loops that were yellow, red, gold, and orange. It was a present I made to give to my mother, and oh, was she proud. And did it make me feel good!"

Those are the words of a man in his late fifties. He has a doctorate and many scientific achievements on his résumé. But when asked about his sense of confidence, he talks about the potholder.

Small things make a big difference.

I still remember the day I carried my chicken home. I carried Rocky, the rooster, in a crate bigger than I was. It was the last day of first grade. All through the spring our class had raised chicks, watching them hatch from eggs until they were almost full grown.

Then it was time for summer vacation. Who would care for the chickens? Everyone in class wanted them, especially the one named Jewel.

Our teacher, Mrs. Lutz, decided that the only fair way to distribute the chickens was to have a drawing. And the only children who could participate were those who brought notes from home saying that if we won, we would care for the chicken.

Clutching my note (my brother, who was in fifth grade, wrote it, and my mother signed it), I waited throughout the day for the fateful drawing. About fifteen of us lined up to draw slips for four chickens. At last the appointed hour, 3:15, came.

I watched, eagle-eyed, as Mrs. Lutz marked an X and the name of a chicken on four slips and only an X on the other slips.

Then she started down the row of children. At that moment I realized I was standing in the wrong place. Sally and Sara Quick, the blond twins, stood before me in line, and they plucked the slip with Jewel's name on it. It was disappointing. They were so happy. But I knew even then that if I were to get any chicken at all, I had to pull myself together.

I was next. Now usually I close my eyes during crisis moments. But this time, as I have at times since then, I kept my eyes wide open, and I concentrated, and then I picked, sliding my hand carefully along the top of the book until I came to a precious slip of paper.

And lo, there it was, "Rocky." Oh, I was proud and happy; yes, disappointed that Jewel was not to be mine, but happy that I was a winner nevertheless.

The end of the school day came, and there I was with my

chicken crate and a feeling of success. I struggled with that big box over the six blocks to my home. My brother came by a couple of times to try to help me with it, but I refused. This was my chicken, my achievement, and I would bring him home alone.

For the rest of my elementary school years, my brother and I raised Rocky and a group of chicks from the hatchery. We lived in a small town, and no zoning official came by to tell us not to do this.

I have never forgotten Rocky and the day I carried him home alone. It is a memory of struggle and success that gives me confidence and motivation to this very day. When I have to do something hard and when I get scared, I think back to Rocky and that crate, and even though it has nothing to do with the current situation, I breathe deeper and think to myself, "I can do it."

That's what every child needs ... experiences that give the message, "I can do it." We all need some version of Rocky in our lives.

CONFIDENCE PRACTICE

Confidence ebbs and flows like a river. It does not run at high tide all the time. There are some days when you know you can manage whatever comes, and there are others when getting out of bed can seem a momentous step. So too with children.

On those more difficult days, it's good to be able to think back to a time when something good happened and you managed well and overcame some odds. It provides the strength to keep going on days when confidence is running low.

Coming up with confidence-building experiences for children can be a challenge. These experiences need to be small enough for children to deal with, large enough to encourage growth, and easy enough for parents to work with.

When children are young, it does not take a momentous act to help them gain confidence. Small actions can have great impact. You can start at home with household objects, such as a telephone or a television.

The telephone, found in almost every home, is ideal for giving children what I call confidence practice. Young children use it to call Grandma or a friend, reaching out socially to get early practice in the art of conversation. Older youngsters use it to keep talking but also to give and get specific information.

Here are three activities, all using the phone, suited for children's needs and abilities at different times in their growing-up years.

TELEPHONE TIME ages 4–6

For this early reading activity, you need a telephone, seven small squares of paper, crayon or pencil.

Tell or show your child your home telephone number. Say each separate number aloud as you point to it.

On separate pieces of paper, write down each number. Now show your child how to put the pieces in the same order (left to right) as your phone number. Let your child read this telephone number aloud from the assembled pieces of paper. Provide help as needed.

As a game, mix up the pieces of paper and let your child put your telephone number together. At first let your child match the papers to the number listed on the phone. Then try this without looking at the phone. Now ask your child to write down the phone number, left to right, on a larger piece of paper. You might want to post this for all to see and admire.

When you are both out together, let your child dial home. Do this when someone is at home to give your child the satisfaction of making contact.

CALLING FOR HELP ages 7–9

This activity helps your child learn to use the telephone to report emergencies. This is especially important when children are home alone. You need a telephone book, telephone, markers, and paper.

Ask your child to find in the telephone book the numbers for *Fire/Rescue* and *Police*, usually listed at the front of the telephone book.

If you don't already have one, make a list of important telephone numbers to call in an emergency, similar to the one that follows. With your child, fill this in and put it near the phone.

Emergency: Dial 911 or 0

Fire _____   Dad's Work _____

Police _____   Mom's Work _____

Friend or Neighbor _____

Take turns explaining what to say on the phone when you report emergencies. *Examples:* Someone at home is hurt; you smell smoke or see fire. When you use the phone in this practice, be sure to keep the contact button pushed down.

(See Chapter 12, "Problem Solving," for a full range of safety activities.)

INFORMATION HUNT ages 10–12

Telephones can give children practice in getting needed information, like when a movie is going to start or how late the library is open. For this activity you need a telephone, telephone book, and newspaper.

Let's say your family is ready to make a major purchase, such as a washing machine. Ask your youngster to check at least two newspaper ads and then make a few calls to get additional information from salespeople. *Examples:* What's the guarantee? When will the washer be delivered? Have your youngsters call at least two stores and compare answers to these questions.

Or perhaps your family is planning an outing: You need directions before you start out. Let children pick a place around town to visit and find out, by calling the bus lines, etc., how to get there, how long it will take, and how much it will cost. Picking up the phone to ask these questions may not be an act of bravery, but it does take a measure of courage, and it helps to build confidence.

We're surrounded by confidence-building "tools." A bicycle is one example. For younger children, it's a matter of learning how to stay on it without falling off. For older ones, it's a means of transportation to school or to pick up a carton of milk at the grocery store. Beyond that, it could be an entry into a bicycle race.

TACKLING TV

Think about the TV set. First a child learns to turn it on. The next step is to figure out what shows to see. Beyond that comes a test of children's confidence when they turn the set off on their own.

A good idea that comes up in most households is that kids really ought to watch less television. Today's children are viewers supreme, tuned into TV on a daily basis for learning and entertainment.

There is an art to using television well, to helping children get the most from it, without the extremes of youngsters who sit before the set six hours a day and parents who forbid any TV for fear that their children will become addicted.

"No TV at all" homes are rare, but where they do exist, it's often because deep down the parents cannot trust themselves with a TV set, afraid that once it goes on they won't be able to turn it off. It's unfair both to turn TV loose on children and to deprive them of it altogether.

Cutting down on TV watching is one of the toughest good ideas to translate into action. Here are TV activities that help children show growing confidence — mastering and manipulating their environment.

OUR TV DIET ages 4–6

This activity gets the whole family involved in making choices about TV watching. You need thinking minds, a television schedule, and marker.

As a family, decide how many hours you will each watch TV. Read the TV schedule aloud with your children. Ask what programs everyone wants to watch. Share your opinions about the shows you like. Circle the shows you pick. Children need to hear your judgments. This helps them build their own critical viewing skills.

Together go on a TV diet. If your children are watching four hours a day now, cut back to three hours a day the first week, two hours a day the second week, and so on.

Set young children to thinking about scheduling their own TV-watching time. Every family works out its own plan.

Here's an example of how one family does it. Parents set the maximum daily watching time: one to two hours a day. (Educational specials, which the parents encourage children to watch, may be exempt.) Children choose any shows — equaling that time period — up to eight P.M.

If this diet doesn't work all the way, it at least does part of the job. It raises the awareness of how much time the family is spending in front of the set. Just learning that number, which is usually higher than we think, is enough to change some TV-watching habits.

TAKING CHARGE OF TV WATCHING any age

This activity actually has youngsters keeping track of the family's TV watching. You'll need a TV set, TV schedule, pencil, paper, and ruler.

Start out by reading the TV schedule together. Pick the programs to watch, alone or together. Then make an easy chart like the one below. Make several copies.

TV Plan

Date	Time	Program Name	Who Watched?

Everyone fills in TV-watching choices, date, and time. Let children who can't yet write dictate their choices.

Post this plan in a special place near the TV set. Nearby keep a pencil attached to a string. After you watch the show, fill in *Who Watched?* In this way, keeping track of what is picked and what is watched is easy.

With your child, decide on a reward for keeping to the TV Plan for at least three days. It might be going on a family picnic or attending a baseball game.

This activity helps families continue their efforts to manage TV watching. You need a TV schedule and markers.

Talk about different family members' interests and hobbies: Skating? Stamps? Cooking? At the beginning of the week, check the TV schedule for any programs that might be related to these. Together circle the programs the family decides to watch. Children circle their programs with one color marker. Adults circle programs with another color.

If someone becomes interested in a new subject after watching a television program, try to find more information on that topic. *Example:* If the program is about computers, check newspapers or magazines for articles on computers.

Television need not be an ogre to be afraid of or to avoid. Activities like these use TV as the resource it really is. (Some of the activities in Chapter 20 address TV violence and how to help children deal with it.)

FROM THINGS TO PEOPLE

In the journey of growing up, children must learn to manage objects and work with people. Confidence comes from both. In the activities that follow, children find out more about their families and themselves, and they get a chance to learn to like each other more.

You'd never guess it from Norman Rockwell paintings of families gathered around holiday tables, but many children pass through a period in their lives when they are somehow ashamed of their family. Some don't get over it. Much of this embarrassment about family may be a normal growing-up rite of passage, when Mother doesn't dress right or Dad never says the right thing. When children want to be just like everyone else, their parents may be different, with "funny accents" or very little money. This "shame" causes a lot of pain for both parents and children. There may be no way to overcome it completely, but I believe that if children knew more about their parents, especially about their early lives, it would help.

My parents have been dead for twenty years. They look out at me from pictures on my wall, but I do not know very much about their lives before I came of age. They came from Europe to make a new life in a new land. I remember a few words of their language, but I know nothing of their early lives.

I regret that we did not talk about their past. I didn't realize how important it was to talk together about this, and neither did they. With my own children, I'm trying not to make the same mistake.

I'M OK, AND SO IS MY FAMILY

Children love knowing more about themselves. Parents like this activity because it not only helps children think seriously about themselves but provides lots of laughs, too. It helps families remember the funny times that sometimes seem funny only in retrospect — the time the big fish got away, along with the fishing rod, or the time friends were invited for a birthday party on the wrong day.

THE IMPORTANCE OF ME ages 4–9

This activity helps children build pride in themselves and their interests. The task is to make a "me" poster. You need markers, poster cardboard or large paper, scissors, paste, old magazines for pictures, and snapshots, if possible.

Together look through magazines. Find pictures of what your child likes — pets, foods, clothes. Cut them out and with paste arrange them on a large sheet of paper. Magazine pictures are fine. If you have extra snapshots, use them.

And be sure to put some words on the poster. Kids might write: "Look at me at four years old!" "See the picture of my brother!" Adults might add: "This is a pretty dress." "Look at the fish we caught."

You might want to take turns and make poster life stories of other family members. Draw pictures of other members of the family and display these about the house.

Hang the poster in a special place for all to see and enjoy. An activity like this one says to your child, "You are special, and your family knows it."

FAMILY MOBILE ages 4–9

This gives children a greater sense of the family along with pleasure in creating an art object for the home. You need a clothes hanger, some snapshots or drawings of the family members, construction paper, paste, scissors, and some yarn.

Mount the pictures of the family on separate pieces of construction paper. Cut a small hole in the top of each paper and thread a piece of yarn through the hole. Tie these to the hanger in different places.

Lo and behold, you have a family scene that you can enjoy and talk about.

NOW AND THEN ages 10–12

This activity helps to get generations talking together, especially about those early years. Everyone was a child once. Here's a way to share some of those memories.

In this activity, the child and a parent or grandparent make a Time Line. It's a way to recapture memories of people at certain times in their lives.

You need a roll of shelf paper or large brown wrapping paper, pencils and crayons, and a ruler.

Decide together with your child when to begin the Time Line. This may be at birth or when school started or some other special time. Decide how much space will be allowed for each year. One inch per year or one foot per year? Draw a line for each one of you.

Now try to remember. What was special about age five? Was that the year you began kindergarten? What about your parents? Was there a kindergarten where they grew up? Did you each have a pet? What kind? Fill in the years as each of you has experienced them. If you don't remember everything, fill in what you can.

Example: This is a very simple version, but it gives you an idea of what a Time Line can look like.

Child	5 years	6 years	7 years	8 years
	I began kindergarten	I got my dog	I went to the circus	I joined the Scouts
Parent	5 years	6 years	7 years	8 years
	?	I started school	?	I got my rabbit

Talk about the memories. Compare similar experiences. Talk about differences. For example, at no time in my life have I experienced such a momentous decision as my parents did when they decided to immigrate to a new, unknown country.

Another way to harvest memories without using a Time Line is to have children interview grandparents and relatives who lived through different periods of American history: the Roaring Twenties, the Great Depression, World War II, or the peace demonstrations during the Vietnam War. Youngsters can record these interviews with a tape recorder if one is available.

These activities provide a framework for beginning conversations. What unfolds are the feelings and the special ties that bind us together.

Young people may want to start their own family archives by putting all these family memories in a book to share with their own children.

WHAT DO I DO RIGHT? ages 10–12

Many of us spend a lot of time telling each other what we do wrong. Here's an activity to help us focus on what we're doing right. You need paper and pencil.

Together think of and write down at least two things you like about yourselves. *Example:* "I have a good sense of humor. I like to share with others."

Talk about what others say they like about you.

Figure out together jobs and activities at home that both you and your child will feel proud of accomplishing. *Examples:* Fixing something around the house, cooking a special dish for the family, teaching the family a new game.

Above all, find some listening time in your daily routine. Even a car ride to the grocery store can be a good time for a chat. Try to set a time every day, if only for a few minutes, to talk about the events of the day.

There are times when children need to share a secret or to ask a question that is bothering them. If you're available to listen to your children when they are young, chances are they'll continue to communicate with you as they grow older.

IT TAKES COURAGE

Just like the old adage "It takes money to make money," we can also say, "It takes courage to make courage." It can take a parent's courage, or at least the control of fear, to show a child how to be courageous.

We want children to be careful but not fearful. How do we work toward this special "recipe"? How do we help children be careful but not fearful?

You teach this on the street as you're waiting for the light to change, on the beach when you're dodging the big waves, beside the basketball court when you yell to your child to go for a big shot.

Little by little you show, you teach, you let children test themselves — first by letting them ride a bike to the corner, then around the block, then to the store, and then on a trip out of town. You work toward a gradual building of the abilities it takes to be courageous and careful at the same time.

I have a problem with heights. When my young children went to the top of the big slide in the playground, my immediate reaction was to shout, "Stop! Come down! You'll hurt yourself!" They were perfectly happy up there high in the sky. I was the one who was petrified. It took some time for me to pull my own courage together, to let them be courageous and free from the seeds of my fear. They needed to be brave, even if I couldn't be.

Take the case of Peter. Peter, a high school junior in his first year as a driver, asked his father if he could borrow the car to take two friends for a day at the beach, three hours away on country roads he had not driven before. His dad was worried. Actually he was scared, but he knew that his son was responsible and that he had shown he was a good driver. The father agreed but laid down certain instructions about when to be back home and what to do in an emergency. Dad was reluctant, somewhat fearful, but knew he had to let go. (Peter made the trip safely, not without a few calls home to ask to stay overnight now that he was "at the beach." This request was denied. The boys arrived home late but very pleased. Dad was pleased with himself as well.)

CONFIDENCE AND EXPECTATIONS

In California a few years ago, a study showed that "ordinary" students could exceed themselves when expectations for them were high.

Researchers went into a school and tested the students for academic potential. They did not tell these scores to the teachers. Then, ignoring the scores, they randomly divided the students into two groups. They told teachers that one group was made up of "late bloomers" whose academic "promise" would be realized that year.

At the end of the year the "promise" was realized. This group was comparable with their classmates as far as could be established, but their teachers had expected them to succeed, and they had. These children got a confidence-building message.

As adults, we know what makes us feel confident. It's when we see ourselves doing things, accomplishing, taking action, and having some things turn out right. Not everything is going to work. But we know that nothing works if we don't try.

That's how children learn — by trying. When they try, they build confidence. It's good to tell kids they're wonderful, but it's not enough. When children see themselves as doers, they develop the ability to do more.

Now — In School	Later — On the Job
Mary is a go-getter, excited about learning.	Mrs. Holbrook always seems to be thinking and planning ahead.

Chapter 4.
MegaSkill Two: Motivation

When they have it, it shows:

You see your children wanting to do things, eager to learn.

They do schoolwork and household jobs without a lot of nagging.

They make plans for the next day, for the next week.

They say yes more than they say no.

Sorry to say, there is no medicine that turns an apathetic youngster into one bubbling with enthusiasm. Parents can help with activities that generate a child's excitement in learning. But children have to catch this fire and start fueling up on their own.

In this chapter are activities that help children gain the sense of discipline it takes to stay motivated, to work against discouragement, and to face competition and challenge.

- How to break down jobs into manageable "bites."
- How to set and keep to time limits.
- How to give yourself a pat on the back for a job well done.

There was a picture in the paper the other day of a ninety-one-year-old woman who had just climbed Mount Fuji.

Now that's what I call motivation. She was quoted as saying, "You always feel good when you've made a goal. You need goals."

Right! But how do you get them, whether you're nine or ninety-one? And what does it take to handle competition, to handle failure, to handle whatever comes?

I believe it takes a special ingredient that's found in motivation. This is the ability to work against discouragement and to keep on going.

Attitude counts for so much. The youngster with an IQ of 160 might not study or get good marks while the kid who keeps plugging away receives good marks and goes on to do what the innately gifted cannot accomplish. Every teacher has students who live out these tortoise and hare stories.

When I look at sports events on TV, as I sit back and watch teams pummel each other, I think, "Gosh, those guys are really motivated." And then I think about the students I've had over the years; some were motivated, and some I just couldn't seem to budge.

How do people become motivated? I think it has a lot to do with catching a feeling of excitement, of some one thing that gets us going, has us saying to ourselves, "I want to learn more about this" or "I want to be better at this."

Certainly we can't catch "fire" for our kids, but they can catch some of our fire or the fire of those in the vicinity. We know that youngsters get excited. They can go wild about the latest music or clothes or movies. What we need to look for are ways to help them get excited about developing a skill that, like a good stock, has growth potential. We all need things we can enjoy learning. We don't have to be precocious math or chess geniuses to catch fire, and the fire does not have to be a bonfire. A slow, low simmer will do.

One way is to share our own excitement. It might be about skiing or cooking or long walks or short stories — whatever it is that excites us. And if we are not excited about anything (which, while we're breathing, is hardly likely), let's find people who *are* excited and put our kids next to them. It might be the neighbor who does woodworking, the dressmaker down the block, the uncle crazy for fishing, the accountant who really gets a kick out of balancing numbers.

Wanda, our bookkeeper, recalls what got her going with numbers. As a child, she sold candy to neighbors and classmates. Her mother gave her big ledger sheets and showed her how to fill them out so she could keep track of the candy she bought and sold. Wanda loved it. She received an allowance, and using her ledger sheets, she was able to tell how much she had spent and how much was left over. Her sister couldn't, and that edge probably added to the excitement. She felt special.

Years later, when she was tested for job aptitude, she learned what she suspected. The answer was, "Finance, banking, and/or accounting." She thinks it all started with the ledger sheets that she loved to fill out.

That's a neat story with the edges tucked in. For most of us, it really doesn't work that way. We have to be exposed to quite a few excitements in order to pick the one or two that get us going.

"COACHING" MOTIVATION

Teachers and parents are like coaches on the sports fields — encouraging, urging, and sometimes pushing. Children have to develop their own sense of direction, but we can show them some ways to light the fire.

This chapter provides activities to help children ignite and manage this motivation so that it lasts and lasts, just as it has for the ninety-one-year-old mountain climber.

BEATING BOREDOM

Children are born motivated, not bored. They come out into the world eager, reaching, looking, touching — and that's what we want them to keep on doing.

Just outside our front door is a world of experiences waiting to delight even the child who complains bitterly, "There's nothing to do around here." What we do doesn't have to be exotic to be exciting. The activity examples that follow prove the old saying, "All you have to do is look." They help children (and adults) see the world with new eyes.

JUST OUTSIDE any age

While your children are young, start to share and discover the joy and mystery of the world: a walk as it's turning dark, a stroll through light rain. Talk together about what you're sensing and feeling. Stay up together to see the moon rise and get up early one day to watch the sun rise. Use a magnifying glass to look closely at those small objects that fascinate small children. Listen to the wind and the birds. Smell the rain and the burning wood in the fireplace. Observation and use of the senses are crucial to a scientist and to a poet.

SHOPPING CENTER STROLL ages 4–7

Most of the time we shop at breakneck speed with kids being dragged along. Try a walk with no other purpose than to show your children some of what goes on backstage at the local stores. Go into the florist's and watch the making of corsages. And go "backstairs" in the supermarket, if permitted. That's where the supplies are kept and where the meat is cut ... where the action that makes the market look good takes place.

SITTING AND WATCHING ages 4–7

There's a lot to be seen and learned while watching the workers at a construction site, at an airport or rail station, or at your own corner.

Look, listen, and talk about what you see. How many different jobs do you see being done? Do you see workers using tools? What kinds? Are others reading plans and blueprints? What do they say to each other? How are they dressed? Do they seem to get along? Who's the boss? How can you tell?

As children watch others working, they become familiar with what jobs are like and what they might like to do when they grow up.

Some of the happiest moments, and the most motivating ones,

are the ones in which parent and child sit together and talk about what they see together as the world goes by.

LOCAL LAW ages 8–12

Lawyers are not just on TV. Every courthouse provides an ongoing display of law in action. And the courts are open to all, usually including children of any age.

Check first with the courthouse information office to see what trials are scheduled, what stages the cases are at, whether there are juries, and so forth. Before going, talk with your children about what they'll see, including the courtroom itself, the judge, the jury, the lawyers for the two sides, and the witnesses. Seeing a court in action is eye-opening for everyone.

GETTING AROUND ages 8–12

Learning to get around without a car can be a valuable lesson. Gather bus route maps and schedules to a place around town. These are usually available by calling the local transportation company. Let children use the schedules to figure out what transportation is available, how much time it will take, and how much it will cost. Destinations might be a library downtown or a movie theater or a park. Once the most economical and fastest methods are identified, put the youngsters to the test. Let them take the trip, if possible, by themselves, or with the whole family.

One of the fastest ways to have youngsters appreciate the service of the family car is to let them take public transportation.

THE FOREIGN TOUCH AROUND TOWN any age

Visit foreign restaurants and stores in your community. You don't have to buy a fancy meal or an expensive souvenir. Just give children time to browse, have dessert, and perhaps buy a postcard.

When you visit a large American city such as New York or San Francisco, be sure to stroll with your children through ethnic neighborhoods like Chinatown, Little Italy, or the Lower East Side.

Even if your town hasn't got a foreign section as such, it probably has a Spanish grocery or just an old-style delicatessen. Buying rye bread in a deli is both educational and nourishing.

All of these activities have provided a platter of experiences, a smorgasbord to delight and excite the eye and the palate. Now comes the time to move children from seeing to doing.

BEYOND NAGGING

How do we get people to do things? Sports people say they do it with inspiration (heroes to be imitated) and with competition (get out there and beat the other guy). Teachers do it with grades. Employers do it with salaries.

How can parents do it?

I'd like to think that nagging works because it is such a handy thing to do. But like millions of other parents, I have found that nagging can do just opposite of what it is intended to do. It can motivate kids not to do things. Cutting down on nagging, in contrast, can be a motivating factor, one that works for both parent and child. Here's an activity that cuts down on nagging because it cuts down on talking.

It uses notes — in words and pictures — as reminders. I wish I had thought of this when my own kids were young. They say I was a terrible nag, and if I had nagged them less, they would have been more motivated.

THE NO-NAG WRITING SYSTEM any age

For practice, announce that for five minutes no one will talk. Instead you will send notes. Try this out at the breakfast table. Write short messages such as, "Please pass the toast" and "May I have my lunch money?" If you enjoy the quiet this brings, you can try this for longer periods and at other times of the day.

Ask your child, "What do I nag about a lot?" The answer might be, "Cleaning my room" or "Practicing the piano."

Children have been known to nag. Tell them what they nag about. It might be about getting ice cream or using the car, depending on the age.

Choose at least one nagging problem that is important to you and your child. Promise each other that instead of nagging, for one whole week you will send each other reminder notes.

Set up a message center for these reminders. A bulletin board in the kitchen or family room is a good place.

Or post reminders around the house. Leave the notes in the bathroom, on the stairs, or in other places where they will be seen. A note left on the pillow always seems to work!

After the week is over, check to see if the messages have worked. If they have, you may want to continue to keep up the writing and keep your voices down.

BUILDING MOTIVATION MUSCLES

There is method and discipline in motivation that can be built from tiny, beginning steps. Here are activities designed to encourage children and imbue them with the staying power it takes to remain motivated.

THE FIRST STEP any age

The old Chinese saying is true: "The longest journey starts with a single step." The first step in doing something can be the hardest.

We need to get children used to taking those all-important first steps. They need to recognize a first step. One way is to tell them about our own first steps: the first date, the first job. If you can remember it, describe your own first day in school, or any first you feel you can tell your children about. You need not have been a first-time success. It may be even better if you weren't. The point is that you tried and then tried again.

Ask children to tell you about any first times they remember. It might be the first day at school, the first grade they received on a paper, the first time they tried to ride a bike or swim the pool.

First steps are hard. We tend to say, "Aw, come on, that's easy," but it's not. Our goal in helping to motivate children is to help them gain the optimism and the courage to take more first steps. That is the lesson we have to teach, and one way to teach it is by sharing our experiences.

Before they do things, children tend to ask two questions over and over:

- How long will it take?
- What was that I was supposed to do, again?

The following activities for young children can help answer these questions.

TIME ME ages 4–6

This activity will help your child better understand the difference between "a few seconds" and "a few minutes." You need a clock or watch with a second hand.

Ask your child to watch the second hand for five seconds. Together count off the seconds. Put this into action. Time it again and see how many times your child can clap in five seconds. Now have your child watch the clock for one minute. Then time it again and see how far you can both count in one minute. Together read a book for five minutes. Time yourselves. How many pages did you read? Hold your breath for five seconds. Let your child time you. Then trade places. Time yourselves as you both say the alphabet aloud. Together time a traffic light as you stand at a street corner. Time two TV commercials. How long did each one take?

As you see, there are many ways to help children get a feel for time. Even as adults we often have trouble knowing how long thirty seconds is. A better sense of time helps us anticipate how much we can accomplish in a day — if only we try.

TELL ME ages 4–9

Teachers in the early grades tell us that children have trouble listening. Perhaps it's because they have been bombarded by so much coming at them all at once on television. Here's an easy activity that can help cut through the multimedia, noisy environment. For this one, all you need are listening ears.

Think of a real job at home that your child can do. It might be setting the table, taking out the garbage, bringing in the newspaper, hanging up clothes. Think of three or four instructions for this job. Ask your child to listen carefully as you say them. *Example:* "Take out four forks, four knives, and four spoons. Put these on the table in four place settings. Put the fork on the left, the knife and spoon on the right."

Let your child give you instructions to follow. They can be as easy or as complicated as you and your child want. In this way, you individualize this activity to suit your child.

By adding pencil and paper, you can turn this into a "write and do" activity. Write down instructions instead of talking about them. Have your child write a set of directions for you to follow.

Hide something and give instructions on how to find it. *Example:* "Take two steps forward, turn right, take three steps back." Trade places and let your child hide something for you to find.

As a special treat, organize an outdoor treasure hunt. Prepare a short list of items, such as a small stone, a branch, a green or red leaf. Give youngsters a paper bag for the collection. Turn this into a game by timing the minutes it takes to find the objects. Use this when you go shopping. At the store, your child can help you find the family's grocery items.

FOLLOW THROUGH

When children see that they can concentrate and follow through on an action, their desire to do more grows.

THIS HOUSE IS A MESS any age

This activity is really ageless. I don't know anyone who responds to the task of cleaning up with joy and eagerness. Maybe it's because we think we have to do everything at once, and we can't. So we feel discouraged.

Just as in teaching in the classroom, where we divide a curriculum into parts, cleaning up a house can be divided into parts. Then the tasks become doable, and while children may not be whistling while they work, they do know where to start.

For the big job of cleaning house, you might do one room at a time or one task, like washing windows, in several rooms. For children, putting away clothes and toys in their rooms can be a first step. This can be followed by dusting and then by vacuuming.

Make the job more pleasant by working with someone else or even to music. Marches are known to be very effective. Rock 'n' roll moves the dustcloth along.

Turn cleaning into a game. Decide how long it will take you to do the job. Then time yourself against the clock.

Set the same task for yourself and your child. You can race each other to see who is the fastest cleaner of them all!

EXCUSES DON'T COUNT ages 7–12

This activity teaches children that work can be organized so that it gets done and that excuses for not doing tasks just don't count — at home or in school or on a job. You need paper, pencil, and a ruler.

Make a chore chart for the hours between five P.M. and bedtime. Ask children to choose a time to do each chore. Write those times on the chart. The chart might look like this:

Chore	Time	Done
Setting the table	5:30	
Doing homework	7:30	

The next day, children do the tasks at the time planned. When they've completed the job, they put a check mark in the *Done* column.

Talk about when they did the tasks. Did they do them all? If not, did they have real reasons or excuses? An excuse might be that they forgot to set the table while playing ball. Talk about using excuses to avoid doing things. Do we know when we're using them?

Look around the house. Think about the chores that need to be done. *Examples:* Clean out the closet, straighten the drawers, weed the garden. What excuses do adults use to avoid these chores?

(For a related activity, see "A Homework System" in Chapter 5.)

A PAT ON THE BACK

Every family needs to figure out what it chooses to reward for doing the dishes or doing homework. Children need our signal. Will they be rewarded for keeping quiet or speaking up? For reading a book or watching TV? For obeying rules or breaking them? And families need their own reward system. It's important that the rules be clear, the system fair and consistently followed. Whether it's a present, a grade, a raise, or a word of praise and a kiss, a reward is very sweet, indeed.

This scene captures for me the power of rewards. It was a hot summer Saturday in a restaurant in a small town. A little girl had just opened the door. Her parents were busy behind the counter. And this child, age eight, was busy, too. Carrying her parents' laundry, she came through the door with a smile on her face that said to all of us, "I'm not bored. I'm happy. I am doing something important." That was her inner reward. Her parents' praise was the external one.

I believe we can help our children understand their strengths. This enables them to feel good about themselves and strong enough to compete with others. Our children need to be able to face competition.

To be competitive, we have to be willing to work hard, but we also have to have a sense of what is special about us. When kids compete in the classroom, it is not the same as competing on the football field. In football, we win or lose. While a lot of talk is given to how we play the game, the result reported on the news is who won and who lost.

In the classroom, there is the possibility for a different kind of winning, based on a child's individuality. A child needs to think about and to hear from parents and teachers answers to "What is special and different about me?" Children who know this are in a better position to compete and succeed than youngsters who do not recognize their unique strengths.

For most of us, there is no one big win and then competition is over. Every day there are wins and losses, and the person who can keep competing without losing heart has more chances to be a winner.

There are some basic principles of competition that every child should learn, or at least listen to. To compete, you have to be able to lose. You have to be willing to fail but not feel like a failure. You have to get up off the floor and try again.

There's a lesson that is taught at every dance recital and ball game. When dancers stumble in the middle of a solo, they get right up and keep on dancing as if nothing had happened. The same is true for football players who miss a touchdown pass. They're competitors because they keep on competing, not because they keep on winning.

We want our children to be competitors who keep on trying. It would be grand if they could always win, but that's not the way it usually happens . . . even for the big winners.

LOSE AND STILL WIN

A successful accountant tells me he learned how to get going and keep going through sports. "To be successful, I have to feel success. Sports has done that for me. While I am in the top 10 percent in native sports ability, my son is in the low 10 percent. But that doesn't mean he can't participate. He enjoys sports and learns from them. I've coached his Little League and soccer games for years. Other parents are pushing to have these kids go on to tougher competition, but I want these youngsters to experience the feeling of success. I know what it did for me. My mother told me, 'You can do anything you want to do.' That's the way I feel today."

In coaching, even when his teams lose, which happens a lot, he talks with the kids about what they did right, about the wins in their loss. Did Tom catch a ball he had never caught before? Did Stephen steal second base, something he had never done before? There is, he says, some success in every loss, and his team members need to know this.

WHAT KEEPS US GOING CHANGES WITH THE YEARS

We have to keep alert to what fuels our motivation motor at different points in our lives. What works at age five won't work at ten or fifteen or forty. A young child may be motivated by the promise of a star on a chart, an older child by a new pair of jeans. A woman of forty-five tells me she swims an hour every morning before work, driving almost an hour to get to the pool. She does this so she won't have to take pills. Every other member of her family takes mountains of pills each morning to keep blood pressure down. As long as she swims, her blood pressure is fine. "I made up my mind I won't take those pills," she says, "and I'll swim the ocean if necessary."

Now — In School	Later — On the Job
Alice likes to do a lot and she tries her hand at almost everything. Alice is a doer. She is ready to do the hard work it takes.	Mrs. Taylor seeks opportunities to gain new skills and knowledge.

Chapter 5.
MegaSkill Three: Effort

We recognize effort when we see it:

> The doctor who takes time to talk to us.

> The waiter who attends to us with just the right amount of care.

> The student who reads a paper over before handing it in.

And we recognize effort when we don't see it:

> The mechanic who lets a car out of the shop without checking to see that all the hoses are attached.

> Household repair firms that make appointments for a certain time and then don't show up.

> Students whose work is so sloppy it can hardly be read.

Do our children know enough about the value of effort and the pleasure of work? What is known about student effort today? What are some ways to encourage it? What about homework, and what is a parent's role? This chapter provides some answers to these questions.

Where do children get the idea that saying, "I'm doing my best," in as plaintive a tone as possible, will excuse them from having to work hard?

Do I sound cranky? Well, maybe I am, but I am also tired of hearing from young people who are doing perfectly inadequate jobs of bagging groceries or writing an essay, "Well, I am doing my best. What more can you ask?"

As for me, a lot. I want more than that pat phrase that gets every adult off their backs. I want their best, and while I don't know exactly what that is, I know when I am not getting it.

When I called for the fifth time to find out where my computer had been sent, I was told by the clerk, "Well, it's not here," and I asked, "Well, where is it?" She said, "I'm doing my best." I said, "Well, you'll have to do better."

An hour later she called back to say it was in her office after all. She just hadn't looked. She had not done her best before, and now she had. I praised her for making the effort. I wanted her to know her best when she used it.

Maybe not knowing what effort feels like is a problem today. If so, it's not just a personal concern; it's a national problem.

Recent research has uncovered a difference between American and Japanese students and their mothers, which I will call the "effort gap." Stanford University researchers asked mothers in Japan and in the U.S. to explain their children's achievements in mathematics. These were their questions: "Why does your child do as well as he/she does?" and "Why doesn't your child do better?" Mothers could respond from among these choices: ability, effort, luck, schooling. The groups of mothers gave very different answers.

American mothers voted overwhelmingly for ability and schooling. Japanese mothers voted for effort. The fifth-grade youngsters in the study shared their mothers' views. The American kids agreed that native ability was the key, while the Japanese kids said that if they did not do well in math, it was because they were not making a great enough effort.

The value of believing in effort over native ability is that you can help children do something about their level of effort. It's fatalistic and harder to help them do something about their level of ability. Ability seems set in stone; effort can be influenced; it's open to change.

What's ironic about the American mothers' response is that the

U.S. is supposed to believe in the Horatio Alger story that hard work, in the long run, pays off, no matter what the odds against you. Instead, our children seem to be getting a contrary message — that they need the ability first.

Can we send our children a message about effort that they will listen to? Research says we can.

In Texas, elementary school children having difficulties with subtraction were divided into four groups — A, B, C, D. Each group worked on its own with a packet of materials. An aide checked the work in groups A, B, and C every eight minutes. As the children came to a new section, the aide gave them the new instructions. To group A the aide said, "You've been working hard." To group B she said, "You need to work hard." Group C received no comment. Group D had no involvement with the aide other than to hear her read the instructions to everyone.

The results make a strong point for telling children they are working hard. The group that was told, "You've been working hard," actually did work harder than the others. They completed 63 percent more problems and got three times as many right on the test that followed this training. They also said that they felt more confident about the test and their ability to deal with the problems they would face.

Across the world, in Australia, a somewhat different strategy resulted in a similar pattern. Aides in this study congratulated the children each time they said that their success in math was due to their own effort or lack of it, instead of blaming it on luck or their ability.

What do these studies mean for families and for effort? They mean that we can talk children into making more effort, that they do not have to be afraid, and that we can help them see that more effort can mean better results. Children can have an effort standard for themselves, and as parents, we can have an effort standard for them.

So how do we do it? It has to be more than a lecture on making an effort. First we may have to help children know what effort is and how they can measure it.

LEARNING ABOUT EFFORT

Effort has its secrets. And we need to let our children in on them. If more young people knew what a significant impact even a little extra effort can make, more of them would make it. For example, in an office, one secretary may jump up as if the seat ejects at five o'clock, no matter what, and another will ask if everything has been done for the day.

Inevitably the questioner is told that everything has been done, thank you. The other does not ask the question or get an answer, but the behavior is noticed. When a pay raise is distributed, chances are that only one will get it. One secretary will be asked to stay on and will move up; the other will be encouraged to move out.

When one waiter makes sure that you are happy with a smile or an "Everything all right?" and the other ignores you, guess who will get the bigger tip. It's no mystery. It's the result of effort.

Those are cases where even a little effort has a payoff. In other situations it takes a lot of effort to see results. Take the case of sports. It's interesting that often in these areas of extracurricular pleasures people expend enormous efforts without having it feel like effort at all. They're working hard and often without a lot of, if any, immediate gratification.

The kid learning magic tricks, the adult perfecting a golf game or struggling with a crossword puzzle, the tennis enthusiast practicing strokes over and over, the aspiring figure skater at the rink at dawn, the marathon runner who practically drops before stopping — these are people making lots of effort, and they think they are enjoying themselves. It feels like enjoyment. The secret is that it is.

We need to let our kids in on this secret. How do we do it? Here are some suggestions on how to give them the opportunity to know effort when they see it and to practice effort on their own.

MY DAY any age

Spend time talking with your children about the pleasures of work and of effort. Try to be as specific as possible. If you enjoy your work, so much the better. If you enjoy part but not all of it, talk about the things you enjoy. Tell about incidents from work, and not all of them have to be heart-warming. Describe the feelings of satisfaction you may get, even after a very hard day. The reluctant customer you were able to woo and win, the copier at the office or the washing machine at home that just wouldn't work until you finally figured out what was wrong, the meeting that got meaner until you told a joke that broke the ice, the memo that got the boss's applause.

The list can go on and on. It's not made up of big things. Sure, if you get a raise, brag about it. But don't stint on letting children in on the everyday efforts and goings-on at work and at home that illustrate effort and the sense of satisfaction that comes with it.

Not all problems are solved quickly or easily. Let children in on your frustrations. Perhaps it's the car that didn't get fixed, the mail that didn't go out, the telephone that stopped working, the meeting that didn't take place, the bus that didn't come on time, the grocery store that was out of milk.

But when you do talk about the day's problems, try to discuss what you are doing and what your children think can be done to solve these problems. Satisfaction lurks in the nooks and crannies of dealing with manageable problems.

Ask children about their day, too. Urge them to follow your lead in talking about the little successes. They should not have to emerge from school with A's to have had a good day. Ask about the bits and pieces of success along the way: the new friend at lunch, the speaking up in class, the locker that finally opened in time for gym. This list can go on and on, too, and it should. It's these efforts that children recognize in themselves that enable them to make more effort.

I think of effort as going that extra mile, not taking the easy way out. It's hard to measure. No one can go 100 percent all of the time, and yet we have to expect enough. Here's an activity that helps children recognize levels of effort all around us.

THE EXTRA MILE any age

Help your children know what we really mean when we say "make an effort."

Take time to point out to children those people who are making that extra effort.

The gas station attendant at a full-service station who actually gives full service, wiping off the windows or even the headlights without being asked.

The supermarket checker who, instead of kibitzing with other checkers, moves directly to take care of each customer without delay.

The salesperson who, when asked if a product is on sale, gives a polite, full answer instead of a grunt that says, in effect, "Why did you bother me?"

You promote your child's sense of effort by pointing to others who are making an effort and showing how much you respect this.

DO AND NOT DIE any age

It is very possible to make an all-out effort and still not win. But that does not mean do or die. One of the major blocks to all-out effort is fear. Fear of doing wrong, fear of not being perfect. The excuse for not making an effort is often this: "If I don't put my all into it, I can always lean back and say I have not given them my best. I'll never know if I could have won, nor will they, because I held back."

Sports is one place where people can't hold back. There are winners and there are losers, but both have to try like crazy.

Together check the sports pages. Almost every day there is a story about athletes who never said die, who didn't give up the fight until the fight was really over, who played the match to the end with all the strength they had.

These are inspirational stories. Talk about them. They are superhuman efforts, not able to be made every day, not expected every day, but they point the way.

HOMEWORK AND EFFORT

I am not a lover of traditional school homework, but I don't hate it, either, except homework saved for Sunday nights, which is a downer. I don't automatically think teachers are better because they give lots of homework or terrible because they don't.

One problem with homework is that subjects are different and students are different, but homework tends to be the same: reading that everyone in the class has to cover and then those repetitive exercises that perhaps only half the class needs. Even those drills are not without some redeeming qualities. They give youngsters who don't need them a sense of being out in front, of having achieved mastery of the material.

The remarkable school success of recently arrived Asian children who came to this country without even knowing English has prompted discussions about nature versus nurture. A Stanford University survey of San Francisco high school students found that Asian Americans consistently received better grades than other students, regardless of the parents' level of education or income. Actually, the more English spoken in the home, the less well the students did in school. Researchers found that Asian parents are able to get their children to work harder.

The Stanford study measured hours high schoolers spend on homework. The differences are startling. Asian American males spend almost twelve hours a week on homework; American white males spend eight, and American black males spend a little over six.

For females, it was found that Asian Americans spend over twelve hours a week on homework; white Americans, eight hours, and American blacks, over nine hours.

Asian Americans also scored higher on other measures of effort, including attendance and paying attention to the teacher.

There are continuing arguments about whether Asians have a higher math aptitude or even higher IQs to start with. The arguments will accelerate with each new study. But while whatever we discover about inherent capacity will be interesting, it will not effect change for other students and enable them to perform better.

What is measurable now, what we can learn from, is the greater effort that Asian American youngsters put into their schoolwork.

A University of Michigan study of elementary school students in the U.S., Taiwan, and Japan found that the American children scored lowest in math. But the study resulted in perhaps an even more revealing finding. It's about homework. American first graders spend about fourteen minutes a night on homework and hate it. Japanese spend thirty-seven minutes and Taiwanese seventy-seven minutes, and both groups say they like homework. What's more, Asian children go to school 240 days a year, while American children go only 180 days a year.

Asians believe that hard work makes a difference, and they let their children know it.

I believe that Americans also believe in hard work, and we have to let our children know that we do.

No Substitute for Hard Work

There is still no substitute for hard work and for the time that work takes. Maybe a lot of our stress is caused by our thinking — children thinking — that there are short cuts for everything and that everything should take little time and be easy to do — if only we knew the short cut. But very little comes easily and quickly.

A recent article about the success of the Japanese in wooing business in China (despite the long-standing enmity between the two countries) points to the fact that the Japanese count on persistence and patience to win the day. They just plain outwork everyone else. They have long-term perspective, and they're persistent. They work long hours; they live in accommodations Americans would not accept. While unhappy American executives might quit, unhappy Japanese executives endure.

I am not making a case for Japanese upbringing and schooling over ours — but they do appear to be able to teach their children endurance, and that is one thing we tend not to teach. Our young people need to learn about endurance and to be taught the importance of effort. Homework gives children practice in making effort.

THE HOMEWORK CONFLICT

Whatever teachers do, there never seems to be a happy medium in homework. Some parents say their kids have too little. Other parents say their kids have too much. I don't necessarily believe kids need to have more homework, but I believe they must pay attention to the homework they are given. Children need to know that their parents feel homework has to be taken seriously. This is true even for homework a parent might think is "busywork" or "a waste of time." Students need to understand that homework is something they must do. It is not an option, even if the assignment is dull or too easy or too hard. If students and parents have an objection to an assignment, they should raise it with the teacher or with the principal, if necessary. But homework, like an assignment on a job, cannot be ignored.

Taking Homework Seriously

Homework is a student's responsibility, not the parents'. I am troubled by homework assignments for children that are really addressed to parents. If it's too hard or too long for a student, it should not be assigned ... unless it's clear that it's an assignment parents and children are supposed to do together. How much does a child learn from a science fair experiment designed by a weary parent at two A.M. when the child is asleep? An honest show of hands at PTA meetings would reveal that many parents are veterans of these late-night projects for which children receive grades. This is no way to teach science or to teach honesty.

As an English teacher, I told my students that homework writing assignments were theirs solely to do, that if parents helped them do the writing, I would never know how to help them. I encouraged them to talk over the assignment and to share ideas with their family, but I wanted to be sure I was reading a student's, not a parent's, paper.

As a parent I worked to follow my "teacher's hat" advice. While I enjoyed hearing my children read their essays aloud after they had completed them, I was not involved in writing them. When it came time for college essays, they wrote and typed their own. I wasn't applying for college. They were.

It can be hard to remember that homework assignments are our children's alone, not ours. The difficulties are theirs, and so are the achievements.

PARENTAL INFRASTRUCTURE

This does not mean that as parents we don't have a role to play. We do — as the infrastructure that makes it possible for children to accomplish their homework. The infrastructure I have in mind is like a bridge or a road that makes comings and goings possible.

Providing the infrastructure in homework means providing the base from which children can operate. It's the atmosphere that promotes study and enables children to be students.

Children need parents who think homework is important, who

let them know this, and who provide discipline that children can follow and that is enforceable.

At least three kinds of parental discipline patterns have been identified, and I believe they are relevant to homework:

Permissive: Adult makes few demands on child and sees child as own self-regulator.

Authoritarian: Adult has set standard of conduct in mind and sets out to shape child to fit it, using force and punishment to curb child.

Authoritative: Adult sets standards and asserts control but sees child's need for reason and understanding.

Parental-authority researchers are all for the authoritative parent. Permissiveness is not as good for children as once was thought. The trick, and it's a tough one, is for parents and for teachers to be authoritative without being authoritarian. It's not easy.

Here are some "authoritative" activities that can help. They provide children with an atmosphere that encourages learning within a structured and supportive environment.

A STUDY PLACE ages 4–9

All children need their own place at home to do homework. Even with this special place, they might still use the dining room table. But they gain a sense of the importance of homework from having a place of their own. Fancy equipment is not needed. Use old furniture. Cut it down to size as needed. You need a table or desk, a chair, a light.

Walk through your house with your child to find that special study corner. It need not be big, but it needs to be personal. With your child, find the furniture needed; check the attic, ask friends, or visit nearby garage sales.

Paint cardboard boxes or orange crates for bookcases. Latex paint is easy to clean. Encourage your child to decorate the study corner; a plant and a bright desk blotter do wonders. Save children's artwork from school for the extra touch.

A study place can be a desk, or it can be a modest lapboard for a child to use atop a bed. What is basic to both is their message that studying is valued in this house.

A HOMEWORK SYSTEM ages 10–12

There is a better way than nagging children every day about homework. This activity enables children to keep track — on their own — of what has to be done. You need paper and a marker.

Use a sturdy, large piece of paper to make a homework chart that can be posted on the wall. Here's what one looks like:

Days	English	Math	Social Studies	Science
Monday				
Tuesday				
etc.				

Each day after school, your child makes checks to represent homework assignments. To show completed homework, the check gets circled. Attach to the chart a marker or pen so that it is always handy.

Talking About Homework

Talk about assignments with your child after they're completed. This is more of a conversation than a checkup. Was the assignment difficult? Easy? Would your child like to know more? Consider follow-up trips to a museum or library. Homework can be a starting point for your child's continuing interests — pursued with pleasure and without assignments.

OUR HOME: A LEARNING PLACE any age

Help your home (even if it's a small apartment) convey the message that people learn here.

You want children to be reading as often and as many different materials as possible. Let there be books and magazines everywhere, including the bathroom. Studies show people do a lot of reading there. These do not have to be the latest magazines or books to be useful. Ask friends and neighbors to save theirs. You can set up an informal exchange so that there is always fresh reading material, just as there is fresh food, in your home. Let your children see you reading, and talk with them about what you've read.

You want children to be writing as often as possible. Put notepads and pencils in a number of places around the house, including next to the telephone, for messages. In the kitchen use them for grocery lists, and keep them next to the bed for putting down that brilliant middle-of-the-night thought.

And you want to show that you value your child's school experience. Use a bulletin board or magnets on the refrigerator to display children's schoolwork and artwork. Or use an indoor clothesline with clothespins. Youngsters enjoy changing these displays themselves as they bring new work home. When parents ask, "What did you do in school today?" children can point with pride to the newest addition in their very own gallery.

STUDYING: A PERSONAL APPROACH

After years of studying students, I am more and more convinced that what works for one person does not necessarily work for another. There are those who have to do it standing up, those who do it sitting down, those who need complete quiet, and those who do well studying with lots of background noise.

Just because children are sitting down and look as if they are reading quietly does not mean they are absorbing the material. Don't let what looks like studying make you think it is studying. Children will evolve their own personal style of study, but it's important that it be shown to work. If children can't pass tests and master the material after studying in complete quiet, they may want to try some background music. If they can't work with noise, they can go to the library. The beauty of studying at home is that children can have their own personal style, as long as it does not bother others.

TIME FOR STUDYING

We know from experience in school that some children are faster to finish classroom work than others. The same is true for homework.

The research on Asian students and math shows that time spent on the task pays off. And as an English teacher, I know that when a student takes time to polish an essay and read it over more than once, it pays off.

When you talk with your children about homework, ask if they think they are putting in enough time to do it really well. When you talk with your children's teachers, ask if they think your child is spending enough time to do the homework carefully and thoroughly.

If your children are now spending more time watching TV than doing homework, they may not necessarily need more homework, but they do need to cut down on TV watching. TV does not help children feel a sense of accomplishment. Help your child spend time on hobbies — perhaps those old standbys, stamp collecting and model airplanes, or cooking or a new sport. These involve effort, and with effort comes a sense of accomplishment.

EFFORT IS PLEASURE

Clearly effort is not all grim and serious. People are made for effort. We function better when we're exerting ourselves. Ask any jogger, swimmer, baseball player. The pleasure of effort comes not just from physical exercise but from mental exercise, too. Our children need to know this.

Talk about the pleasure a writer gets, an artist, a mathematician, an accountant. There is real pleasure in working with our minds.

It may be harder to feel a rush of pleasure after finishing ten pages of homework than after jogging ten blocks or swimming ten laps, but our children need to know that even their homework can bring them pleasure. It is the pleasure of using oneself, of accomplishment.

Our children need to know that effort is the path we take to achieve mastery — and mastery is one of the greatest pleasures of them all.

Now — In School	Later — On the Job
Becky gets her assignments in on time.	Ms. Stein meets her deadlines through effective resource management.

Chapter 6.
MegaSkill Four: Responsibility

Check yourself. When you hear yourself saying or thinking about your children,

"Why are you always late?"

"Where have you been?"

"Why can't you start acting more grown up?"

you are hearing the need to help your child become more responsible.

When you hear yourself saying about your children,

"I can count on you,"

"You are reliable and dependable,"

"When you tell me something, I can believe you,"

you are hearing yourself praise your responsible child.

This chapter is about developing self-discipline in children. It's about children knowing what they have to do and gaining self-respect from doing it.

At the age of twenty-four, Paul is one of the most responsible young men I know. He is a topnotch printing salesman, a father of three, and a man of his word.

I asked him how he got to be so responsible.

> My parents gave me a motorcycle when I was thirteen. They told me I was to care for the bike, that I was not to ride it on the public streets, and that I was to walk it to the biking trails. But I didn't always do what I was supposed to.
>
> One day as I came roaring over a hill in the middle of a street, a policeman was waiting for me. I'll never forget the ride to the station in the back of the police car and the meeting with the judge. I received a Juvenile Two form for unauthorized use of the road, my parents were angry, and I was scared.
>
> My dad said, "I hope you learned something from this." And I did, but it was probably a very risky way to learn it. I learned that there are authorities out there to enforce rules, and you'll be caught — maybe not today, but they will catch you.
>
> But that motorcycle kept me out of trouble, too. It kept me in the fresh air, getting mud all over me in the fields rather than getting into drugs on street corners. I subscribed to all the magazines on bikes and read them cover to cover — even when I wasn't reading all my schoolbooks.
>
> My parents probably put more trust in me than they should have. They were determined to force me to learn to be responsible.
>
> For my own kids, I'd be less risky, probably get them a dog instead of a motorcycle.

For many parents, giving a teen a motorcycle is both out of the question financially and unsuited to how the family lives.

So it's good to know that responsibility and reliability and trustworthiness can be taught quietly and at home. When I thought about the activities that are useful in teaching responsibility, I realized that they can seem an odd combination. Some are as straightforward as learning to sew on a button or to get up on time. Others are as complex as what it means to cheat on a test or lie to a friend.

Children will probably learn to sew on a button faster than they will grasp abstractions about truth. But the underlying willingness and readiness to be responsible can be strikingly similar for both.

The activities in this chapter seem so unrelated that I began to question putting them together. Then I remembered the broad definition I had chosen for responsibility — *doing what's right.*

Teaching children to be responsible involves finding ways to help children feel competent, to know what's right and to do what's right. If children need to wake up on time, you show them how to use an alarm clock and expect them to use it. If a child lies to you, you let your child know that lying is wrong and that it works to destroy the precious trust you share.

Our children become responsible through an accumulation of experiences. The value of mixing tangible activities — using buttons and alarm clocks — with family discussions about an intangible abstraction, such as truth, is that buttons and clocks provide immediate, positive payoff for responsible actions. The payoff on the abstractions can take a lifetime to assess.

Here are some starter activities that span the broad MegaSkill of responsibility. They include the following:

- Taking care of children's own property and others' property.
- Carrying out home and school tasks.
- Encouraging children to think about choices and values.

It can be helpful to think about personal responsibility in this way:

How to enable children to *do for themselves*
and
do for the family.

The following activities widen children's sense of responsibility from self to family, and each reinforces the other.

HELPING CHILDREN DO FOR THEMSELVES

Children need to learn to take care of themselves — even if parents have nothing to do all day but take care of them. When children hang up their clothes or wash their feet, it does not seem like schoolwork. But this practice in self-reliance carries over to the classroom.

Let's start with some activities that help children learn to take better care of their bodies and their clothes.

BODY BEAUTIFUL ages 4–9

For this activity, you need a marker, a pencil, and paper.

Talk with your child about personal cleanliness and why it's important. We're not talking "too clean." We're just talking clean, such as "not smelly." And, it can be pretty easy.

Talk about washing face and hands, combing hair, and brushing teeth. Include any other parts of the body that children tend to get dirty.

Together make a list of what needs to be done to be clean before going off to school. Post the list in the bathroom.

If you and your child like charts, post a simple one like the one below. Your child checks off this chart in much the same way that a pilot goes over a checklist before takeoff. Attach a marker to the chart so that it's easy to do the checking.

Looking Good	Sun.	Mon.	Tues.	Wed.	Thurs.	Fri.	Sat.
I brushed my teeth.							
I washed my face.							
I washed my hands.							
I combed my hair.							

To provide incentive, especially at first, you may want to think of a small reward. It might be a new brand of toothpaste that your child picks out or a new toothbrush or a special brand of soap.

Check the chart daily at first, then weekly. Pretty soon you won't need a chart. The idea is to make good grooming your child's habit.

Clothes may or may not make the man, but taking care of them helps make the all-important inner man or woman. When children are young, taking care of their own clothes may be among the few areas in their lives in which they can practice responsibility.

Picking Them

For this activity, you need ordinary clothes. Pencil, paper, and tape for labels are optional.

With your youngster, put clothes together in places where they can be found. One way is to label the outside of dresser drawers.

Talk about appropriate clothes to wear in different weather. Turn this into a game. Pick a thick sweater and ask, "Do you wear this on hot or cold days?" Do the same for shorts, mittens, and so forth.

Before children go to bed at night, ask them to think about clothes to wear the next day. Let them lay out these clothes in advance. Ask your child to check to see that the clothes are clean and ready. This can save time and stress in the morning.

Washing Them

Mom and Dad are not the only people at home who can wash clothes. This is a skill everyone can have, including young children. For this activity, you need some dirty clothes, soap, water, and perhaps a washing machine.

Pick up any detergent box. Reading it together with your child will immediately broaden your child's vocabulary with words like "formulated" and "cycle."

Whether you are washing an item by hand or in the machine, with your child move through the process step by step, preferably with one or just a few items, treating spots first, if necessary. Talk about separating colors, then talk about the temperature of the water, then the soap suds, then the machine instructions, then the rinsing, then the hanging up or the machine drying. Go through all the steps with your child watching and helping.

Now, with you close at hand, let your child take one dirty item all the way through, either by hand or by machine. What precautions need to be taken? How will you know it's worked?

It may take time to graduate to the washing machine. Next to learning how to drive a car, learning how to use a washing machine and a lawn mower are the most responsibility-building tools in any home.

An iron is also a responsibility-teaching tool. Because we iron less with today's no-iron fabrics, I sometimes tend to overlook it. Show children how to iron safely. Lower the ironing board and give children the chance to show their stuff.

Fixing Them

What I especially like about this sewing activity is that it not only teaches responsibility but also builds children's hand-eye coordination, an essential for learning to read and write. You need needle, thread, scissors, buttons, and children's clothes that need repairing.

With your child, pick an item that needs a button sewn on. Together select the necessary tools. Look for a needle with a large eye. Show your child how to thread it. Take time to illustrate how to do all this safely. Then show step by step how to sew on a button.

Now watch as your child replaces a button on some old clothes. Don't expect the job to be perfect, and resist doing it over. Children need practice to master this skill. Wearing a crooked button in this case is a mark of honor for both girls and boys.

With some colorful fabric scraps, you can help children move to making gifts and other items around home. For example, a bright patch on blue jeans is easy and fun. Placemats, book covers, and banners are other easy-to-do items. Personal hand-sewn gifts from children are especially appreciated, and they cost only a few pennies.

A SPECIAL PLACE ages 4–9

Here's a responsibility builder for the early school years. It calls for setting up a special home-school box to help children keep track of their belongings.

Children generally come into the house and toss their school things every which way. In the morning, with everyone rushing off to jobs and to school, these things are hard to find.

You can hear your child now: "I can't find them anywhere."

("Them" can be anything from mittens to pencils.) And hear yourself saying loudly, "Well, keep looking until you do."

You need a cardboard box big enough to hold supplies and some clothing. Add some magazine pictures, markers, glue, and scissors, and you're ready to make a Special Place.

Children decorate these boxes with pictures, words, artwork, and their own names in big, bold letters.

This box goes near the front door or in your child's room. When your child comes home, the box is the first stop for school items, hat, toys, glasses. It is the last stop on the way out the door in the morning. Finished homework and supplies needed for school are put in the box at night, ready for the next day.

As a reward for your child using the box, put in a note every few days, praising your child's responsibility: "Hi! This is terrific. Love, Dad." "See you at six P.M. to go to the game. Love, Mom."

At the very least, children now know where their things ought to be. Moreover, the box cuts down on family nagging in the morning. If a little box can help do that, it's got to be worth trying.

P.S. Older youngsters, even parents, can use their very own boxes. I've got one near my front door for my glasses and car keys. It's invaluable on mornings when my head is in four places at once.

Now that we've covered some do-for-myself activities, we'll move to giving kids practice in doing for others.

HELPING CHILDREN DO FOR THE FAMILY

As parents, we keep saying it — our children need to learn to be responsible. We also have to watch that we don't undermine our good intentions. Our urge is to protect, perhaps even to overprotect. At times we become responsible for our children, often to protect them from unpleasant consequences. We turn in their library books; we feed their pets and water their plants. Sometimes we even do their homework for them. But that doesn't work for very long, and it does not help children grow up.

Overall, responsibility means that we can "count on" our children and they can count on us. Here are some "count on each other" activities.

PROMISES! PROMISES! ages 4–9

When asked to do a task, children often make promises. They may not fully realize what keeping these promises involves. Their intentions are sincere. They want to please. Here's a way to get children talking about promises and consequences. All you need are thinking minds.

Talk about what happens when people don't do the things they are responsible for. *Examples:* Plants that don't get watered wilt. Animals (and children) that don't get fed whine. Garbage that isn't taken out smells.

Ask children to think about what would happen if parents decided they didn't want to shop or cook meals, if the bus driver stayed home, if the movie projectionist didn't show up for work. Should people do only tasks they like?

Discuss the effects on others when tasks are not done. Is it fair? Is it responsible? Is that why carrying out promises is so important?

TAKING CARE OF THINGS any age

Children have been known to be careless about property — their own and others. Expensive items can find their way quickly to the junk heap. That's what can happen if parents don't find a way to help children be responsible for caring for what they are supposed to care for.

This activity can help. You need thinking minds, paper, and pencil. Talk with your child, preferably before buying a costly gift, about what is reasonable to expect in the way of care for this gift.

A pet is a good example, even if it doesn't cost money to start with. A pet needs daily care. How much is your child willing and able to do? Get these understandings ironed out in advance so that there will be fewer misunderstandings later. Write down what you have both decided on, and post this list in a prominent place.

Or you may be considering a home computer. These are fragile machines that need careful operators. Make sure that children know what is expected. Take them with you to the store. Read the operating manual together. Go over the steps one by one. Children need to know not only how to run the machine but how to care for it.

In every home there is some property that is "out of bounds." It might be medicines, Mother's make-up, china, records, or a treasure box in your child's room. Make a pact with your youngster. You will leave your child's treasures alone in return for the make-up and medicines being left alone. Designate these "untouchables" and keep to the bargain.

DON'T WORRY: YOU WON'T BE LATE any age

This activity helps teach children the importance of showing people that they can be depended on, rain or shine. We parents go to work even when we don't feel like it. We call our employers when we'll be out sick or when we are late. Children need to know this and need to copy our behavior.

This activity helps kids learn to wake up on time on their own. You'll need an alarm clock, paper bag, and a piece of paper for each family member.

Write "wake up" on one piece of paper and "wake *me* up" on the others. Put the papers into the bag. Everybody picks one piece. The person who picks the slip marked "wake up" will do the job of waking up the others the next morning.

The people who pick the papers marked "wake *me* up" choose the wake-up time. It might have to be early — early enough for everyone to get to work or school on time.

The "wake-up" person sets the alarm clock for five minutes before the wake-up time. You'll find out the next day if the "wake-up" person was dependable. What happens if the "wake-up" person is late? Will someone be late to work or school?

Do your children wake themselves up regularly? If not, invest in an inexpensive alarm clock for each child right away.

Talk about how people worry when those they are expecting are late. Children worry when employed parents are late coming home for dinner. Parents worry when children are late coming home after a movie. Talk about what to do to cut down on each other's worry. Is there anything that can be done to help us be prompt? This is an investment in other people's feelings.

WHAT DO I DO? HELPING CHILDREN THINK RESPONSIBLY ABOUT CHOICES AND VALUES

There are daily dilemmas in life that virtually every child will face. What do I do when ...

I see others cheating on a test?

I find money?

I know a friend has done something wrong?

These are tough questions. They test our children's ability to tell right from wrong and to do the right thing. And they test our parental ability to help children figure out how to handle these problems in such a way that children feel comfortable with their decisions.

Children need to know what parents think, but moreover, they need to know how to figure out where they themselves stand. This takes time, and it comes through discussion, the chance to open up and talk honestly with parents and close friends. It takes asking questions ourselves: What are the choices? What are my values? How do I want to be treated? What kind of person am I? What kind of person do I want to be?

Most of us want to be good; we want to do the right thing; we want to feel good about ourselves. As children grow and define the kind of persons they are, they need encouragement and support in following their impulse to do the right thing. The people most responsible for providing this support are parents.

This takes discussions around the dinner table and while driving in the car; it takes time, but it's worth it. It means talk and a lot of it, but it also means action. As parents, we don't have to be angels, but children need to see parents who are honest, who have respect for laws, who wear seat belts, who do not take drugs.

All the lectures in the world will do no good if children see that it's just "talk." It's hard, if not impossible, to hold children to certain rules when parents brag about breaking laws. It's hard also when parents seem too good to be true. Have we never been tempted to do anything wrong? It can help when we tell about a temptation and how we handled it.

I have my own story about shoplifting. It's my "Sen-Sen story," and it must have impressed my children, because whenever I start to tell it, they say, "Oh, not the Sen-Sen story again!"

I was eight years old, and I was in a drugstore, waiting to make a purchase. As I stood at the counter, I picked up a small packet of Sen-Sen (a tiny package like a sugar packet) and held it in my hand, reading the instructions. Sen-Sen, for those not as old as I, was one of the first breath fresheners on the market. Whether I needed a breath freshener in those days I am not sure, but after walking out of the store with the item I had bought and paid for, I looked down into my hand and found that I was still clutching the packet of Sen-Sen, which I had not paid for. What to do? I walked back to the drugstore, told the druggist what had happened, and paid for the Sen-Sen. I am not sure I ever used it, but I do know I feel virtuous about it to this very day.

Not all such stories have happy endings. Teachers are finding themselves caught in problems involving cheating. It's hard to know whether there is more cheating in school today. Possibly it's discussed more openly because cheating is seen as a reaction to stress, and we talk more about stress than before.

To be sure, cheating occurs in many more places than in school. But school is a place which in large measure determines students' future success in academics and in personal values. That's why "looking the other way" is a real disservice to children. How to handle cheating and cheaters continues to be a problem. To report them or not to report them, to punish them or to counsel them — these are continuing dilemmas for students and teachers. The bottom line is that adults must be responsible so that children can be responsible.

I LOVE YOU WHEN YOU BEHAVE YOURSELVES

Responsibility is really a two-way street between parent and child. MegaSkills are not just for children; they're for parents, too. I remember a message from my own children that reminded me of my own responsibility, which I was not meeting.

I have this tattered and faded sheet of yellow paper upon which a six-year-old's wobbly print calls out firmly: I LOVE YOU WHEN YOU BEHAVE YOURSELVES!

That note was written by our daughter while an argument raged between her parents in the next room. What that argument was about I cannot recall. What I have to remember, thanks to that note, is that we were behaving irresponsibly.

The note was a "responsibility reminder." It came from a child, so it probably had greater impact than most parental reminders. I'd like to say that this sweet note prevented all future acts of irresponsibility. It didn't. But I'm sure it helped. It's good to let our children know that we parents need MegaSkills reminders, too.

Now — In School	Later — On the Job
Stan keeps coming up with new ideas that the class really likes.	We depend on Mr. Johnson for his creative thinking. He moves the whole office along.

Chapter 7.
MegaSkill Five: Initiative

When you hear yourself thinking or saying to your child,

"What a good idea!"

"You're our spark plug,"

"You're pulling us along,"

"You're always thinking of something new,"

you are hearing yourself praise your child's initiative.

This chapter is about generating and harnessing initiative. It's about energy, vitality, interest. It's about the organization it takes to get started and keep going.

Initiative starts with a good idea, but the idea is not enough. You have to do something to make things happen. Even after you hit a home run, you still have to run around the bases.

Initiative is grounded in first steps and follow-through. Activities in this chapter give children opportunities to build interest and gain practice in taking the initiative to put good ideas into action.

I'LL TRY IT!

You don't have to go outside your home to give your child a world of experiences that build interests and lead to school achievement. These experiences give children ideas on which future interests are built.

I remember how I felt when I tried science in the kitchen with my young children. Let me tell you, they were not the only ones learning. We watched water come to a boil. We timed how long it took to make macaroni soft. We defrosted ice cubes in the sun and in shade. We put wooden and metal spoons into hot water and then touched them, sometimes with a burning surprise. And we talked about what we were learning. My children still remember these special times, and so do I.

Children who have visited their parents' workplace or have watched the sun rise or have taken a bus to the other end of town are children who, when thinking about taking a new or first step, have a better chance of hearing a soft inner voice say, "It's OK, you know about that," or "It's like what you did last week," or "It's not so different from what you did before." "You can handle it!"

The activities that follow are especially appreciated by younger elementary graders, but older children who have not had these will enjoy them, too. My own kids, now grown, still remember our special "science times" in the kitchen and in the yard. *One warning:* My kids say I lectured too much about what they were learning. So try to avoid my mistake and enjoy these moments together.

Employed parents, fathers especially, may think that to make up for lost time with the kids, they need to sacrifice, to do activities like going to museums or the zoo or a show. Not so. There really is great educational value in activities such as going with children to the bank and to the grocery store ... or even down to the basement.

MACHINES: LOOK AND LISTEN ages 4—9

Use the house itself. Go down to the basement and take a look at the furnace. How does it work? What are all those pipes for? Don't forget those plumbing pipes. It really is a shame that some are not exposed so that children can see the activity beneath the walls.

Kitchens make noises. Listen and name them — the refrigerator's hum, the stove's purr, the fan's whoosh.

Look at a bicycle. What's the importance of the wheel? Peek beneath the hood of the family car. Can you name the parts?

Take a good look at all the appliances at home. You might want to tackle the bigger question of where all this electricity comes from in the first place. When traveling past a power plant or a dam, you might mention that little old toaster at home.

MACHINES: PLEASE TOUCH ages 4—9

Oh, the joy of taking things apart and maybe even putting them together again. Here are some activities in which you can put parts together wrong and still enjoy them. You need a working flashlight with batteries, a small machine that is broken and dispensable, and some tools.

How do flashlights work? Find out what happens when one battery is taken away or put in upside down. The beauty of flashlights is that they can be made to work so easily.

If you have a small, broken machine, such as a clock or pencil sharpener, and you don't care whether it works again, try this wonderful activity: Put the machine and some useful tools, such as a screwdriver, on a table. Allow your child to take the object apart. Stand by in case you're needed, but do let your child try to put it back together without your help.

WATER, WATER EVERYWHERE ages 4—9

Water is great for stimulating scientific thinking. For these activities, you need water, ice trays, salt, an egg, and some dishes.

Put water into an ice tray and set it in the freezer. How long does it take to freeze? Try this with different levels of water in different sections of the tray.

Put a few ice cubes on the table. How long do they take to melt? Why are they melting? Put them in different places around the room. Do they melt faster in some places than in others?

Salty and fresh water: Make some salt water by adding a couple of teaspoons of salt to two cups of water. Fill an ice tray with this water. Fill another tray, but for this one use tap water only. Put them in the freezer and check them after a few hours. What do you see? Is the one with ordinary tap water frozen? Is the salty one jellylike?

Float an egg in both salt and fresh water. Which water holds the egg higher? Salt water is more buoyant. From that you might go on to discuss salt in the Dead Sea and how easy it is for people to float there.

Evaporation: Put some water in an open dish in a sunny place. Let your child make a mark to show the water level. Use another dish with an equal amount of water, and put this one in the shade. Which one dries first? Watch what happens, and talk about what you see.

HOT AND COLD ages 4–9

Stand by as your children try this activity. You need water, macaroni (or spaghetti), and two pots. Put some water in one of the pots and bring it to a boil on the stove. In the other pot, put a larger or smaller amount of water. Try to use a similar degree of heat and the same size burner. Watch to see how much faster or slower it takes different amounts of water to boil.

Put macaroni in boiling water on the stove. What happens? Ask children to carefully check how much time it takes for the water to boil, and watch the boiling process. Plunge in the macaroni and watch what happens next. Then you can eat the experiment.

To check on temperature around you, use a house-and-garden thermometer. What happens when the thermometer is in the refrigerator? In the freezer? Atop the radiator? In the sun?

LIGHT AND SHADOW ages 4–9

For these activities, you need a light, objects of different shapes, a mirror, a glass of water, and a spoon.

When are shadows longer and shorter outdoors during the day? On a sunny day, go outside at different times and stand in the same place. Check to see shadows grow longer and shorter.

Use a strong light bulb indoors. Try some shadow play on a dark background. Try making different shadows with squares, circles, and other shapes. What happens when children jump, skip, wave hands, wiggle feet?

Use a mirror to catch light from the sun. Then move the mirror, throwing the light in different places around the room.

To illustrate how light passes through air and water at different rates, try this experiment. Put a teaspoon in a glass of water that is two-thirds full. Looking at it sideways, children see the "disconnected" parts of the spoon.

A CAN AND A STRAW ages 4–9

You need a can of juice, a can opener, a plunger, water, and straws.

Open a can of juice on one side only. Try pouring. Nothing comes out. Why not? Make another opening. Again try to pour. What happens and why?

Attach a plunger to a wall. It sticks. What holds it there? When will it fall off?

Using straws, suck up water. What holds the water in so that the straws can be twirled about without losing the water?

PLANTS AND HOW THEY GROW ages 4–9

Taking care of plants is a visible cause-and-effect experience. What do plants need? How do they change when they don't get what they need? For these activities you need plants and aluminum foil.

Put two similar, healthy plants side by side. Let your child water one plant but ignore the other for a week or two. What happens?

Using aluminum foil, cover the leaves on one side of a sun-loving plant. Keep this covering on for a week. What do the leaves look like when you take off the foil?

This adventure of growing things can be enjoyed in a window box or on vast acreage. Green beans will almost always come through, and carrot tops like nothing better than to show off with green growth.

DON'T WORRY any age

In a number of these activities, you are raising questions to which you might not know the answers. You and your children can go to the library to look up the answers later. The important part is for children to be interested enough to want to know and try more.

LET'S GET ORGANIZED

There are mornings when you wake up and you just know it's a day to get organized. Children get those feelings, too. That initiative needs to be captured before it evaporates.

Not only do the following activities for very young children teach organizing skills, but they also get needed jobs done at the same time. Take classifying and categorizing, for example. This next activity will eliminate that mess you've been avoiding for months.

NUTS AND BOLTS, PINS AND NEEDLES ages 4–6

For this activity, you need a toolbox, jewelry box, clothes drawer, sewing box, or bookcase.

- With the toolbox, ask the children to sort nails according to length.
- With the jewelry box, children can separate necklaces, rings, and earrings.
- With their dressers, children sort their clothes (otherwise known as cleaning out drawers!).

- With sewing boxes, children separate thread, needles, pins, etc.
- With the bookcase, books can be sorted in many ways: by size or color or in more abstract ways — books children like or dislike, funny books or sad books.

It may not be immediately apparent, but classifying is a key skill in the three R's. Students need to be able to identify things and ideas that go together.

EVERYTHING FITS ages 7–12

This activity gives somewhat older children practice in putting things in order. Use the kitchen cupboard or refrigerator, the family linen closet or a closet in your child's room.

First talk about a good way to organize the shelf or closet. In the kitchen it might be by putting containers of the same size together or by putting certain foods together. In the bedroom, it might include sorting socks and making sure they are in pairs. In the closet, all shirts might go together, with pants at the other end.

Let your child organize at least one shelf in the order you have both decided upon. The system may not last, but for at least a day or two the results of this activity provide solid satisfaction.

IT TAKES PLANNING!

Any parent who has suffered through setting up an elaborate easel for a child who says, "I want to paint," and then hears, "I don't want to paint," a minute after the easel has been put up, will want to be able to say as soon as possible to their dear, dear child, "Honey, you know how — do it yourself. OK?"

The sooner children get used to taking initiative, the sooner they will be putting up the easels for themselves.

When my children were very young, if I announced that we were going on a trip, the kids would be at the door, and even if it was midwinter and they didn't have their coats on, or if we were going to spend a week away, they would delightedly announce, without an ounce of preparation, "We're ready!"

Of course, they were ready; they didn't have to do anything. But it wasn't long before they did. That meant packing their own bags and doing anything else that was needed to get ready, including ironing! This activity helped.

GATHER AND GO ages 7–9

Teach children how to collect and organize materials. Start a project, big or little: a puppet stage, a dog house, a party, baking cookies. Talk with children about what they will need. (Young children will need your advice.)

List what you have to purchase and what is already at home. Then, with your child, collect the essentials before you start the project.

For another version of this activity, have children collect information about something they want to do or learn more about, a skill or hobby: how to bake a cake, how to start a rock collection, how to tune a guitar. It's good to *know* before you *do*.

KNOWING WHAT'S WHEN

A calendar in every household is an essential piece of equipment. Yet all by itself, an ordinary household calendar cannot help children become organized.

The extra-ordinary calendar below motivates everyone in the house to use it, as a reminder and as a way to be in touch with other family members.

WHEN DO WE HAVE TO DO WHAT?
THE FAMILY CALENDAR any age

Children seem to be forever forgetting things, especially dates and responsibilities. This activity provides a memory jogger. You need a calendar, markers, or crayons.

Get a plain calendar with large squares for each day. Start any time. Talk about the days, weeks, and months spread out before you.

Start filling in the squares with special days, such as birthdays and upcoming events. Include medical appointments and team practices.

Let your child decorate the calendar. Find ways to personalize it, with special colors for each family member, for example, or with drawings or pictures for special days. Use the calendar for generating children's suggestions; for example, list special foods children want or ideas for places to go on family outings.

Use this calendar to write special messages to each other. Of course, there will always be: "Mom, I need lunch money" or "I really do need those new jeans." But remember, praise is a miracle worker. Here are messages everyone likes to get: "Joe, I like your smile." "Mom, thanks for helping me with my homework." "Dad, you make terrific spaghetti." "Sally, you ride your bike well."

(See also "Vacation Family Calendar" in Chapter 19.)

STRIKING BACK AT SICKNESS

Even when children are home sick and in bed, their initiative can make the day brighter and help them feel better. Sure, there are days when nothing but closed shades, long naps, and lots of TV will do. But there are other days in the recuperating period when new skills and interests can be found and developed.

Children will be interested in different kinds of activities, depending on their age. Readers will enjoy the daily newspaper, lots of magazines, and books from the library. Keep in mind that everyone, young or old, enjoys being read to.

Stock a young child's bedstand with provisions for arts and crafts — crayons, paper, scissors. And don't forget puzzles, old greeting cards for collages, and games.

Preschoolers can dictate stories to their parents or older brothers or sisters and then illustrate their own books. They can also dictate letters to grandparents.

Elementary graders enjoy pasting up family photo albums, bringing together the snapshots lying about in an old shoe box. Boys and girls can be taught to embroider, knit, or sew doll clothes. And there's always string and card tricks and paper folding, including making paper airplanes.

Equip your child's bedroom window with a bird feeder, thermometer, and even a weather vane, if possible. While in bed, children can use pencil and paper to keep records of the number and kinds of birds that come and how the temperature and wind change during the day.

Use a notebook with the hours of the day listed on the left-hand side of the page. Attach a pencil to this pad so it doesn't get misplaced when the covers are jostled. Every hour by the bedroom clock, your children can record the temperature, the direction of the wind, and the number and colors, if not the kinds, of birds they have seen. You might want to provide a bird watchers' guidebook.

Set up a bulletin board close to the bed, and a radio, too. Children can post interesting articles, the radio log, or pictures clipped from the newspaper.

Once out of bed, youngsters can work on their cooking, practice learning to type, grow seeds in jars. Activity possibilities are almost endless. Yes, TV is nice when children are sick, but it's the wise parent who seizes on these other learning activities for passing the time.

School should not be forgotten, especially if your child is out three or more days. Contact the teacher to make arrangements for keeping up with the class.

If children are being cared for at home by someone other than you, be sure this person knows about the activities you've planned with your child.

YOU'RE IN MY SPACE!

All those magazine-pretty houses with separate quarters, even whole wings, for children are nice. But for most families, living in apartments or small houses, even a playroom is a dream, and life among all those things children accumulate and argue over is a nightmare.

We can spend days sidestepping the stuff on the floor and screaming at the kids while they scream at each other. Or we can take the initiative to make living together a happier experience.

First ask children what they think ought to be done to clear up the mess. *A warning:* They may be quite content with their mess, so parents need to be prepared to point to the real problems experienced by the rest of the family.

Ask your children which of these ideas they'd like to try first.

- **Provide some kind of work space, no matter how small, for each child.** This can vary from a lapboard that children use while they sit on the bed to a piece of furniture to a drop-leaf shelf that is attached to the wall, if apartment regulations allow.

  Try the idea of a small piece of colorful rug for a young child's work area on the floor. This helps cut down on the tendency for children to covet the same work space, even in big rooms.

  To make communal work space for young children doing artwork, put a heavy plastic tablecloth over the dining room table and an old shower curtain or newspaper beneath.

- **Give children a place to put their possessions.** This should be an "untouchable" place. No one is to disturb these things. The children's end of this bargain is that they have to put the things away neatly. This place could be a box or drawer that fits under a bed, or a shelf above it.

- **Label toys with the child's name when these cherished items are brought into the house.** This way there need be no argument over who owns what.

- **Provide pegs so that children can hang up their own clothes.** Also, make sure that shelves are reachable so that children are able to put away toys when they're finished with them.

- **Use what's in the apartment.** Put a piece of wood on top of a radiator (except in winter), and you have a shelf. Place a large sheet of wood or Masonite over a bathtub, and you have a good-size work area. And use wall space. Hang pegboards to hold carpentry tools and toys.

Organizing our houses in these ways enables us and our children to be ready, to be prepared to take advantage of good ideas when they strike.

JUNK DAY any age

Some things that look like junk in a child's room are really "treasures." But other stuff is really junk, and kids think so, too. Given some incentive, children will be ready to give it up. This activity rewards tidiness and provides some math practice, too. You need large grocery bags and a room with junk in it — often a child's bedroom. A bathroom scale is also useful.

Give your child paper bags and these instructions: "Today is junk day. Go through your closet/drawers/bedroom and take out all the junk or give-aways that you want to get rid of. I pay for junk!"

When your child presents the bags, look through them together to determine if everything in the bag is really ready to leave home. Take the real junk and give-aways to the bathroom scale and weigh each bag.

Offer your child so much per pound. This can be determined by both of you. *Example:* Fifteen cents per pound for six pounds of junk equals ninety cents. Let children figure out what's owed them, and then have them deliver junk to the trash can and give-aways to a special box.

We all know that one person's trash is another's treasure. Getting treasures organized is a way to enjoy them more.

OFFERING WITHOUT BEING ASKED ages 7-12

This activity provides practice in offering to help without being asked. All you need are jobs to be done around the house.

Ask children to choose one job that they're often asked to do. Examples might be taking out the garbage, cleaning their room, washing clothes. Suggest that for two days they do this task before someone asks them to do it. Talk about it. Did they get the task done before someone reminded them? Did it make them feel good? Did they offer to help others? How did they feel?

Take a poll of all family members. Ask which household jobs they like and dislike the most. To show your get-up-and-go and generosity of spirit, try one person's most disliked task for one day. Who knows — one person's dislike may be another's like.

ORGANIZED BUT FLEXIBLE, TOO

There can be a danger in being too organized. I have been in houses so neat, so clean, that I was afraid to put my shoes on the carpet. I have been in too neat, almost sterile classrooms.

We need room in our lives for dirt, for accidents, for changes, for silly mistakes, for missed appointments, and for children who get sick at the last minute.

When I complain to one friend, a very wise woman, about an unpleasantness in my day that I had not planned for or even thought about, she says, "Gosh, that's an interesting challenge." I try to remember those words, even as I gnash my teeth, and somehow it helps.

Now — In School	Later — On the Job
Alan has patience. He wants to keep at a task until it's done.	Mr. Johnson is a man who finishes what he starts. In our business, we call him "the closer."

Chapter 8.
MegaSkill Six: Perseverance

When you say these words, you know you are trying to teach perseverance:

"First you have to try, then you have to persist."

"If one way is blocked, try another. Go around, go beneath, go over."

"It's not enough to start — you have to finish."

"Even when you feel like quitting, don't."

"Keep at it; you'll get it."

There will always be others who are more talented than we are, who are better looking, who have more education. Even with these benefits, they still need perseverance in order to accomplish and to create.

That's what this chapter is about — how to help children get into the habit of following through and finishing.

Perseverance is what some say separates the men from the boys and the women from the girls. It's the steps that follow initial actions.

It almost always takes *more* than:

just sending out résumés to land a job.

just opening the door to have a successful business.

just winning one presidential primary to become president.

Perseverance is the *more* — it's the difference between those who try and those who succeed.

Some people may experience overnight success, but most of them, when the story is revealed, admit that it took a long time and a lot of practice to achieve that overnight success.

We can help our children become perseverers. But this task can be more of a challenge today. Children see everything happen so quickly, or so it seems. I had to wait hours for Jell-O to gel. Even ice cubes freeze faster today.

I'm generally fond of the faster pace of life today, glad for instant Jell-O and sometimes even for instant mashed potatoes.

But my own experience has shown that of necessity some goals take longer to accomplish, and that to get there we have to keep working at them. I'm not sure that our children have as many patience-building experiences as they need to prepare them for those long-range goals.

What is worrisome is that we seem to accept the fact that our children have short attention spans. TV shows made for children — even educational ones — are actually built on that premise. No segment is to be longer than a certain number of minutes or seconds. Instead, we should emphasize building our children's level and length of attention and their ability to concentrate over a period of time.

Words such as these encouraging comments do help, and children need them:

"I know you'll make it."

"You're doing a great job."

"You signed up for those lessons, and you need to see them through."

"It will get better. You'll get the hang of it."

It often, however, takes more. Beyond words, there are experiences that by their very nature teach perseverance. They can't be done in a rush because they demand a level of detail and a passage of time. I've chosen the following activities because even as they teach perseverance, they also get some very important jobs done around home.

ASSEMBLING LOOSE ENDS

Some of the hardest jobs, the ones that never seem to get done, the ones we avoid doing for as long as possible, involve keeping track of things and putting the pieces together. Here are some activities to make these seemingly impossible jobs a little bit easier to handle.

OUR VERY OWN PHOTO GALLERY any age

This activity reinforces family feelings and keeps track of precious moments that are too important to lose. You need a notebook or photo album, family photos, and pen and paper for writing captions beneath the pictures.

On a large tabletop, distribute pictures so that they can be talked about individually. Figure out a way to organize the photos. Most of the time, it's done in chronological order: What happened first? Second?

Attach the pictures to the album pages, along with captions (explanations) that children can write. *Example:* "I am in my first bathing suit." Young children can dictate these lines. Not only does it take time to do this activity, but the activity itself illustrates the passage of time.

You might want to make up a yearly collage of family photos and put it in a frame. One wall can be the family gallery. As the years go by, these memories become even more precious.

FAMILY DIRECTORY ages 4—9

This activity combines writing and alphabetizing practice for children in a task that cries out to be done — assembling important family telephone numbers. You need a store-bought or homemade telephone book for the phone list, and pencil or pen.

Find all the important telephone numbers that would be useful to have in one place. Include numbers of the school, the car repair garage, the pizza parlor, along with the usual emergency numbers. (See "Calling for Help" in Chapter 3.) Ask your child to think of names of family members. Remember aunts, uncles, cousins, and friends. Use scrap paper at first to list these names.

Names are easier to alphabetize when all names beginning with the same letter are listed together. Put the last name first. Help your child alphabetize this list. Double-check this sheet. Then enter the names and numbers in the family telephone book.

This home directory can be decorated with pictures children have made, or they can cut out from magazines pictures that show families doing things together. Put the directory in a handy place, and encourage family members to add new numbers as needed.

HOME HEALTH RECORDS any age

This activity pulls together in one place important family health records. In most homes, these are every which place, and it's hard to remember who got what shot when. This activity helps make sure the information gets collected in an ongoing way.

You need the family's health information records. These can include summaries of clinic visits, immunization dates, and physical, dental, and eye reports. You also need a notebook or folder for each family member.

Find your youngster's health and immunization records. If you have no records, call your doctor to have them sent to you. Together make a record of childhood diseases and immunizations for each child. Here's a sample chart.

Immunization Record: Johnny   *Date Received*

Diphtheria-Pertussis (Whooping Cough) _____

Tetanus (DPT) Vaccine _____

Oral Polio Vaccine _____

Measles Vaccine _____

Rubella Vaccine (German Measles) _____

Mumps Vaccine _____

DPT Boosters   (1) _____   (2) _____   (3) _____

Oral Polio Boosters   (1) _____   (2) _____   (3) _____

Talk with children about changes in their weight and height as they grow older. This helps them understand the pattern of growth. Talk about the various childhood diseases they've had, and how each disease made them look or feel. You might even have a snapshot of Sally when she had the mumps.

LEARNING TO WORK AND WAIT

Time is a big element in perseverance. Children can practice getting beyond the need for immediate gratification, showing that they are willing to work and wait for results.

Among activities that call upon children to wait are growing plants, watching their weight, learning a new skill, and preserving their health.

OUR SPECIAL GARDEN ages 4–9

Everyone enjoys watching seeds sprout and come up through the earth. When they don't, we can start again. The important point is that this activity helps children get practice in finishing a project they start. You need two or three packets of seeds, small pots or milk cartons cut down, a ruler, and, depending on the season and your household space, a sunny windowsill or outdoor garden.

Buy seeds or use seeds you have saved. Empty a few on the table beside each packet. Ask your child to look at the seeds and examine their size and color. Feel how hard they are. Talk about the differences. Ask children to fill each pot with about two inches of soil. Plant a few seeds in each. Place the pots on a sunny windowsill. Together read the directions on the seed packet. Talk about what you have to do to be sure the seeds grow.

Water the seeds as the directions say. Then, day by day, watch for the seeds to begin to sprout. Seeds grow slowly. It will take about ten days to see them.

Plants have a way of saying, "We love you and we care." Share one or more of these homegrown plants with a sick friend, a neighbor, or an older person in a nursing home.

KEEPING HEALTHY: AN EVERYDAY JOB

Getting and staying healthy is an ongoing job that takes daily perseverance. At the same time that so many Americans are on the health kick, others are ruining their health with addictions that cripple the body and the mind. The following activities help promote the real pleasure of good health.

Even kids know it's no fun to be sick.

GOOD AND GOOD FOR YOU ages 4–9

This activity helps young children get into the habit of eating healthy rather than junk foods. They learn that good food need not be boring. You need pencil, paper, a bathroom scale, and nutritious snack foods.

Talk about the reasons to eat right — good looks, more energy. But do more than talk. Actually try out some new, better, different snack foods at home.

Nutritious snack foods include carrot sticks and raisins, bananas rolled in chopped peanuts, celery stuffed with peanut butter, tomato or cucumber slices topped with cheese, raw vegetables with cheese dip, raisin and nut mixes.

Check family weights. Who's the heaviest? The lightest? Try recording weight changes in a week's time. This is good math practice, too.

Ask your child to think of good, interesting food combinations to try. Add these to the grocery list. Set aside part of a refrigerator shelf for children to use for these special snack foods. In this way children can make their own healthy snacks.

EXERCISE PLAN any age

Children spend a great deal of time sitting, and it's bad for their health. It takes some effort to plan and carry out a family exercise program. This activity can help. All you need are thinking minds. Willing bodies come later.

Together talk about what would be a realistic exercise plan for the family. Think about these questions: Do we prefer to exercise alone or with other people? Do we prefer to exercise indoors or outdoors? How much time can we spend on exercise daily?

List one or two exercises each person can do regularly. *Example:* Jog fifteen minutes daily in front of the TV set. Take the stairs at the office instead of the elevator.

Think of what you do that may hurt your health: Smoking? Drinking? Not eating fresh fruits and vegetables? Can you name one thing you will try to start doing? Make up a plan for a week-long, practical exercise routine. Figure out a reward if you stick to the plan. Then plan for the next week, and the next. Children will be inspired by your perseverance.

FALSE FRIENDS: ALCOHOL AND TOBACCO
ages 10–12

Youngsters sometimes give in to pressure from friends to smoke or drink or take drugs. These are dangerous to their health and prevent them from using their minds well and excelling in sports. Being informed and aware of the negative effects of alcohol and tobacco can make it easier to resist these temptations. This activity helps youngsters face up to the problems of drinking and smoking. You need newspapers, scissors, and good conversation.

Together talk about as many reasons as you can think of why people drink and smoke — boredom and curiosity, for instance. How can we avoid these traps? It's not easy. Getting involved in sports or club activities can help.

Be sure your children know what you think. Remember, they see what you do. It's harder to make a case for not smoking when parents are heavy smokers. What we ask our children to do is what we must be willing to do. That involves sacrifice. But it's worth it.

Often there are articles in the paper about rising sports stars who get hurt not on the sports field but with drugs in their homes. Over a period of a week, cut out newspaper articles telling about these athletes or about accidents or fires caused by drinking or smoking. Talk about these. Could they have been avoided? Does your family know of an actual case of someone who was hurt because of alcohol, drugs, or tobacco?

Look for ads that show glamorous people drinking and smoking. Is what they say true? What don't you and your youngsters agree with? Try to listen more than talk. Try to create a climate where your youngsters' views can be expressed and discussed.

GRIN AND BEAR IT

When children hang up their clothes or put away the dishes — and keep doing it night after night — it does not seem like schoolwork. But it is, in a most fundamental way.

Making a bed regularly or taking the dog for walks conscientiously has a lot to do with success in school. School achievement depends on a child's ability to see a job through to completion. Taught this early, children will continue to want to complete a job and will get pleasure from doing it.

PRACTICE MAKES ALMOST PERFECT any age

This activity helps children understand that learning something new and difficult takes practice and time. You need thinking minds.

Talk together about activities that you each do in free time: swimming, sewing, bike riding, reading novels. Try to remember when you learned to do these and how long it took to learn. Did you make mistakes? Do you still make mistakes?

Each of us has a lot to learn and a lot to teach. Choose something that you each do well. Think about teaching this to a friend or to a member of the family. Teach one thing at a time. If it is baseball, it might be how to hit the ball. If it is sewing, it might be how to thread a needle.

Increase the difficulty of what is taught each time. Try to offer helpful, not harmful, criticism. Helpful tells what to do *without* tearing down the learner. Avoid put-downs: the goal is to build up.

Make some realistic choices about what new skills to tackle and about how to teach them. A teenager, for example, might want to learn how to drive a car but may need a teacher or a car to practice on. Ask friends or family members to help, if necessary. This builds team spirit into the effort and passes along experience and skills from generation to generation.

WHAT'S SO EASY ABOUT INCOMPLETES?

Students can get into the habit of taking an incomplete and of not finishing what they start, but it's not necessarily the easier way out.

Some may think it's easier to do an incomplete job than a complete one. I am not sure. When I see students who have to think of all kinds of excuses for why their papers are late, I see them squirming and feeling uncomfortable; think of the effort they're putting into coming up with the excuses. I wonder if they wouldn't find it faster just to do the complete job.

I am not convinced that we always have to finish what we start, but we have to learn to finish many things. A lot depends on the situation: As an adult, if I don't like a book that I am reading for pleasure, I'll stop reading it. But as a student, I have to finish all the assigned readings, and as an employee, I have to finish tasks assigned to me.

When I was a child, I was given piano lessons. As the old saying should go, you can lead children to the piano, but you can't practice for them. Maybe I sensed that piano playing was an option in my family. What was not an option was doing homework and getting it done on time.

Every family needs to decide on its own options. But there should be some that children know they have to complete. For example, if they sign up on their own for tennis lessons, they should not be able to quit after the first lesson. Just as you can't expect penicillin to work after the first dose, your children need to understand that they need to give things a chance to work. And when they do this, they need and deserve praise!

IT TAKES TIME

Rome wasn't built in a day, but if you are a watcher of TV, as our children are, you might believe it was built in an hour, or in a miniseries, at most.

Perhaps more than other generations, our children need to learn that things don't happen all at once, and sometimes not even very quickly. Reaching a goal may take time and long days of effort and continuing work, but it's worth it! Practice may not *make* perfect, but it *makes*, it builds, it creates, it accomplishes, it completes. And in doing that, it makes us feel good about the job and about ourselves.

Chapter 9.
MegaSkill Seven: Caring

Are you worried about your child's ability to care about others, to show affection, to be thoughtful? If so, you'll hear yourself saying or thinking:

"Don't be so selfish."

"You've got to care about other people."

"Do you think you're the only one in this world?"

"Do you think you are the only one in this house?"

This chapter is about how to help your child practice caring. It's about consideration, about being interested in others, about listening to and learning from them.

I, I, I. Me, Me, Me. These aren't musical notes. They're the sounds children make — before they get tuned into You, You, You, and Us, Us, Us.

When I put "caring" on the list of MegaSkills, I had to face the question of how caring fits into the definition of MegaSkills. How does it, like the other MegaSkills, help children learn and want to keep on learning more?

Caring, I believe, belongs on the list not just because it's "nice," but because caring helps us learn from each other. It enables others to help us. People don't function well in isolation. Caring connects people. It gives us and our children a sense of community.

Knowing how to care is especially needed today. Children reared in smaller, separate households may need to learn caring more than those who come from larger families and who know from birth that they aren't the only ones around.

Growing children are naturally wrapped up in themselves and in their needs. But parents and teachers can teach caring in ways that are meaningful, even to the young.

A WORLD OF CARING

Most of us live, work, and care in the concentric circles of family, friends, school or job, and community. These are like circles made by a stone tossed into a pool, causing new, ever-widening patterns. The center is the family, and it's in the family that children learn caring skills for the other circles in which we live.

In this chapter are personal caring activities within the family and with friends, and broader caring activities that extend beyond the home to the wider community. These activities emphasize "talk" — sharing ideas and feelings, using small moments to connect and communicate.

FAMILY NOTES ages 4–6

Tell your child that each day for three days, you will send each other notes. You need pen or pencil and note paper.

Each note will be a special message that will say something nice. The "something nice" will be something true that one of you has noticed about the other. It might be, "You have a nice smile" or "Your dinner last night was very good" or "I like the way you cooked the chicken." Let children who do not yet write dictate their messages to you. Children enjoy figuring out nice things to say. Not nice things might come to mind first. After a few laughs, the kids settle down.

Decide on a place to exchange daily notes. You can put them on the refrigerator, stick them in lunch bags, or pass them out at the dinner table.

As a special touch, ask a surprise "mystery guest" to send your child a note. It might be a message from a best friend, from grandparents, or from a neighbor.

HOW DOES IT FEEL? ages 4–8

This activity helps children get a sense of how other people feel — an essential for work in school or out. All you need are thinking minds. This is a "talk about" activity.

Start by helping young children describe someone else's appearance. Ask your child to describe how a certain person — a friend or a teacher — looks. Use drawings. Where adjectives fail, a picture usually helps. Even when children are not artistic, they are generally more confident at first with drawings than with writing.

Ask "how do they feel" questions. *Examples:* "Jane has just won a race. How does she feel?" "Bill has just fallen down. How does he feel?" "What might each of these friends do, based on how they feel?"

Tell children to try to visualize themselves in your place. How do parents feel when mud is tracked into the house? How do parents feel when they have to nag children about homework or chores?

Trade places. Try to put yourself in your child's shoes on the first day of school or when the big test comes back or when kids are picked or not picked for a team.

Children will believe you really do understand when you share some "emotional" memories of your own — not just what happened on your first day at school, but what you felt.

GREETINGS FOR FRIENDS AND NEIGHBORS
ages 4—8

This activity has children making greeting cards. It gives children a chance to be creative, even if they don't think they're artistic. It saves money and lets friends know how much you care. You need paper, pencil, scissors, markers, old greeting cards, and magazines.

For ideas, you and your child might take a few minutes to look through the greeting card section in a drugstore or stationery store. Decide who needs a greeting card. Does someone need cheering up? Is a friend having a birthday?

Together pick someone to receive a homemade greeting card. Fold the paper so that there will be a front, back, and inside for writing a message. Cut out a picture from a magazine or draw a picture for the front of the card. Ask your child to think of and write a message. For ideas, read old greeting cards and look in poetry books. Then address, mail, or hand-deliver the card.

Some of the people who would most appreciate those greetings may live nearby. Do you know a senior citizen who is living alone? Do you have new neighbors who have just moved in?

Not only will the greeting be welcome, but it is a good way for your child to get to know the neighbors and for the neighbors to get to know and care about your child. (See "Our Block" in this chapter.)

HOW CAN I HELP? ages 9—12

Right near where each of us lives is someone who can use the help your child can provide. It doesn't have to be a big kind of help.

Do you have an elderly neighbor or relative living nearby? Suggest that your child perform an essential task for this person on a regular basis, once or twice a week. Depending on your child's age, it could include some marketing, going to the post office, answering mail, or reading the paper aloud.

Of course, it helps to know and trust the person your child is helping. Start by asking your friends for names of people they know and can vouch for.

ALL IN THE FAMILY ages 9–12

To know how to behave, it helps to know how we affect others, especially family members. This activity helps youngsters get "feedback" from the family about their behavior. You need thinking minds. This is a "talk about" activity.

Let family members "rate" each other. The object is to think positively and to avoid put-downs. What you hope to build is more of an "I care about how you feel" atmosphere at home. This can be done anywhere — at the dining table or in the car. Ask:

"How well do I listen?"

"How well do I help around the house?"

"Do I ever make you feel sad? How?"

"Do I make you feel happy? How?"

Think of two things that make each of you happy and two things that make you sad. Think of at least one thing you can do easily that would make your family happy.

Talk about these and about how easy or how hard it is to make other people happy. Small things can go a long way. A kiss, a cookie, a flower, an encouraging word, can give a big, quick lift. Children need to know this so that they can form the habit of making other people feel good.

ABOUT OURSELVES any age

This activity helps children learn more about others and share more about themselves. This is a personal activity, so you may want to save it until you have warmed up with a few of the other, more impersonal activities. You need pencil and paper.

Finish these sentences separately and compare answers.

I am happy when _____ .

I am afraid of _____ .

I am sad when _____ .

It's funny when _____ .

My favorite things include _____ .

When I am alone, I _____ .

I really care about _____ .

Talk about your responses. Share a few examples of happy and sad times. There may be some tears and more than a few laughs. It can be a very special moment.

OUR BLOCK ages 4–6

Young children especially need to know their neighborhood and their neighbors. This is important for their physical safety as well as for emotional reassurance. Help children know who lives where by drawing a neighborhood map together. You need paper, scissors, markers, ruler.

In the middle of the paper, draw your own home. That is the center of your child's world. Mark it with an *X*. Then list all the names of the people who live next door on either side. If you don't know them, make a note to find out their names and introduce yourselves.

Then extend the map to include the entire block, the route your child takes to and from school, and the route to and from the grocery store.

Draw with a free hand. Don't worry about exact distances between places. Fill in street names and telephone numbers for places and neighbors. Use a telephone book for information and a community map if one is available.

Post this map for everyone in the family to see. If you and your child have not yet taken a walk around your neighborhood, make a date to take this walk very soon.

FROM ONE TO ANOTHER any age

This activity helps youngsters appreciate differences among people. You need thinking minds for this "talk about" activity.

Think of ways in which people make themselves different. Examples include the way they dress, the way they talk, the way they do their hair, the way they have fun.

Think of ways people make themselves similar. Examples might be the way they dress, the way they talk, the way they do their hair, the way they have fun. (Notice that they are the same.)

Can each of you think of someone who has difficulty getting along with people? Could there be reasons for this that no one knows about? Is there anything you might do to help this person?

Talk about handicaps and about people who have them. Help children build a sense of empathy, of understanding what it's like.

Together read aloud some stories about the bravery of the handicapped. Better yet, make sure your child has some firsthand experience with a handicapped person at school or among your friends, relatives, or neighbors.

Making fun of differences is known as childish, but it may be childish because no one has bothered to talk with children first.

PEOPLE SCAVENGER HUNT any age

Together go on a people scavenger hunt. You need thinking minds.

Do you know anyone who speaks another language? Has been in a play? Has a relative who is more than ninety years old?

Think about someone you saw recently who is different. *Examples:* A street person carrying old bundles, a person in a wheelchair, a blind person. Try to imagine what it feels like to be that person. Talk about the problems these people face and how they cope with them.

Seek out people from other countries to talk to. Many of our own communities have become miniature United Nations. Help children take advantage of this opportunity by talking to neighbors who may be immigrants. When you hear a foreign accent, take time to stop and talk. Ask what we need to know about their native country, and share a tip or two about what they need to know about the U.S.

WHO CAN HELP ME? any age

There is always something that other people can help us with. But first they have to know we need help. For this activity you need paper and pencil.

Make two columns on the paper. At the top of the left column, write: HELP NEEDED FOR. At the top of the right column, write: WHO CAN HELP? Post the paper. Those who can help will put down their names.

Examples: Mom's clock might be broken, and a friend who comes to visit and who knows how to fix clocks offers to help. Sally may need someone to help her check the spelling on a term paper, and her older brother offers to help.

The idea is to get children in the habit of using skills to help one another. This puts some organization into the give and take needed to manage a household.

HEROES AMONG US any age

This activity encourages kindness and provides reading practice, too. You need newspapers, pen or pencil, and scissors.

Cut out newspaper articles about heroic acts by ordinary individuals. *Examples:* Someone rescues a person from a fire; a neighbor stops a robbery; a youngster saves a child from being hit by a car.

Think about and remember a time when you were particularly helpful to someone. Share your memories with each other. Talk together about good deeds that have been done by other family members. Don't forget grandparents and great-grandparents.

Think together about one or two caring, unselfish people, famous or not, whom you admire. What do you like about them? Are there ways to become more like them? What have they accomplished? Share these thoughts and think about realistic efforts that each of you can make to be more like these heroes.

THE GIFT OF TIME any age

Gift giving provides an opportunity to think about what would make someone else happy.

Talk about gifts that people love to receive but that don't cost much money, if any. Think about making gifts at home. What materials are needed to bake cookies, to sew a potholder, to construct a model plane?

Think about the people you'd like to give to and what would

suit each person. Pool ideas and make some choices. Try to think of gifts that aren't "things." You might share a special skill in order to help someone.

For children, it might be: "I will play ball with my younger brother for one hour." "I will make my sister's bed for three days." "I'll weed the garden for Mom for a week." "I will polish the car."

For adults, it might be: "I will read to you for at least fifteen minutes every night before bed for the next week." "I will take a walk with you this weekend."

Some of the best things between parent and child are still free! And one of the best and most surprising things between brothers and sisters is the caring they can show toward each other.

When Brian was nine, illness forced him to be bed-ridden for six months. Every day, his sister, Eve, age seven, would come bouncing in from school, ready for some outdoor play. But first she would go in to see Brian and ask, "Want to have my day?"

Then she would launch into funny vignettes about classmates and teachers and special events. They would laugh a lot. It was a good time for both of them — the giver and the receiver.

Where had this little girl learned this secret for sharing her day? It was what she saw at home. Both of her parents worked. When they got home, they each told a story from their day, usually a funny one. She listened and she learned.

CARING AND LISTENING

Children truly need people who care about them. After my mother died, my father had to be both father and mother. It was very hard for him, not only because he commuted to work three hours every day, but mostly because, until my mother's death, he had not been involved in taking care of his children.

Friends told my father about Millie, an unmarried, middle-aged woman who had just come from England to work in the U.S. and who needed a place to live. Millie wanted a family. She probably wanted to get married and have her own children, but what she got was me. We had an extra bedroom in our house (my brother had gone off to college); she moved in and started keeping an eye on me. Maybe the real purpose was to get my father to marry her.

That didn't happen, but what did happen was that Millie cared for me at a time when I felt very uncared for.

Millie did not try to function as my mother, but she showed me in many ways that she cared. She worked in a dress store that had discounts for employees and their families. I was often there, trying on dresses, and I bought some with the discount she got for me. We went out for dinner and the movies together when my father worked late. She needed my companionship, and I needed hers.

Millie was lonely for England and her sister's family. I can still see the mirror of the dresser in her bedroom. Tucked in the edges around the glass were pictures of her family and friends. They stared out at her every time she stared in. When I went away to college, she put my picture up there, too.

Now, decades later, Millie is gone. And I remember her presence more than anything she did for me. She was there when I was alone, and she listened. When it comes to caring, that's the bottom line.

Now — In School	Later — On the Job
Jim stands up for himself, yet he works well with the group. He doesn't always have to get his own way.	Mr. Samson is a loyal member of the company team, working with and on behalf of the other members of the firm.

Chapter 10.
MegaSkill Eight: Teamwork

We know team players when we work with them:

They don't always have to get the credit.

They have spirit, and they share it with others.

They laugh with others, not at them.

They pitch in and make sacrifices.

They are helpful, not helpless.

This chapter is about building a child's ability to work with others, as part of a team, cooperating to achieve a common purpose.

Teamwork is essential not just on a sports field. It's essential in business and in a family.

The activities in this chapter build children's abilities to cooperate and to be part of a team.

It's not easy. An uneasy balance exists between individualism and group work in this country, especially in our schools. Students are expected to perform and to be graded as individuals, competing rather than cooperating with each other.

It's different outside the classroom walls. On the football field, not even the best player can win the game alone, and an orchestra needs a stage full of cooperating players. Job evaluations make it clear that to receive good "grades," employees are expected to work together, collaborating to get the job done.

Teachers increasingly emphasize the need for teamwork, but the school as an institution is basically just not a hospitable place for this. That's why it is so important for parents to pay special attention to teamwork.

WORKING TOGETHER

There are few cows in the backyard for our children to milk. While there are still chores for kids to do, with dishwashers and washing machines, there are fewer of them. So increasingly, the only way children can succeed and feel needed is to bring home top grades from school. All children will not be able to receive those good grades. They need other ways to show that they can accomplish. Activities at home, even chores, can help. They provide a sense of getting things done, and they help children feel more needed, more important in the life of the family, even when they gripe.

Together and Alone

There are at least two kinds of teaming — one, where we are next to or near each other, doing the same job together, as in a bucket brigade to put out a fire, and another, where each of us does a different job as part of a larger team effort, such as cleaning the house.

In looking back, I don't think I did enough of the bucket-brigade kind of teaming. In our house, we usually divided the labor. There I was in the kitchen, scrubbing, while my kids were down the hall, vacuuming. They didn't actually see me doing my job. And I didn't see them.

There is something special about being in the same place, doing a job together. Before sending children off to do a job on their own, I'd start by having them do jobs right with you, next to you. This isn't just to keep an eye on them; it's to build the spirit and the sense of teaming, to see ourselves accomplishing a task together.

My friend Ruth remembers bringing her children up on the roof with her and her husband, and together they tackled the job of repairing roof shingles. The children passed the nails; they held the ladder; they felt part of the team.

This same spirit prevails when families bake cookies together or read aloud to each other or change a tire together or shovel snow together or rake leaves together.

Most of the time, most people like to be with other people. We get strength from each other. We don't feel so alone. But today more than ever, it is not always possible to be together. To accomplish a large task as a team, we divide the labor, and each of us goes off to do part of the task. This is the way we make dinner, run a house, or manage a business.

My own children disliked housework chores but found them more agreeable when we were all in the same room together, one doing the dusting, another doing the polishing or the sweeping.

Outdoors, they loved to rake leaves, but not alone. They liked it when we did it together, one holding the bag, another putting in the leaves. It's the being together that they really liked.

My children do not have pleasant memories of the Saturday mornings when I insisted that they check the chore chart before going out to play. This was especially hard when the other kids were waiting for them outside, without having done their chores at home. I will be forever grateful to the "really mean mother" on the next block who didn't let her children go out to play until they had cleaned their rooms and taken care of the chores for the rest of the house.

My own mother was a compulsive cleaner, plumping up the cushions on the sofa, for example, the minute someone got up from sitting there, and not leaving the house for a family outing until the kitchen floor had been cleaned, even if it was clean to start with. So I was reluctant to be too clean. Maybe that's why I did not insist that my children's bedrooms look the way I liked. I tried to be content with a shut door so that I did not have to see their version of order, which I called mess. Even so, there were times when my children felt I was too demanding, and I was.

I think we all would have been better off with more do-it-together activities, especially at first, and a more democratic approach to handling tasks. The activities that follow do divide the labor, but they still build the important feeling of teamwork.

WHEN THEY SAY, "LET ME!" ... LET THEM

Many young children plead to do chores around the house long before their parents ask them to. Young children will beg to fix dinner or wash the car. Parents often turn down these offers because letting your children help usually means more work — at first.

It's true. It does take more time and patience to teach children how to work, to show them a job step by step, to encourage them, and then to step back and let them take over. It's easier to do the work for them.

But as with much of parenting, efforts when children are young are an investment in the future.

REAL WORK, NOT MAKE-WORK ages 4—6

Talk with your children about jobs that need doing at home. Ask what they think they can do. It can be surprising how willing and eager they are to tackle jobs ... when they're still young and not expected to enjoy working.

Set attainable goals with your child. Start with easy tasks and work up to harder ones. *Example:* A four-year-old can bring in the paper every day and wipe the kitchen table.

Turn jobs into games. Set the same task for you and your child. Race each other to see who wipes the table or retrieves the newspaper faster. Chances are, your child will win, on the up and up.

Remember, show children how to do the work — but do *not* redo their work. *Example:* The first time a child uses a vacuum, show how to do it and what to pick up. One mother turned a six-year-old loose without instructions, and within thirty seconds a new baby bib was in the sweeper. It was a lesson for both of them.

DIVIDE AND CONQUER ages 7–9

One of the best ways to organize a household task is to divide it into parts. Teach children to accept and carry out household responsibilities as a member of the "family team." You need paper and pencil.

Pick a job that has several parts. A good example is preparing a meal. What do you do first? What do you do second? Your list might look like this:

Plan the meal.

Shop for groceries.

Prepare the food.

Set the table.

Clean up afterward.

Ask everyone to choose from the list one job to do. Some coordination is needed, just as if the family were a football team driving to the goal line. A team spirit is built when each person does part of the bigger job. And don't forget to pass around a heaping helping of praise!

ORGANIZING HOUSEHOLD CHORES ages 10–12

Here's a writing activity that helps family members remind each other in a positive way about jobs that need doing at home. You need paper and pencil.

Together make a list of all the jobs that need to be done around the house. You might separate them into weekly jobs and daily jobs.

Weekly Jobs: Doing laundry, vacuuming, grocery shopping, mowing the lawn.

Daily Jobs: Cooking dinner, making beds, taking out garbage, feeding pets.

Decide together when jobs will be done and who will do them. Write down names next to the jobs. Family members can switch with each other later. Try to avoid labeling work as "girl's" or "boy's."

Talk about a job a youngster usually does around the house, such as setting and clearing the table, and a job an adult usually does, such as washing clothes. If possible, trade places and do each other's jobs at least once. Did you do these jobs differently or the same way?

LET ME HELP YOU!

When children say to a brother or sister, "Let me help you," it's music to a parent's ear. But it's a tune some of us don't hear very often.

To spur these generous outbursts, think of ways to do activities together.

Use stories to make a point about helping one another. Among the classics for young children is "Cinderella." Those mean stepsisters who never helped got their comeuppance, and Cinderella, the great helper, got the prince. Real life isn't a fairy tale. But we know that teamwork is highly rewarded in sports and business. Point to the examples reported in the media. For older children, tell the story or show the film *It's a Wonderful Life.* In this classic, Jimmy Stewart sacrifices for his family, stays home from college, and manages to keep open a small bank that helps poor people get homes. With the help of an angel named Clarence, he learns that he has indeed lived a wonderful life.

TALKING AND THINKING TOGETHER

In teamwork, not only do you have to do things together, but you have to be able to think as a team.

The goal is to help children express their thinking so that the family as a team has a better understanding of the "wave lengths" everybody is on. In this way, we generate respect for everyone's ideas.

WHAT DO WE THINK? ages 7–9

Help children practice finding out what others think. Take a poll at home about household products. You need pencil and paper.

Ask your child to take a poll on a product the family is using, such as toothpaste or soap suds. Should we buy more of this? If yes, why? If no, why not? What could the family buy instead of this product?

To do this, your child must be a good listener. When everyone has been polled, ask your child what he or she has learned. Does the family like these products? What changes are asked for? Talk about the poll results at the dinner table.

As a reward, on the next shopping trip you might buy some of the new products the family suggested. In this way your family sees its wishes come true.

WHAT ARE WE WATCHING? ages 8–12

This activity helps youngsters ask questions and get answers about a subject on which everyone in the family has an opinion — TV. By hearing how others use TV, children develop their own judgment about whether a show is worth watching. You need paper and pencil.

Decide with your youngsters on two or three adults to interview about their TV watching. (These might be a parent, a neighbor, an aunt.)

Together think of three questions to ask. Your youngster should write them down and leave space for the answers. *Examples:* "Do you watch TV each day?" "For how long?" "Do you have favorite shows?" "To improve TV, what would you change?"

Talk about the answers your youngster receives. Suggest forming a team effort to keep each other "on the road" to more activity and less TV watching.

WHAT'S YOUR OPINION? ages 10–12

Yes, we can. No, we can't.

Children often disagree with their parents about rules, seeing only their own points of view.

This activity makes it easier for children to see both sides of an argument. It teaches them to think as a team member. All you need are thinking minds.

Choose one rule that causes family arguments. *Examples:* When to do homework? How late to stay up on school nights? What TV shows to watch?

Ask your child's opinion of the rule. If it's about bedtime, that opinion might be, "Having a bedtime is a bad rule. Kids should go to bed whenever they want." Ask your child to give at least two reasons for this opinion. These might include, "I miss the best TV shows when I go to bed early." Listen carefully.

Now ask your child to give two arguments for the other side. One might be, "Kids need sleep to keep awake in school."

Coming up with pro and con arguments is an excellent way to help children learn to consider alternatives before making a decision. While your child is working on these pro and con arguments, you do the same. Explain your points of view. Talk over your differing opinions. Does everyone have good points? Do you need to change any rules? Actually, children have been known to be very reasonable team players when they get involved in helping to make family rules.

MONEY — DIVIDING AND SHARING

A handy tool in teaching teamwork is money. It can prompt families to pull together to save it, figure out how to divide it, and get together to spend it. Here are three activities that illustrate this.

DOWN THE DRAIN AND OUT THE WINDOW any age

This activity helps children team together to save family money on utility bills. Children may be wasting electricity and water without even knowing that they cost money. For this activity you need some utility bills.

Take a house electricity tour. Check whether lights, radios, or televisions have been left on. Talk with your children about ways to save on utility bills, such as turning off the air conditioner when nobody is home or lowering the heat at night when people are sleeping.

Take a house water tour. Think of all the ways you use water — for dishes, for bathing, for cooking. Then talk about ways you can conserve water.

Look at the bills in the next few months to see the results. Use a set of bills you and your youngster can follow.

WHAT'S MY SHARE? ages 10–12

This activity gives children practice in learning about and paying their fair share of a bill. It builds a child's sense of individual responsibility within the family's larger financial effort. You need newspaper, paper, and pencil.

Think of at least one thing the family wants or needs. Find an ad for it in the newspaper. Pretend that everyone will share the cost of this item equally. *Example:* The family decides to buy a new record. Perhaps it costs eight dollars. If everyone in the family shares the cost, how much will each have to pay?

Think about your own daily living costs. Lunch and bus fare are good examples. Calculate these for a one-week period. Are there ways you can save on these costs?

You might think even bigger. How about a pretend vacation? Figure out where to go and how much the holiday will cost. Look in the newspaper travel section. Pick a spot. Read the ads and see if you can get an idea of how to plan a family vacation you can afford.

SHOPPING AROUND ages 7–12

This activity helps children learn how to compare prices in order to shop carefully for an item they want. You need newspaper ads for new products, classified ads for used items, and pencil or crayon.

Ask children to select an item to "buy" from a newspaper ad and from a classified ad. This might be a bicycle or a television set. Together mark the ads that sound like the best buys. Talk about the items and urge the "consumers" to discuss the ads with other members of the family. Which do they consider the best buys?

Compare classified prices on really large items, such as houses or cars. This helps children begin to think about big sums of money. Go to an auction that is advertised. Visit some garage sales listed in the paper. These are fun, and the prices provide math practice. You don't even have to buy anything!

LEARNING ABOUT TEAMWORK

Good examples are good teachers. The news media provide us with examples, many bad, but some good. Use the good ones to show children how people working together can make a real difference.

And look to the living examples you have near you, perhaps right next door. These are neighbors, friends, relatives, who, if prompted, have a great deal to share and teach your children about how they work with others in the community and on the job.

PEOPLE HELPING EACH OTHER ages 8–12

You need current newspapers, a television, pencil, and paper.

Together find at least two articles that tell of events affecting families in a foreign country. *Example:* A drought in Africa leads to food shortages.

Talk about these events. Could they happen here? Together look in the paper or think about a situation that affects the area in which you live. *Example:* A neighborhood school closes. Talk about this. What, if anything, can you do about it?

Ask your youngster to pick a news event to follow for several days. Try to find a topic that involves people helping each other. Follow it in the paper. Listen to the radio. Watch the news. Discuss it together.

Take action: Help your child write a letter to the editor about something affecting families in the area. *Example:* Suggest an after-school center for kids. Explain that this is one of the ways to make your opinions known and to change other people's views.

HOW HAVE OTHERS HELPED YOU? ages 10—12

Many of us owe a lot to other people. These are our "mentors," people who worked with us, helped us along. Often these are our parents, but not always. A mentor might be a friend, a co-worker, or an older person who became interested in us. This is a "talk about" activity, designed to help children learn about the people who have guided them in the best sense of teamwork.

Invite a few friends in and ask them to tell your children about the big influences in their lives. Trade places and share your experiences with their children. Sometimes we listen better when the story is being told by someone we don't know as well as we know our own family.

And your children may even pick up some new mentors.

WHERE TEAMWORK IS TAUGHT TODAY

Among the most vivid examples of family teamwork seen today are the small businesses run by families of newly arrived immigrants. Everyone appears to be working together. Whether that can be or will be continued as these families become "Americanized" is unknown. To someone like me, who was raised in the Depression, when we did spend time working together in the store — not always harmoniously — watching such closeness brings back bittersweet memories. This teamwork may look better than it actually is. And the current situation for most of us, where the lack of teamwork is lamented at home and at school, may look worse than it really is.

Among the most visible and positive signs of communities caring about children — and among the most successful programs — are clubs or groups designed specifically to help youngsters grow up. I'm talking about the Four-H Clubs, the Boys Clubs, the Scouts, the Big Sisters and Brothers, the athletic leagues, and the church groups. These groups exist in almost every community, small and large. The MegaSkill they teach remarkably well is teamwork.

It may be a problem for employed parents to find the time to participate with children in these groups. But just as banks are now open at different hours and doctors now accommodate working parents' schedules, it is likely that these groups can also work out ways for busy parents to ensure that children can come to the meetings and to be involved themselves. My advice is not to assume that it can't be done.

When your children want to join, it's a good sign. You may need to ask around to find out about these groups and where and when they meet. First check with your school, then with a nearby recreation center. The local United Way or Community Chest office is another good source for information about these groups.

HUMOR HELPS

Working together with others, whether in small or big organizations, can be a headache.

We all have moments, often at meetings, when we want to stand up and shout, "I quit!" or "All of you are fired!"

That's what I do in my daydreams and my nightmares. At difficult meetings I have found another way. It seems to help — because it's humorous.

In the meeting room at my office, I keep a very large aspirin. It's about six inches across, and I found it one day at a specialty store in New York. When the meeting is going nowhere and everyone seems to be getting a headache, I thrust that aspirin onto the table, and we all get a big laugh. It helps.

I believe that having a sense of humor about ourselves is an essential life skill, even if I haven't classified it as a MegaSkill. There's a big difference between laughing at ourselves and laughing at others. Laughing at ourselves without tearing ourselves down is what I think of as a sanity keeper. It's a connector, a bond to other people and their experiences.

If we can gain some perspective in the middle of an argument at home or on the job, we're bound to see something funny in the scene that will give everyone a good laugh. It might come right then or a day or a week later, but it's delicious at any time.

THE IMPORTANCE OF TEAMWORK

When I asked a top-management public relations executive what his firm looks for most in new employees and in advancing others, without hesitation he said, "People who can work with other people. We need people we can count on, people who are loyal, who are team players."

Jobs today depend more than ever on people-to-people skills — not just in public relations, but throughout the economy. Projections indicate that the majority of job seekers will find this to be increasingly true.

Beyond the practice of the activities in this section, the daily news is filled with articles that can supply ongoing discussions about teamwork. Teamwork pervades all sections of the news, from the sports pages to the business pages. Everyone, it seems, is working as a member of a team, including scientists. Rarely can one person perform a major task completely alone. Writing a book might be an exception, but publishing it requires people working together. The challenge is to ensure that every member of the team has the opportunity to contribute.

The search is for team players, not as yes people but as strong contributors helping one another to be stronger.

Now — In School	Later — On the Job
Joan knows how to divide her time so her assignments get done, and she still has time left to read over her papers before handing them in.	Dr. Thornton has the ability to keep things in proportion. Even when the pressure is on, she doesn't get rattled. She keeps on doing her work carefully.

Chapter 11.
MegaSkill Nine: Common Sense

Do your kids have common sense? If they don't, you are not alone. We all want our children to:

- Know about cause and effect, including understanding that what they say will have certain effects on others.
- Show balance and judgment about handling the irreplaceable resource of time and the scarce resource of money.

This chapter provides practice activities to help children develop this kind of common sense. Gaining common sense is an evolving, long-range process. When parents ask in exasperation, "Where in heaven's name is your common sense?" the truest answer a child can give is, "It's coming."

Common sense is not so common. A reason children may not be using common sense is that it is not a sense we are born with. It is built through experience and practice.

I pride myself on my common sense today, but I didn't always have it.

When my brother, age eleven, invented a chair that would go to the top of the tree next to our house, he asked me, age seven, if I wanted to ride in it. I was delighted. The next thing I knew I was rising into space. The chair was attached to ropes that my brother and his friend Ivan had thrown around one of the tallest tree limbs. They were experimenting to see if they could pull on the ropes to carry me and the chair to the top.

It worked. The chair and I reached that limb. But I looked around from my perch in the sky and I began screaming, "Let me down! Let me down!" Hearing my pitiful pleas, they let go of the ropes. We all learned about gravity very forcefully and very quickly, especially me. Had I not landed on the grass, I would have been in pieces. I think my fear of heights began that day. I ran crying into the house to complain about my mean brother, and my mother asked, "And where was *your* common sense?" I didn't know, but I think at that moment it was more in my hurting bottom than in my head.

Can we teach common sense, or at least a few of the basics, and avoid our children having to learn it all through bitter experience and trial and error? I believe we can.

Unlike a subject such as reading or math, common sense has no curriculum. The best we can do is to find areas in which common sense is needed and then figure out ways to give children practice acquiring it. That's what I've done in this chapter, with activities in very different areas for which there is wide agreement that common sense is needed. Inch by inch, we coach children to common sense.

GATHERING INFORMATION

When you have common sense, you try to see more than one point of view. When you have common sense, you have perspective.

To get this, children need to know how to acquire information, and not just from textbooks. Information helps kids make decisions and avoid hasty conclusions, as enticing as they might be.

In this section are activities for gathering information not only from things around us but also from and about people.

The activities may look like fun. Actually, they are, but they're more. They help reinforce children's innate information-acquiring abilities.

THE CAREFUL EYE ages 4–9

Look around the room and ask children to name everything they see. This activity builds observation skills. At first the list may be short, but encourage children to name everything from floor to ceiling.

Put several objects on a table. Ask youngsters to look hard and then close their eyes. Remove one or two of the objects. Let children name the things you took away. Turn this game around and ask your children to play it on you.

Ask children to observe everything on their way home from school to see how many things they never noticed before. *Examples:* a broken tree limb or a stop sign.

Noticing is important. One of the fathers in our program, now a single parent, says of himself, "I noticed everything at work and nothing at all in my relationship at home." Noticing in relationships is discussed later in this chapter (see "People Common Sense").

MEMORY STRETCHING ages 4–9

To encourage information gathering, try questions like these:

Does your back door swing in or out?

Do you put your right or left sock on first?

Who's the slowest eater in your house?

What did you have for breakfast? For dinner last night? Go back meal after meal to see how far you can remember.

Ask your children to make up questions for you to try to answer. You'll probably have more trouble answering these questions than do your children. It's an exercise in humility, even for high-powered executives.

GUESSING ages 4–9

Everybody has to be able to guess. The fancy word for it is "hypothesize." The better guesses are ones based on as much information as you can pull together beforehand. For this activity you need a yardstick and a scale.

Ask "guessing" questions and let children ask them of you. How wide is this room? How long is the driveway? Get out the yardstick and check these guesses.

Talk about weight in general terms. Then guess how much different things weigh. A typewriter? A book? Mother? Brother? Put them on the scale and check.

These activities help children make judgments based on what they know to be facts or guesses.

CHECKING ages 7–12

Checking is common-sense practice, and it can be taught in a straightforward way with a series of questions.

Have we checked to see, for example, that:

There's gas in the car before starting out on a trip?

There are no cracks in the eggs that we buy at the supermarket?

The seams are tightly sewn in clothes we're planning to buy?

There are no cars coming before we start across the street — even if the light is green?

We can get children in the habit of doing these checks. With all the checking in the world, there will still be plenty of surprises, but some of the everyday, unpleasant ones can be avoided this way.

To keep kids on their toes, try this. Show youngsters the good side of a wormy apple. Ask, "Is this a good apple? Can you eat all of it?" Then turn the apple around. It shows children they have to know both sides of the question. It's a trick with a valuable lesson.

USING CLUES ages 4—8

Help children use clues. This is an easy activity that gets children used to seeing small but important details. This ability is important in reading, mathematics, and science, and it's basic common sense. Use any day, any house.

Begin by saying, "I'm thinking of something — an object — that is in this very room." Then give hints, one at a time. Tell about the object's size, color, or use. *Example:* If you are thinking of a saucer, you could say, "It's the size of a big pancake," "It's blue and white," and "It is used under a cup." After each clue, let your child try to guess the object. Continue giving clues until your child guesses it. If necessary, make the clues more obvious. Switch places. Let your child give you clues. Explain that the purpose is not to fool but to give just enough information so that the object can be named.

Try describing an object in another room. Ask children to guess what it is. Have them go to that room to check the accuracy of your clues. For example, was your description of the sofa's color accurate? For variety, send your children into the room to draw the object that's been described. Try trading places for these activities, too.

ASKING QUESTIONS ages 9—12

This activity gives youngsters practice and confidence in getting information from people around them every day. This is a "talk about" activity.

Ask parents, relatives, and neighbors about their jobs. How did they choose them? Do they enjoy what they do?

Talk about how jobs have changed over the years. What jobs did your grandparents and parents hold? Where did they live? Is it really all that different today?

"Using Clues" and "Asking Questions" illustrate differences in children's abilities to gather and understand information as they grow older. The older youngster's activity asks that the child have a sustained information-seeking conversation with another person, perhaps even leading the conversation and keeping it going with questions. When youngsters can do this, they show growing maturity.

PEOPLE COMMON SENSE

There is such a thing as people common sense. It involves concern for others, but it also means seeing things from other points of view, putting ourselves as best we can in other people's shoes.

To help children do this, here are scenes of real people having a choice of what to say to one another. Common sense dictates that one of the three choices for each scene is the preferred response. It may jump right out at both you and your child.

What Should We Say?

Read these scenes aloud with your children. Before reading the bank of possible answers, think of what you might answer. Ask for your children's answers and the reasons why they picked them. If the answers seem obvious, so much the better. The curious thing is that while we "know" the right responses, we often have trouble using them. Getting into the habit helps.

1. The Report Card. Anne had always received top grades — all A's and B's on her elementary school report card. For her first report card in seventh grade, she brought home three C's. Her father looked at the card and felt these words rising in his throat: "How could you get these C's?" Instead, what do you think he said, and why did he say it?

   a. "When are you going to settle down?"

   b. "Your sister never even got one C."

   c. "Being in a new school is hard. Soon you will get to know your teachers and the other students, and it will get easier."

2. The Kitchen Floor. Tom, age eight, came in to get a cold drink from the refrigerator. The floor was still a bit wet from the scrubbing Mom had given it that morning. With the bottle of juice in his hand, Tom slipped, and sticky liquid went flying everywhere. Mom walked into the once-gleaming kitchen, now a mess again. She felt like screaming. Instead, what do you think she said, and why?

    a. "Why are you so clumsy?"

    b. "OK, accidents will happen. I'll help you clean up this place."

    c. "You're always doing things like this."

3. The Boy Next Door. Leah was only nine, but she really liked Michael, the boy across the street. The boy's family had been away for a year in South America. In the month before their return, Leah had crossed off each day on the calendar. She told that to her friend Margo. Finally the big day arrived. There they were. Leah and Michael said hello shyly. Margo was there, too, and what do you think she said?

    a. Nothing.

    b. "Boy, did Leah miss you!"

    c. "Leah's been counting the days."

4. The Rained-Out Birthday Party. Amy had been looking forward to her tenth-birthday picnic for weeks. The morning arrived, and with it, the beginning of a daylong rain. Her brother Sam, age fifteen, who was helping plan the party, woke her. What do you think he said?

    a. "Why does something like this always happen to us?"

    b. "Don't worry. We're going to have a great time inside."

    c. "I'm never going to help you with a party again."

5. The Bike Race. David was participating in the fifth-grade bike race. He had trained with his father for months. As he started, his bike went over a rock, and he pitched sideways. When David picked up the bike, he saw that the bike frame was out of alignment. His dad was on the sidelines. What do you think he said?

    a. "Let's get a tool so we can straighten the frame, and you can use the bike for the next race."

    b. "We might as well go home."

    c. "Why did you have to do that?"

Answer Key

The answers below are so commonsensical that they make us wonder why we ever use put-downs. Maybe we need to practice these positive answers aloud so they come out more easily.

Scene	Response
1	c
2	b
3	a
4	b
5	a

WHY WE SAY WHAT WE SAY

Talk together about why people say what they do. Without using a fancy vocabulary, talk about motives, defensiveness, and hostility. Make up your own scenes with new sets of responses that include both words and actions.

Children benefit from hearing parents' answers and by practicing positive responses themselves. It's never too early or too late to start.

COMMON SENSE ABOUT TIME

We never have enough time, or do we? We encounter either a drought of nothing to do or a deluge of too much. Children always seem to be at one end or the other. They say, "I'm bored, there's nothing to do," or "Gee, I don't have time to do that," especially when "that" is a chore around the house. The activities that follow attempt to give children some common sense about time.

HOW MUCH TIME? any age

For this activity you need pencil and paper.

Take time to talk about how the family spends time. *Examples:* How much time do we spend watching TV? How much time do we use for sleep? How much time is spent on jobs around the house? How much time for homework or activities with friends or for talking on the telephone?

You're estimating, not measuring. You're making educated guesses based on the time you spent yesterday or last week. Jot down these different estimates next to each person's name.

This can be the beginning of your discussion about time. The activity gets children thinking about how they spend time without making judgments about whether they spend it in the right ways. Actually measuring the time spent and making judgments about it can come next.

HOW TIME FLIES any age

Time may fly, but it can be measured. The ultimate goal is to try to manage it. But first let's see how we spend it. You and your child will each keep track of your time for one day. You need two pieces of cardboard — one for each of you — a ruler, and a pencil or marker.

Draw a very large circle on each cardboard. Tracing that circle against a big round plate helps. The object is to mark off this circle into twenty-four equal parts, one for each hour of the day. First divide the circle into four quarters. Each of these quarters represents six hours. Within each quarter, you and your child should mark off six equal spaces, like slices of a pie.

Pick any day, preferably a weekday. You can do Saturday or Sunday later. Start by shading in the hours spent in sleep, then the hours spent at school or on the job. What's left? Time alone or with friends? Time spent in travel? Time spent on homework or chores? Time before the TV? Time for meals? Time for hobbies?

These pictures of your days will be interesting to compare and will give you both a lot to talk about, and maybe even to complain about.

MY TIME WISH any age

For this activity you need the time circles from "How Time Flies."

Take your time circles and see what you would change if you could. What's your ideal day? Would you spend more time sleeping and less time traveling? Would you spend less time eating and more time on hobbies? Would you spend less time alone and more time with each other? Talk together about these ideal days. See what little changes you can make to bring your current days more in line with your ideal ones.

TIME YOUR PLAN ages 7–12

This activity provides practice in making a plan. You need paper and pencil.

Ask children both to think about what they would like to do and to predict the times they will begin each activity. Saturday is a good day to try this. Together write down the time your child thinks each activity will begin. *Example:* Wake up at 8:00. Get dressed by 8:30. Finish breakfast by 9:00. Play baseball at 9:15.

As children begin an activity, they write down the time next to the prediction on the plan sheet. How close are the estimates to the actual times?

This planning practice can be very helpful in a couple of ways. It helps children begin to manage their time, to take more control over how they spend it. And it helps give children step-by-step skills for handling major school assignments with distant due dates, such as term papers, which just can't be done (well) the night before they are due.

DELICIOUS TIME

There is increasing concern that we overschedule our children, that we want them to be busy all the time, that we "hurry" them along to adulthood before they have had a chance to be children.

I don't think children need be busy or even look busy all the time. The same is true for adults. Both children and adults need time for looking at clouds, for taking a bubble bath and reading a potboiler, for playing with a pet, for sitting with each other, even when we're not talking. This is time for what used to be called smelling the roses.

The common-sense activities provided above give us not only a better sense of how we spend time but also a better chance of saving more time for those delicious unstructured hours.

MONEY COMMON SENSE

Money isn't everything, but it is a daily concern of families, and it's useful in developing common sense. Giving children practice with money is important because it gives them a sense of competency that carries over to their other work, in school and out.

Kids do funny things, even with their allowance. Maybe that's all right, but I have this attitude about wasting money: I don't like it. Neither does my husband. I asked our younger daughter recently if she remembered wasting money when she was young, and she said she certainly did, and we certainly got angry.

It seems that when she was six, she invested her entire weekly allowance of seventy-five cents (not a small sum then) in chewing gum. Perhaps worse yet, she opened all the packages and put the naked little gums out on a plate in the center of the dining room table. I don't recall this at all, nor does my husband. But our daughter tells us that when we came home from work and saw the dried-out gums, we both became angry and used such famous parental comments as "Have you no sense?" and "Why did you do this?" The upshot was that her allowance was cut back to thirty-five cents, since it was apparent that she did not really need the larger sum and had only wasted what she had left.

In retrospect, we probably overreacted. What our child did was precocious (gum hors d'oeuvres), but it was foolish. Maybe it was then that I decided she ought to learn about the value of money; the activities in this chapter are the result. In her mid-twenties now, our daughter reports that she has learned about money. She says she never unwraps gum until it's ready to be chewed.

Handling money is serious business, but it can be taught in easy, commonsensical ways.

MONEY IN PRINT AND IN POCKET ages 4–6

This activity helps children reading newspaper ads figure out both how much one dollar buys and the different ways that pennies, nickels, dimes, and quarters add up to a dollar. You need newspaper grocery ads, scissors, glue, paper, and a variety of change: five nickels, five dimes, four quarters, and the more pennies, the better.

Ask your child to look with you through the ads to find items that can be bought for a dollar or less. Cut these out and paste each ad to a separate piece of paper.

To teach children how to make change, try this. Put pennies, nickels, dimes, and quarters in different sections of an ice cube tray or an empty egg carton. Hand children a quarter and let them give you that amount back in different coins. Use this with other combinations. As a reward, let your child buy a surprise, using the correct coins, from a vending machine.

As a variation, use children's allowance to teach number combinations. One week, present a dollar in four quarters; the next week, in ten dimes, and so on.

YESTERDAY AND TODAY ages 7–9

This activity gives children a clearer understanding of daily living costs and how they have changed over the years. It also helps them get to know about your childhood. You need grocery receipts, current bills, and paper and pencil.

Gather together some household bills. List each service and the amount owed. Put the name of the bill on the left side of the paper. Put the cost on the right side.

Fold the paper so that the cost side is hidden. This turns the activity into a game.

Ask your child to predict the amount owed for each bill. Write down the guesses next to the items. Then unfold the paper to show the actual costs. It may surprise you that your child has very little idea of the costs of rent, groceries, and telephone use.

If sales tax is charged in your state, explain the tax and how it works.

Talk about how prices have gone up since you were a child. Share your memories. *Examples:* "I remember when candy bars cost five cents" or "I remember when seeing a movie cost much less than a dollar." Tell what you saved for when you were a child and how you did it. If you had an allowance, tell how much you received.

On a trip to a grocery or department store, talk with your child about how you used to be able to buy more with the same amount of money not so long ago. Of course, don't forget to mention that salaries are now higher, too. Sharing these memories is a good way to help your child know you and your past better.

EATING WELL FOR LESS ages 4–9

This activity helps children practice math by planning nutritious family meals that cost less. Use newspaper grocery ads, pencil, and paper.

Talk together about what the family might eat this week. Make up a menu of meals for two days, with your child taking charge of the choices for one meal. Check the advertisements together for coupons or sales on these or substitute foods.

Judge with your child the amount of food needed. Total the prices for the planned meal. Divide by the number of people who will be eating. This gives the cost of the meal per person.

Together check your cupboards and refrigerator before going to the store. See what you have on hand. Let children go to the store with you, if possible. Let them choose certain foods and pay for them. Two tips: Remember to go grocery shopping when you're *not* hungry. If your stomach is empty, you'll buy more than you need. To find the best buys, use unit pricing, which helps you and your child compare prices on the same types of food offered by different companies and in different-size boxes or cans.

At home, put a sign on the cupboard or refrigerator. It might say, "(Child's name) found best buys for our meals this week and saved us money." (If you know how much you saved, indicate the amount.)

CLOTHES FOR LESS ages 10–12

Preteens buy clothes a lot, or at least they want to. They might as well know how to save money on them. This activity helps. You need store catalogues, newspaper ads, pencil, and paper.

Pretend you each have $250 to spend on clothes. Pretend you have absolutely *nothing* to wear. Make up a complete winter wardrobe from top to bottom. Use newspapers and catalogues. Compare "purchases." How well did you do?

Talk about the advantage of buying clothes and other items out of season. Think of an item each of you wants. When would be the best time to buy it? How expensive is it? Set up a plan for saving (at home or in a bank) so you will have the money when the time comes.

Each of you make up a clothes budget. Include your total monthly income from allowance and any jobs. Figure out when you'll be able to buy the item you want. Make sure there is a little left to put away.

SAVING AND BANKING ages 10–12

This activity helps youngsters learn about bank accounts and provides tips on how to save money. You need pencil, paper, and perhaps even money with which to open a savings account.

Visit some banks to get information and pamphlets about services. Read the information together and discuss it. Decide which bank is most convenient. Which offers the highest interest rate? What are the bank's charges? Consider opening a savings account for your child. (The bank may require a minimum balance.) Let your youngster answer the bank officer's questions and fill out the application. Try to see that the bank statement is addressed to your child or you and your child jointly. It is important for your child to read and check the statement.

For a special item your youngster wants to buy, suggest a savings plan. You could work out a "matching grants" arrangement. For every dollar your child puts in the bank toward the item, you might give a dollar (or part of a dollar). This can inspire your youngster to a greater savings effort. Help your child set goals for regular deposits. How much will be added each week or each month? Will there also be regular withdrawals? Talk about any basic expenses you expect this savings to be used for.

JOBS AND MONEY

Parents have been worrying more and more about the impact on teenagers of part-time jobs that take too much time away from schoolwork. The money earned from these jobs is often spent not to help out the family at home but to buy teenage luxury items.

Preteens need to have impressed upon them that schoolwork, now and into their teen years, is their main job, and that it demands and deserves a great deal of time. Most jobs they would be able to get as teenagers, as young and inexperienced as they are, would not provide them with much opportunity for learning. It is more important for young teens to do well in school than to spend a lot of time on a job.

ARGUMENTS ABOUT MONEY

People probably argue more about money than anything else. While many of these arguments are really about money, I suspect that many are really about other things, such as self-respect, power, recognition, affection, and security.

I remember an all-evening argument with my husband when we were first married. It was over a two-dollar can of furniture polish that he had bought and that I thought we didn't need. In retrospect, I don't think the argument was about the two dollars. I think it was about values and whether that purchase showed that we shared the same set of values.

I was never able to bring myself to use that can of polish, and I don't think he used it, either. When we moved several years later, I saw it sitting alone in the back of the cabinet under the sink.

Maybe some good does result from arguments about money. Maybe they give us a chance to know more about each other — and ourselves. My daughter remembers that when she was five, she had a boyfriend, also five, who lived across the street. He never had any money. She had an allowance, so she bought him treats every time the ice cream truck visited the block. He said he would pay her back, but he didn't. We moved a few blocks away, but she never forgot his debt.

When she was ten years old, she walked back to his house and said, "Michael, you owe me sixty cents." He paid her almost everything he owed, but she's sure that the moment signaled the end of their friendship.

They had grown apart, and it probably wasn't because of the money at all. But arguments about money have the strangest way of being about more than money, a common-sense lesson she learned at an early age.

Chapter 12.
MegaSkill Ten: Problem Solving

Do your children say "I can't" instead of "I can"? Children are not born problem solvers. They learn how, and they show they're learning when they:

Know how to ask questions and get answers.

Have the ability to identify and face a problem.

Generate ideas that could be solutions.

Show that they can make a reasonable decision.

The activities in this chapter are designed to encourage children's problem-solving abilities, helping them put what they know and can do into action.

A special section focuses on safety, an issue of great concern to families today. We cannot be safe for our children. They have to know on their own the questions to ask and the steps to take. They need to be able to deal with problems and potential problems calmly and effectively.

The smartest thing I probably said to my children when they were growing up was, "Try to be one of those people on whom nothing is lost." I think one of the James boys said this — not Jesse, but Henry, the writer.

Problem solving depends on not losing ideas. It requires thinking. When I taught in high school and even in graduate school, the hardest question I could ask students was, "What do you think?"

Because they had so much trouble, I began to consider how thinking could be taught, not just in the classroom but in the home.

Thinking is not a subject all by itself — it's what you *think about* that is the subject. We need children who can begin to think about serious subjects; with encouragement and the proper skills, they can do this.

My recipe for problem solving is made up of two basic ingredients:

- Practice in asking and answering questions.
- Practice in making decisions.

That's what the activities in this chapter emphasize.

It's intriguing that these activities cross age and ability levels without a scratch. I've used many of them with success from the elementary grades to graduate school. Of course, the results are different. We should expect college students' responses to be more sophisticated and complex than those of second graders — but sometimes they aren't.

QUESTIONS, QUESTIONS, QUESTIONS

Asking and answering questions takes a lot of practice and time. In school, children don't really get enough practice. There isn't much time for "thoughtful" questions and answers. Sure, children answer true and false questions and questions for which there is one correct response, such as, "What is the longest river in the world?" But what they need more of, and what schools — for very good reasons — have trouble providing, are thought-provoking questions, such as, "What do you think about . . . ?" or "How could this be made better?" or "What would you do to organize this differently?"

These are open-ended questions. They are not used as often in class as even many teachers would like. There are lots of reasons.

They take a lot of time; there are no "right" answers; they often elicit "I don't know" from students; and they might generate answers that teachers find troublesome to hear and difficult to handle. I have asked a number of them in my time as an English teacher, and sometimes I berated myself afterward for not going for the multiple-choice, single-right-answer quiz.

THE "THOUGHT-FULL" HOME

There is a growing movement afoot to encourage more "thought-full" schools, but it will probably take more time than today's students can wait for.

What parents don't have to wait for is the "thought-full" home. By this I mean a home where children get the practice they need in asking thought-provoking questions and in coming up with "thought-full" answers.

Any parent can do it ... and do it now.

First, it means asking questions that you really want answers to and that you really care about hearing the answers to.

For younger children, you might ask questions about the stories you read together: "What do you think will happen next?" "How do you think the story will end?" "What makes you think so?"

For older children, you might use situational questions. When the TV konks out, ask the kids, "How do you think we should handle this?" "Should we get it repaired?" "Should we buy a new one?" "What do you think?" "Why?" (Also see "What's Your Opinion?" in Chapter 10.)

When the TV is on, you might ask, "Should we turn it off?" "What is this show telling us?" "What are we getting out of it?" "Should we think of doing anything else instead?"

Second, it means listening to children's answers, even forcing yourself to listen, if you have to. If necessary, ask your children to remind you to listen when they find you aren't. We're not talking about thirty-minute presentations, but answers that may extend over a minute or two.

Third, it means letting children know how really smart they are. Preadolescents may know more about the working of a TV set than any parent suspects. We have to be sure that our children know when they give us their thoughtful answers that we are not only listening but learning.

Fourth, it means letting your children ask you questions that they want answers to and your taking the time to respond thoughtfully. They might ask why they have to do the chores at a certain hour every evening or what is making you so upset about their hair style or their friends or their report card.

Fifth, it means that your children listen while you talk and that just as they are expected to keep within reasonable time limits in their answers, so are you.

THE "CREATIVE TOUCH"

Even though all problem solving is creative, some questions elicit more "creative" answers than others. When you ask a child, "What do you wish would happen?" you can expect a more imaginative answer than when you ask about the broken TV set.

You can spur children's inventive thinking with questions that limber up the brain. Ask how many things can be made from a paper plate. From a rubber band? From a paper clip? How can ordinary stairs be improved?

Encourage children to imagine. What would happen if the automobile had not been invented? A whole new world opens up. Ask children to name five inventions the world could use that have not been invented yet.

Try designs on paper to elicit ideas. Put a blob of ink on paper, fold it, rub, and blot. Ask children to tell you all the things the blob reminds them of. Trade places and try it yourself.

Place circles or squares or triangles of various sizes on a sheet of paper. Then ask children to name and draw as many different objects as they can think of using these figures.

Help children think ahead about what they would change and what they would do if they had their wish:

What do you want more time for?

How would you use more money?

What is a waste of time?

What makes you feel really happy?

How do you wish the family would be different?

What would you like to keep always the same?

Whom would you like to be friends with?

What would you like to do tomorrow? Next week? Next month?

Encourage children to ask you some of these, too. The list is as endless as are wishes. Asking the questions may be one of the first steps in having these wishes come true.

YOU KNOW MORE THAN YOU THINK YOU DO

For some people, the hardest answer in the world is "I don't know." But for many children, I think one of the easiest answers is "I don't know."

We can't let our kids get away with this. They are smart. They know more than they think they do. Street-smart kids, for example, are problem solving all the time. They get in the classroom, and they're often struck dumb. They need the chance to show what they know and how they go about solving problems. Home, where there is no worry over wasting classtime and covering a certain curriculum by the end of the month, is a good place to let kids show what they know.

What you'll be talking about for the most part are open-ended questions. There are no right answers. You are not in the classroom, so there are no other hands waving in the air, no other children eager to give the right answer. It's a relaxed atmosphere of give and take. It's a time for exchanging ideas, feelings, hopes, dreams. It's a time that only a "thought-full" home can provide.

MAKING DECISIONS

Decision making is not easy, but it becomes less painful as children:

- Become increasingly aware that they can help to solve problems.
- See that a problem can have more than one solution, but that one may be better than others.
- Learn about restraint and to think about a problem before taking action.

Not to Decide Is to Decide

Decision making generates a lot of fears. I know it does for me. Years ago, I brought home a poster that was helpful to me. It said, "Not to Decide Is to Decide." Finding this in a bookstore made me realize that I was not alone. Since they had printed so many of these, other people must have been having the same trouble. This was comforting and provided me with more courage to make decisions.

Involve children actively and early in decision making, especially in family decision making. They can be active participants or can just listen in. In this way they come to know, and to identify with, the process we adults go through making up our minds.

THINKING AND CHOOSING ages 4–7

Children can use practice making small decisions before they have to make large ones. You need thinking minds.

Ask your child to pretend the following things are happening:

- You can't find your key and no one is home.
- You get lost on your way to a friend's house.
- You are teased on your way home from school.

Ask children to think of as many ways to solve these problems as they can. Don't reject any ideas, even if they sound far-fetched.

After they have mulled over three or four different solutions, let them pick one way that seems best.

For more ideas, try out these scenarios with your children:

- Mother calls you to go on an errand to the neighbor's house next door. But before you start out, a friend comes by and says, "Let's play." What do you do?
- You're in a terrible hurry to get to a costume party, and just as you're putting on that special costume, it rips. What do you do?

Let even young children decide how to arrange their own room or at least part of it, and include your child in the choosing of the decor and furnishings.

Ask for children's ideas to remedy a problem they cause (not necessarily at the time when you're upset about the mess). *Examples:* Mud on the floor, coats not hung up, milk left out. This way, instead of having a solution imposed on them, children have a hand in making it — and, we hope, a stake in seeing the solution work. (For more examples, see the special section on safety that follows this chapter.)

DECISIONS AREN'T EASY ages 9–12

As kids grow older, they need to be aware of the many decisions they make every day ... about clothes, friends, jobs. You need thinking minds.

Talk with your youngster about some important decisions you have made in the past. *Examples:* Buying a car, changing jobs, getting married. Tell about the things you considered before making these decisions. Were there good and bad consequences? Were you happy with your decisions? Would you make the same ones again?

Making decisions usually involves looking at the pros (the pluses) and the cons (the minuses) of a situation. Together consider the pros and cons of skipping school, eating a lot, spending money. What is gained? What is lost?

Whenever possible, try to let your youngsters bear the consequences of their own decision making — good *or* bad! Talk about what could be done next time.

Encourage children to become planners: What would they do if they were teachers? Fathers? Mothers? Exchanging roles gives them a glimmer of teachers' and parents' points of view.

Ask for children's advice in choosing the best place for a vacation. Discuss the reasons for their choice and the factors that determine the ultimate decision, such as time and money. Children need to face these realities of life. Providing this practice will help.

THE MATTER OF CHOICE

Since choice is basic to problem solving, real choices must be available to children. For young children, limit the number of possible choices. Don't give children decisions to make that you believe are yours alone. There is danger when children are given decisions to make that are really not theirs to make or when children are told they can make the decision and then find that their parents really didn't mean it.

Choose the real decisions that children can make and be prepared to live with their decisions. The ones our children make are not always the ones we would make. If you say, "This is *your* decision," you have to mean it.

Special Section:
Safety — Everyday Problem Solving

SUPERVISING THE "LATCH KEY" CHILD

Security is safety, but it's more than that. It's feeling safe. Many young children say they don't feel safe at home when an adult is not there.

Studies show that children feel safer and less alone when they *feel* supervised.

While it is still impossible to be in two places at one time, there are ways to help children feel supervised, even when parents are not at home.

Children need to know that parents care about what they are doing.

Just being home doesn't always do the job. It's possible to be at home all the time and not have children feel that their parents care.

Use your problem-solving abilities to come up with ways to make sure your child knows you are supervising — no matter where you are.

Examples:

Set up a call-in, check-in time as soon as your child gets home from school.

Leave messages for children all around the house: on the calendar, the front of the refrigerator, the pillow, the back door.

Use a tape recorder or answering machine to leave and pick up messages from one another. Hearing an adult voice is helpful in itself.

Make sure that children know what they are supposed to do. Go over their after-school time with them the night before.

Ask around to see if there is a neighbor — perhaps a retiree at home — who can be called — just in case.

Help brothers and sisters get along without your being right there to break up fights.

It can be more dangerous for siblings who don't get along to be home together than for one of them to be home alone. It's comforting for parents to think the darlings at home are taking care of each other. But that's not always the case. Efforts need to be made to help siblings be civilized; these include providing separate activities that keep kids out of each other's hair, and separate study areas as well.

(See also Chapter 24, "Parents and At-Home Child Care." Tips provided for helpers can also be useful for children on their own.)

Make sure that the house is safe and that children know how to keep it safe. The activities presented later in this section focus on basic household safety strategies.

ON THEIR OWN IS NOT LEFT ALONE

Children need routines to follow, limits that they understand and that can be enforced, and structure for use of their time. This is the essence of feeling secure, of feeling supervised, of feeling cared for. This is what parents can provide, even from afar. Studies of children who report in to their parents after school and who say that their parents know where they are all the time indicate that they feel well supervised. And they behave that way.

WE CANNOT BE SAFE FOR OUR CHILDREN

Children have to know the steps to take on their own to be safe. Of course, we can and should warn kids not to step in front of speeding cars and to turn off the stove after using it. But children have to do these things themselves. We can't watch kids from morning to night to prevent them from doing something unsafe.

One way to tackle this problem is by building children's own safety habits. Without becoming overfearful, our youngsters can be taught about decisions they need to make to protect themselves.

WHAT'S THE PROBLEM?

A solution is good only when it's carried out. It doesn't help when the front door is not locked, when heaters remain on after children have departed the room, or when purses are left out for all to see. That's why it's important for children to be part of the problem-solving process. They're the ones who will be putting the solutions into place.

Take children through these activities by asking questions before coming up with solutions. You can ask the following questions first or go straight to the solutions suggested in the activities. In any event, make sure that your children know the problem they are being asked to prevent. Here's a four-point system to try:

1. What is the problem?
2. What solutions can we try?
3. What are the good and bad points of these solutions?
4. What do you think of the solution in this activity?

Helping children go through some step-by-step thinking is just one way to get them into the habit of problem solving. This is not an automatic, sequential program. Good ideas can come in the strangest way, like bolts out of the blue. When faced with decisions, many of us say, "I want to sleep on it." Somehow or other, good ideas germinate in the middle of the night, and by the next morning, we know what we're going to do. It's not clear we have employed step-by-step reasoning to get there; it seems that some wonderful, mysterious process is at work.

THINKING THROUGH A PROBLEM: STEP-BY-STEP EXAMPLE

Here are questions keyed to the system above. They can lead you through the activity "Warning, Warning," which follows. The activity is about poison prevention.

1. Children accidentally eat or drink poisons and dangerous medicines lying around the house. Many youngsters become ill and die.

2. What can we do here at home to prevent this from happening? Let's name a lot of ideas.

3. Are there any good or bad points about the ideas we've listed? For example, if we are going to hide everything, will we be able to recognize new, dangerous medicines or products in other settings?

4. How about giving the following activity a try? In a few weeks, we'll check to see how it's working. (*Note:* To check, you bring in a new medicine and see how your children handle it. Can they tell it's dangerous? Where do they want to put it?)

Make up your own questions as you work through all these safety activities. In this way, your children will know that they

have a role to play in keeping themselves and their home safe —
and you will feel a lot safer when you are away from home.

WARNING, WARNING ages 4–6

Children have ways of finding everything, so it's best to instill in
them their own understanding of how to prevent poisoning. This
activity helps children recognize the warning labels on medicines
and household cleaners at home. Early readers get practice reading the labels. You need a sturdy box with four or five household
products and medicines. (Use only those with warning labels.)

Take one product out of the box. Help your child find the warning label and say it or read it aloud. Point together to the words
that mean WATCH OUT. Some of these are *caution, poison, danger,
warning, hazard.* Point out the skull and crossbones symbol.

Ask your child to read the labels of the other products in the
box and to list these words. Talk about why these cleaning products and medicines are kept out of reach.

Discuss what can be done if these products or medicines are
swallowed accidentally. The labels tell us what remedies or anti-
dotes counteract the poison.

Put your child's list of warning words in a special place for the
family to read. The refrigerator door is a good place. Make warning signs for your house. *Example:* "Poisons are stored in this
cupboard."

Remind your children to take medicine only with your approval.
Twice as many children die accidentally from taking drugs and
medicines as from swallowing household cleaners.

HOUSEHOLD DANGER SPOTS ages 4–6

Here's a way to help children learn how to recognize home repair
danger spots, so that when they see one, they'll avoid trouble and
let you know what needs to be fixed. You need ordinary household
objects, including paper bags and rags.

Take a walk around your home with your child. Check in each
room to see that electric cords are not frayed, that throw rugs

don't slide, that old papers, rags, and paints are stored properly, that sharp edges of knives and tools are covered.

Make a list of items in the house that need to be repaired. Separate the list into two sections — those that can be repaired at home and those that have to go to the repair shop. If items are repaired at home, try to involve children in helping.

APPLIANCE CHECK LIST ages 4–6

This activity helps children learn how to use appliances safely. Have children find lights and appliances with OFF marked on them. Practice turning appliances on and off. *Examples:* Light switches, record players, irons, portable heaters, televisions.

Show children how the stove is turned off. If the stove is not to be used at all, explain why. Talk about why children should never play with matches.

Together with your child, make an OFF chart to post near the front door. Here's a model to follow:

HAVE WE REMEMBERED TO TURN OFF:

_____ TV?   _____ Heaters?

_____ Stove?   _____ Lights? (Leave hall light on for safety.)

_____ Other electrical appliances?

Note: Use symbols on the list for children who cannot yet read.

KEYS TO THE KINGDOM ages 4–6

You need working locks and keys for this activity.

Take a walk around your house. Show children how to lock and unlock all doors and at least a few windows. Point to exits to use in case of fire or other need to escape.

Let children try using all house keys. Have keys made for each family member and put these in special places for safekeeping.

Try to make your home as burglarproof as possible. Make sure there is a strong chain on the front door so that it can be opened only partially. Many parents tell children never to open the door for people they do not know.

Tell children never to enter the house after school if the door is ajar, a window is broken, or anything looks unusual. Give instructions to go to a neighbor's or to a store, then to call Mom or Dad and wait for an adult to arrive before returning to the house.

COMMUNITY SAFETY TOUR ages 4–6

This activity helps children feel at home in the community, and it teaches them the meaning of important signs, even if they can't yet read them. You need thinking minds, paper, pen, and some change.

Walk with your child or drive through your community. Point out the many signs you see. Which are the signs for safety? What do the other signs tell you? *Examples:* BUS, YIELD, WALK, and CAUTION are some signs that children need to know.

Show safe and less safe places to walk. Identify and introduce yourselves to neighborhood safety personnel, such as policemen and crossing guards. Talk about safe places to go in case of danger. *Examples:* a neighbor's house, a business office.

Prepare a safety kit for your child to take everywhere. It can include an identification card, a list of important telephone numbers, change for several phone calls, and perhaps enough money for bus or cab fare. Tape the kit inside your child's lunchbox or knapsack.

DEALING WITH STRANGERS any age

Children must learn to protect themselves against strangers at home and on the street. Here's how. All you need are thinking minds.

Give instructions to your children on how to talk to strangers on the phone, at the door, and on the street.

Make up a set response to use on the phone: *Example:* "My mom can't come to the phone now. May I take a message?"

Teach children how to take careful telephone messages that include the caller's name and phone number. Buy a phone pad or make one out of scrap paper. Practice handling phone calls. Use a play phone or the real phone. Take turns being the caller and being the child at home.

Warn about accepting rides and gifts from strangers. In view of the tragedies that have occurred, be absolutely firm in your warnings. Do not assume that children know the dangers. Role play some typical situations such as, "Do you want candy?" "Can I give you a ride?"

It's wise to avoid calling attention to money. Advise children not to carry thick wallets and to keep them out of sight. Girls who carry shoulder bags should hold on to them firmly. If youngsters are carrying large amounts of money, tell them to divide the money and to carry it in at least two places.

STREET SMARTS ages 10–12

Safety rules have a tendency to be overlooked by older youngsters — once they feel old enough to take care of themselves. Use thinking minds for this one.

Talk together about at least three things to increase safety outdoors. *Examples:* lock cars, keep personal items out of sight in parked cars, avoid deserted areas.

Ask family and friends to tell about one special safety rule they practice at home or outdoors. Are there any good ideas your family had not thought of?

Use city transportation schedules to figure out a trip to a specific destination, such as a concert hall. How long will it take? Is it a safe place to go? What safety precautions, if any, are needed?

IN CASE OF FIRE any age

Help your family know how to leave the house quickly and safely in case of fire. You need thinking minds, pencil, and paper.

Show children the emergency numbers for Fire, Police, and Poison Control listed in the front of the telephone book. Tell children to dial "0" for the operator in case of an emergency. For children who can't read, make a picture chart with the numbers. Buy a small fire extinguisher to keep in the kitchen and a smoke alarm for your home.

Practice leaving the house quickly, using different exits. Make these sessions family affairs so that everyone will know exactly what to do in case of fire or an accident. Practice until you are sure children understand what to do.

Children are much more likely to stay calm in a crisis if they feel they know what to do.

SAFETY: AN ALL-AT-ONCE SKILL

One of the differences between teaching about safety and teaching about money, for example, is that you really can't teach safety in stages, waiting for children to grow up and handle more complicated details. A six-year-old needs to know as much or almost as much as a twelve-year-old. It's as if you want to teach everything at once, especially now that young children spend so much time alone at home.

Children don't know all the safety problems and hazards in advance. They don't start out knowing which items at home are poisonous and what to do in case of fire. And you don't know when and if they will face such problems. Thanks to the growing number of good books on children's safety as well as to the activities in this section and others that you will think of, your children can be prepared.

Chapter 13.
My Children: What Are We Going to Do with Them? Everyday Q and A

Nobody said raising children would be easy. Here are some complaints I've heard across the country from parents about their children. Take a look at these answers and see if they help:

Q: My children never feel that anything they do is good enough.

A: Check to see how your family feels about its successes. Is there a tendency to feel that nothing is quite good enough? This is self-defeating.

Try with your children to set up daily situations in which they succeed. Have they learned to swim? Are they able to locate a needed number in the telephone book?

Take pride in their successes. Guard against, "Oh, you can do that better," and "What, not finished yet?" Success ought to feel good.

Q: My children can never seem to make up their minds, or else they say, "I don't want to."

A: Give children practice in making decisions. It helps if they make small decisions before they have to make large ones.

Encourage children to make a list of pluses and minuses when they are trying to make up their minds. Perhaps their decision has to do with going to a movie. A plus would be, "I like it because I can be with friends." A minus would be, "I don't want to go because I'm saving up money for a bike." How do they add up? Encourage your child to choose the more reasonable decision and to try to stick with it.

Keep using this method. Eventually this kind of careful decision making becomes a good habit.

Q: My children never finish anything they start. It takes a lot of nagging both to get them to start and to keep them at it.

A: Make sure that you convey to children your expectations that they will start and complete the task or project. Be optimistic, and check that your children have what they need to complete what they are doing. It may take them longer to do a project than it takes you, so be realistic about the time they will need.

Encourage them to tackle projects suited to their age and ability. Help children to think in terms of first, second, and third steps. After they start, encourage them to keep going, taking one step at a time.

Q: My children don't seem to be able to do things as they ought to be done.

A: Sometimes when we ask people to do things, we have preconceived ideas of how the task should be accomplished. *Example:* "Please wash the dishes. Oh, you should do the glasses first and be sure to soak the silverware before washing."

Remember that one method may work best for you while another method works best for someone else. As long as children get the job done, there's no reason why they have to do it your way. They might even come up with some good suggestions for parents.

Some tasks do need to be done in a specific order, such as those for baking a cake. But if directions are not absolutely needed, as in dishwashing, for example, let children do the task well in their own way.

Q: My children seem bored. What kinds of activities will make them more enthusiastic?

A: Help children feel successful. Provide jobs and activities they can do and will feel proud of having accomplished. These include building something needed around the house, taking care of a special corner in the garden, cooking a meal for the family, teaching the rest of the family a favorite game.

Q: The house in which I grew up was not as messy as our home is today. Why do things seem more chaotic nowadays?

A: When you were a child, you didn't have to worry about the bills, the plumbing, the car, and the house. Your parents handled these things. And it probably didn't bother you when your toys were out of place. As an adult, your standards are different.

Nowadays, too, the pace of life is faster. Mothers often work outside the house; household help is scarce. Try not to let a little extra dust bog you down. But keep clear a pathway to the door, in case of fire.

Q: Family life seems to demand much more effort than my job. Why?

A: Do you have a secretary at home who picks up after you? Files papers? Takes phone calls and handles mail? Probably not. That may be why you're bothered about the daily details in the household, like the empty refrigerator, the dirty laundry, and a baby sitter needed for Saturday night.

Also, you're more personally involved at home than at the office. If the children don't listen to you, you have to work it out with them. If people at the office don't listen, they can be fired. Kids can't.

Q: Sometimes I feel I can't do anything right. The kids get irritated. I get upset.

A: You can start by letting your children know that you — an adult — also have needs. You need praise, encouragement, love — and criticism and put-downs hurt you, just as they hurt them.

Sometimes put-downs can get to be a habit. So get yourself and your children more accustomed to making such comments as, "Nice going!" "That's the way!" "Great." Parents have a right to feel good, too.

Chapter 14.
My Parents: What Are We Going to Do with Them? Everyday Q and A

Children have complaints about their parents, too. And some of them are valid.

Here are some I've heard that have a ring of truth. If any hit home, share them with your children and see what they think. They may have some to add to the list.

Q: My dad tells me one thing and my mom tells me another.

A: Ideally, parents should talk to each other first before they tell children what to do. Parents don't necessarily have to agree, but they need to be aware that they are giving different messages.

One parent may be more lenient, the other stricter. Can there be a happy medium? Talk the problem over at a time when everybody is in a good mood. Find a clear direction that you can follow.

To be honest, there may be other reasons for parental differences. Parents may have grievances with each other and not with their children. Children can get caught in the middle. Being honest and talking things over can help.

Q: My parents always expect me to do what they want, but they don't listen to what I want.

A: Set aside a brief time every day when you and your parents can sit together and talk. Perhaps during dinner or right after dinner would be a good time.

Be sure to tell your parents how you feel and what you want. *Example:* "Mom, I really don't like going to the grocery store for you when I just get home from school. Can I go after I've had a snack?"

Try to work out solutions together. A parent might say, "That's fine, but you need to leave in time for me to have the groceries to prepare dinner."

Q: My dad doesn't spend time with me. He's either at work or watching TV.

A: Maybe your dad doesn't know that you want him to spend time with you. You have to tell him, "Dad, I really want to play Ping-Pong with you," or "I need your help with my history homework tonight."

Q: Mom and Dad sometimes yell at me when I have friends over. Now I don't want to bring anyone home.

A: How do you act when your friends are over? Do you act the same way toward your parents as you do when you don't have friends in? Sometimes children are ruder to their parents when they have an audience.

Parents, too, can be more impatient when there are extra people in the house. Your parents may not be aware of your feelings. Sit down with them and tell them how you feel. Then you'll be having those friends back soon.

Q: My parents never let me do anything around the house. They say that I'll do it wrong or that I'm too young.

A: Show your parents that you can take responsibility. Ask them to let you cook something in the kitchen with them. *Examples:* "Will you make spaghetti with me?" "Let me plan dinner for Sunday." When your parents see you complete these tasks, they will feel you are ready to take on more responsibilities.

Be sure to put things away. If you're working in the kitchen, clean up the dishes and wipe those counter tops. Picking up after yourself is part of finishing a job, and it tells your parents that you are ready to do more.

Q: My parents don't seem to take me or what I say seriously. How can I get them to think I'm smart?

A: Start by taking yourself seriously. Show that you can start a task and finish it. Set standards for yourself. Show that you can concentrate and that you're not afraid to try things — even if you don't always succeed. *Example:* If you've cooked something for dinner and the recipe has flopped, avoid saying anything like, "Oh, well, I'm only a kid." Say, "I'll figure out what went wrong and do better next time."

Q: My mother is always on the telephone. I never get to talk to her.

A: You can (nicely) interrupt someone who has been on the telephone a long time. Some families write notes to tell the person on the phone that they are needed. Others have posters or signs that they hold up. The poster might read: WE NEED YOU. Yelling is not the way to do it.

Also decide as a family if anyone will take calls during family meals or other family times. You might tell callers that you can't talk now but will call them back later.

Q: My parents say they will do something; then they say they're too busy to do it.

A: Everyone gets too busy sometimes and forgets things. Parents may need reminders. Try posting a message where they're sure to see it. *Example:* "Mom, remember my physical for camp." Or draw a picture telling them what you want. *Example:* "Dad, here is a picture of you and me taking the hike that you said we would take when the weather got warm."

Q: My parents always remind me that I'm the oldest and most responsible. I feel that I have to do everything better than other people. This makes me nervous, and sometimes I'm too scared to do anything.

A: Sometimes parents depend on older children too early and too much. Parents may almost automatically start to think that you ought to be able to do things well — even perfectly. That can make you scared. If you are so scared of failing, you may stop trying. If you're not trying, you can't fail. Right?

Wrong! Everybody needs to keep on trying. But older kids may need to remind their parents not to overload them with too many tasks or unrealistic expectations.

Section C.
Strengthening the
Three R's at Home

Introduction.
MegaSkills and the Three R's:
Chicken and Egg

What comes first — the chicken or the egg? When it comes to MegaSkills, it doesn't matter.

From eggs come chickens, from chickens come eggs. And so with MegaSkills and the academic skills. One leads to the other. They go back and forth in an ever-renewing, exciting cycle.

Educational life for children is school, but it is more than school. In this section are activities that empower children to use what they have learned in school in their lives beyond the classroom. They do not take the place of school homework, but they make homework more manageable for children to do and want to do on their own. They fire up children to want to learn more.

They set the base for learning all through life!

The child who learns to write can prepare an essay, conjure up a story, and, later on, create a love letter.

The child who reads can handle a test, devour a novel, and, later on, understand an insurance policy.

The child who learns math can figure out the text problems, bring home the right change from a grocery errand, and, later on, manage the family budget.

The three R's are tools that use the capacities and qualities of MegaSkills, inside and outside the classroom.

Chapter 15.
Reading: When Will
My Child Read?

As parents, we may do some things wrong, but if we have helped our children gain a love of reading, we have done a lot of things right.

We have given our children trips to the farthest reaches of the earth and to the sun and the moon and the stars.

We have opened the doors to knowing their own heart and the hearts of others.

We have given them maps for their voyage through life.

One of the early children of divorce, my husband has bitter-sweet memories of his childhood. One memory, however, remains forever sweet. His mother would come home from work and read to him almost every night before he went to bed. It turned him, he says, into a lifelong reader — an enduring present from his mother.

When children go off to school, almost the first question parents ask teachers is, "When will my child read?" Ideally, the answer is, "All through life." But it's natural to feel anxious. Reading is the make-or-break R. It's the one academic skill that children are expected to show that they have mastered, at least minimally, by the end of their first year in "real" school.

This is hard on children; it is hard on parents; and it is hard on teachers. Rather than dwell on how to change the time schedule within our educational system, this chapter focuses on how to help children take the magnificent, liberating leap into reading successfully — because most children will be able to read and will want to read.

We know a lot about reading. We know that the vast majority of children take to it like ducks to water. But unlike ducks, who keep swimming for the rest of their lives, many youngsters do not keep on reading.

A major concern about reading is not how to teach children to read but how to ensure that they will continue to read, enriching and broadening their skills and interests.

Let me tell you what's in this chapter and what's not. It contains many activities for home use that help to build children's love of reading and learning. This chapter assumes that parents know the importance of reading aloud to children. What many parents may not be aware of are other everyday activities that help with reading. It does not contain a simple answer to the question of whether children should read before entrance into regular school. There is no simple answer; experts often oppose each other. This chapter also does not contain a discussion of phonics versus the look-say method of teaching reading. It's my view that in teaching you need to take advantage of all the methods you can lay your hands on to suit the changing needs of every child, every day.

This chapter is mostly about young readers before they read and as they start to read. I concentrate on the young because of the enormous pressure on children to learn to read as they start schooling. I also focus on the young because of the enormous pressure on parents to do something to help their children read — pressure that often results in the home doing the school's job.

Parents can do a lot to help children read, and this does not mean using flash cards and workbook exercises. There is a world of ways to encourage reading at home without the use of the traditional school methods, which I believe are best left to the school. Children need a different, informal, individual reading environment at home.

Most parents will happily read to children, but some cannot. My own immigrant parents were not able to read aloud in English to me, and I did not understand Polish or Yiddish.

The language of theirs that I *did* understand was that reading was important. That's the message every parent must and can give. It's a message that comes through in simple activities like matching shapes and listening to sounds. It's a message about the beauty and wonder of language.

BREAKING THE CODE ages 4–6

To read, a child recognizes shapes. The alphabet is a collection of shapes that stand for sounds. To read, children see similarities and differences among shapes. Here are some easy shapes games.

Shaping Up

Cut out from colored paper, or even newspaper, large duplicate circles, squares, rectangles. Put one of each shape on the floor. Ask your child to find and put the matching ones on top of them. These are just shapes, not alphabet letters.

Move to asking children to match smaller and more intricate shapes, including parts of alphabet letters. Then make duplicate alphabet letters — capital ones and lowercase ones. Make the letters large. You might want to start your game with three, extend to ten, then fifteen. As your child gains mastery, all twenty-six can be matched in one game.

Then ask children to match groups of shapes that form words — small words like "cat," "dog," "bag."

Play similar matching games with numbers, starting with one and working up to a hundred, if your child is so inclined.

Children really interested in these shapes games may want to trace or make their own games of model letters to play themselves or to give to friends to play.

Finding Shapes

Look around your rooms to identify shapes all around you: the circles in glasses, the rectangular tables, rugs, and windows.

Let 'Em Eat Shapes

Here's a tasty accompaniment to these activities. You need bread, peanut butter or some other spread, and a dull-edged knife. Cut the bread into different, duplicate shapes. Ask children to find a pair of matching shapes, put spread on one piece, and place the matching shape on top for a tasty sandwich.

These activities are great for older children to play with younger children in the family and those for whom they babysit. They're easy and cost no money.

LISTENING TO SOUNDS ages 4–6

To read, children also have to be able to listen. They need to hear the sounds the shapes make. Try thirty seconds of silence. Then have children tell you what they hear: a car down the street, a bird twittering. The moment of quiet is wonderful, too!

Name that Sound

Children close their eyes and tell what sounds are being made. *Examples:* a key jangling, the click of tongue in mouth, water running in the sink. Then turn the tables and let your child play this game on you.

Rhythms

Tap out rhythms with a fork on a table top. Ask children to repeat the rhythm back to you. Vary the style: slow, fast, loud, soft. Use more complex rhythms and patterns as your child's responding abilities develop.

Phonics Bingo

Combine heightened listening ability with alphabet sounds. To help children associate sounds with letters, make a grid of consonants on a piece of cardboard. Here is a sample:

S	D	F	M

Keep the grids simple at first, with perhaps only three or four letters. (The more recognizable, noisier consonants are *B, D, F, J, K, L, M, N, P, R, S, T, V, Z.*) Call out a sound and ask players to cover the letter with a button, bean, or small cardboard circle. Say the sound with a word. *Examples:* "puh — 'pat'"; "mmm — 'mat.'"

Rhyming Games

Use rhymes to build children's sense of the different sounds that words make. *Examples:* "Ball, tall, fall. Which bounces?" "What is a word that rhymes with cat and is used with balls?" "I see something on this table that is round, white, and rhymes with fish."

The Daily Rounds

Take time on errands to point to letter sounds in the signs seen each day. *Examples:* S — STOP, STORE, SCHOOL; B — BUS, BANK, BEAUTY SHOP; F — FIRE, FLOWERS; G — GO, GAS, GROCERIES.

Reading is all around us, all the time. While riding in a car or bus, read the signs aloud and encourage children to sing them out as they see them.

Stop/Look/Rhyme

"Sock" and "clock," "bed" and "head," "floor" and "more" — rhymes are all around the world, even in the bedroom, and they're good for going to sleep with and for learning to read.

Encourage your child to say words aloud with you. Children who speak and write well enjoy the sounds words make. A baby babbling in a crib begins a love affair with words that need never end.

MYSTERY WORD BOX ages 4–9

I think that just about the best reading activity I did at home with my children was one we called the "Mystery Word Box." It was a vocabulary activity, but it was more than that. It was a bedtime activity, a parent/child lovefest — and it was about words.

We used a recipe card file box, three- by five-inch index cards, and alphabet dividers. It worked like this. Each day, my daughter, who was five at that time, got to pick up to five mystery words of the day. She didn't have to know how to spell them or what they meant. She could choose any words that she had heard and that appealed to her in some way. The mystery lay in what words she would pick. My job was to write them down in big print on the cards. She would say them aloud, "reading" them from the cards. We would talk about what they meant, and then she would file them away in the box.

I remember only a few of those words — how I wish I had saved that box. It would have been better than a time capsule. What I do remember is that the words were emotional or funny sounding — words like "love," "death," "accident," "crocodile," and a word from *Mary Poppins*, one I still have trouble spelling: "super-califragilisticexpialidocious."

During the day I would sometimes find my child on her bed, the contents of the mystery word box set out before her. These were her very own words, and she would be playing with them, saying them aloud, caressing them with her voice. Some days she would put the cards around the wall of her room so she could look at them at night as she went to sleep.

This word box is really a treasure house of favorite words. They become a child's very own precious possessions, and delight in these treasures lasts a long time.

TALKING AND READING

When children are young, reading is not a quiet, solitary activity. It tends to be an activity that generates lots of talk between parents and children. It's the talking and reading together early that helps to ignite the desire to read alone, later.

Take any day, any time, any place. Try any or all of these activities.

Hidden Letters

All around the kitchen, from the cupboard to the refrigerator, from the stove to the sink, there are letters: A's, B's, F's, P's — on the soup cans, on the cat food, on the cereal box, even on the soap.

Make a game of finding these letters. Tell children to find (without tearing up the place, of course) five A's or three C's or any combination appropriate to your child's skills. Start easy and build up to letters that are harder to find. Children can then write down those they find or just share the objects on which the letters had been "hidden." You're building reading observation skills as well as having fun together.

The Grocery Store Eye

Reinforce your child's concepts of color, shape, size, and numbers with this activity at the store. While shopping, ask your child to locate a box of soap powder — perhaps a large orange box with blue letters. Then ask for eggs in a white container or green beans in a yellow can. With a little practice, your child will be able to locate and bring you the right item. For children who can read, provide a shopping list.

Dishes: Stack and Sort

Would you believe that putting away dishes teaches reading? It does — by teaching classification skills. Match plates with others of the same size, forks with forks. This is similar to recognizing the same alphabet letter in different words.

Labeling Home Objects

Just as in the schoolroom, where teachers label doors and desks, parents and youngsters at home can label beds, sofas, rugs. *Note:* Masking tape leaves no scars on walls and furniture.

Dress Me

There are words attached to clothing — "shirt," "blouse," "sock," "shoe" — and words attached to body parts — "foot," "arm," "head," "knee." The bedroom is a fine place to learn these words: Say the words aloud as clothes are put on and taken off. Print the words on large pieces of paper. A large poster with a child's silhouette on it can be tacked onto a bedroom wall to carry the words for parts of the body, and it's comforting for children going to bed to see "themselves."

Roomfuls of Words

Look in newspapers and magazines for pictures of furniture and objects that belong in different rooms of a house. Divide a large piece of paper into sections labeled LIVING ROOM, BEDROOM, KITCHEN. Children paste the pictures of the furniture in the appropriate section, or "room." This builds vocabulary and teaches classification skills.

Story Telling

Almost any time can be story-telling time — only let your child put the ending on the story. Tell a story that poses a problem, and let your youngster tell how to solve the problem. If necessary, use plot ideas from stories, perhaps from "Cinderella" or "Jack and the Beanstalk." Be sure, however, to stop before the end. Once children get the hang of making up stories themselves, encourage them to come up with plots that you'll have to solve.

Turn waiting time into reading time. Look through the pictures in the magazines you find at the doctor's office. Remember to take along storybooks or magazines whenever you might have to wait.

Scavenger Hunt

Make up some home reading games, and encourage children to do the same. In our house, "Scavenger Hunt" was made up by our older daughter (age eight) to provide reading practice for her sister (age six). She wrote out clues and deposited them around the house and yard. The younger child delighted in finding them and kept asking for more of this reading "work."

Read and Do

Give each child a list of things to do. *Example:* "Roll up a sheet of newspaper, fold it in half three times, tie up the roll with a piece of string." These can be far-fetched, plain fun, or actual chores that have to be done around the house.

Letter to My Child

Letters that you write to each other and actually mail or just slip into your mailbox are another good reading device. These, too, can gradually be made more challenging to read.

Send your child a letter in which you "hide" new words. Keep most of the letter in easy language, but insert several new words that your child has to find and ask about. This pairs the delight in new words with the joy of receiving a letter.

Cooking Up Directions

You don't just cook a dish — you have to read directions to know what comes first, second, and so on. Select a simple recipe with your child — perhaps Jell-O, instant pudding, or canned soup. On every package is a set of directions: Either read them aloud to the pre-reading child or ask young readers to do it on their own. You're coming up with a tasty dish and reading at the same time.

Morning Messages

Leave notes for each other. Children enjoy receiving surprises and take pride in writing notes to someone else. Here's one you might tape to the bedroom light switch: "Dear Susan: When you get up, please gather up the things lying on your floor. Put them away where they belong. Love, Mother." (*Note:* I can report that while these items are not always picked up, children do get practice in reading.)

The message should be written so that the reading is well within your child's ability. For a very young reader, it could be: "I Love You. See You Soon." One morning when I got up later than usual, I found a note slipped under my door: "Mother, don't worry. I have had my meal and I have gone out to play. Love, Jessica." (Jessica had just turned seven.)

READING: A HABIT any age

Not even the best school can take care of all a child's reading needs. A diet of textbook reading has not been known to turn people into lifelong readers.

Visual, listening, and talking activities prepare a child for reading, but children need to *want* to read. That is where the home environment supportive of reading comes into play. The object in teaching reading is not to turn out readers who read only when they "have to" but to turn out readers who enjoy reading and who continue to read even when the homework is over. Here are some ways parents can encourage reading above and beyond the school assignment.

My Reading Corner

All children need their own bookshelf and reading light. They need not be elaborate or expensive. A bookshelf can be a painted crate or cardboard box. The point is to make reading convenient and enticing and, above all, to build children's images of themselves as readers.

Pleasant Dreams

Encourage your children to decorate their sleeping area. The more appealing it is, the easier it may be to get children to go to bed. Ask your children what will make their sleeping arrangements more comfortable. *Example:* an extra pillow can make reading in bed easier and more enticing.

Carry Books Along

Try family read-alouds on summer picnics or even while you're driving in the car. People can get carsick when they read, but some find that they can build up a tolerance and that it is a good time for reading.

Take Turns

Try reading aloud to others who are doing household chores. Or if all else fails, have children read to you while you're cleaning the refrigerator.

Reading with Kids

Everyone reading this book probably knows how important it is to read to children. Even so — and I don't want to forget to say it — you may have to *make time* to do that reading. I did not say "find time." Reading is so important that it is a matter of *making* time, not finding it. Even five to ten minutes a day can make a big difference.

But instead of always reading to children, read *with* youngsters who are able to read. Take roles in plays; act out dramatic poems. When possible, tape-record your voices to give reading added glamour.

Let your children dictate stories to you and then draw pictures to accompany the words. They'll be able to "read" their words back to you. Older brothers and sisters can take turns as secretaries.

When children read on their own, it's tempting to say, "Thank goodness, we can forget about this now." Reading, however, is more than a skill. It needs to be nurtured and encouraged to have continued meaning in your child's life.

The Library

Try to go with children to the library at least once a week. Give youngsters unhurried time to browse, to make book discoveries. Let them take books home, even if you think them too hard, too easy, or not "worthwhile" reading. You can quietly check out another book considered worthwhile or just the right level; bring it out if the ones your child has chosen do not work out.

Check Appendix B for MegaSkills book selections compiled by the Association for Library Service to Children / American Library Association. They illustrate MegaSkills found in stories and novels for children. Encourage your children to try some of these, and use them for read-aloud times at home.

WHY BUY?

Why bother to buy books when you can go to the library and take them out for free? Probably because borrowing is not really the same as owning. (We don't use the rationale of "why buy?" for records.) Some books should just always be around the house, like old friends, to be looked at, to be underlined or starred if a reader feels strongly about a part, and to be read over and over. Many parents have noticed that their children do read certain books over and over, and they ask them why. The answer is, "I like them a lot." Which is all the more reason to have those special books around.

Thanks to public libraries, a home library need not be vast or expensive. But choosing books to stock the home larder can be difficult, just because there are so many to choose from. Where do you begin?

Start with the Children

If they are already reading, they may already have some favorite books, books they'd like to own. If children are not yet reading, ask what kinds of stories they especially like: What subjects? What would they like to learn more about?

Talk to your child's teachers or the school librarian. They often have lists of good books and are delighted to share them. Look carefully at school book fair displays and take notes about those books that interest you and your child. It's helpful when schools and organizations set up samples of good, inexpensive home libraries for children of different ages.

Do some comparison shopping before buying. Books, like dresses, come in different prices. One publisher's edition may cost $4.95 while another edition of the same text sells for $8.95. You may choose the more expensive one because of its illustrations and paper quality. Sometimes the less expensive can be the better buy, comparing favorably in pictures and type sizes.

Look for books that have an appealing "come and read me" look. In nonfiction, check for up-to-date accuracy; look at the copyright and revision dates on the front inside pages. Read a few paragraphs to see if the writing style is clear.

Find books that tie in to your child's interests and needs. A very shy child may gain more than good reading from a book about a shy child who found courage to do some big deed. You can also find books about youngsters of different racial and cultural backgrounds with whom children may identify.

When the books are bought, a parent's job is not over. Books can often use introducing. Even for children who already read on their own, it can help to read a first chapter aloud. And if you know something about the book, you can entice your child to it, just as when friends tell you about a good book they've read lately. The first and last chapters and jacket or back cover blurbs usually provide enough clues to help parents lead youngsters into it.

The Home Reference Shelf

It is probably wiser and cheaper to wait until children are able to read at the middle elementary school level before investing in a set of encyclopedias. In this way you can buy a more advanced set that will last longer. The value in having different reference texts at home, such as almanacs, is that children get used to using more than one book for research material.

READING TROUBLE? CATCH IT EARLY

Children want to read, and they will if they can. If children aren't starting to read by the end of first grade, then there is some reason why, and it's not because they are "lazy" or "ignorant." Either the instruction is not appropriate, or the child can't handle what is being taught.

The situation needs thorough examination. Often the causes are physical. Poor eyesight is obvious but sometimes overlooked. Subtle coordination problems that may occur even in "athletic" children can be a cause.

Both parents and teachers need to watch for early signs of a child having reading difficulties. Many of these difficulties are now commonly classified as dyslexia. For any number of reasons, the child is unable to break the reading code. Fortunately, a growing number of programs and organizations (see Appendix C) are available to help.

Some children's inability to read can be connected to poor self-esteem. Children may see themselves as people who can't do things. Home activities help children see themselves as people who can accomplish things. Self-esteem is crucial for the child to feel like a doer and to be a doer — in all activities, from learning to jump rope to learning to read.

WE ARE NEVER DONE WITH READING

After children learn the basics of reading, some go on to become voracious readers, devouring everything from novels to almanacs. Others go on to become specialized readers, reading a diet of biographies or history or even poetry. The great majority go on to become readers of newspapers, magazines, and cereal boxes.

But there isn't a person who can be done with reading.

We all need to keep on reading, even to protect ourselves. Reading can be more effective than a weapon. Our children will need to be able to read forms and contracts before they sign them. They will want to read movie and play reviews before spending money at the theater. They will need to read about supermarket specials to save money at the store. This is functional reading. It doesn't elevate or inspire, but it's part of the daily routine, like brushing teeth.

I don't know how some people can get through breakfast or start the day without reading or at least taking a look at the morning paper. I grew up before television became a morning companion. For me, reading a paper in the morning makes me feel ready for the day. I'm so addicted that when I don't have the actual day's paper, I will scavenge through the garbage to find an old edition that I will read again.

CHILDREN AND PARENTS: READING TOGETHER

Teachers can teach children to read, but they cannot keep them reading. Encouraging children to continue reading is the job of the home. Setting an example helps. Children — at least when they are young — imitate their parents.

My father was surrounded by newspapers wherever he was — they were next to his bed, on the floor by his reading chair, in the car, in the bathroom. I feel sure that's how I came by my own addiction. It seems natural to have reading material by my side at all times. Once a habit takes hold, it's hard to break it. Becoming addicted to reading is one of the better habits.

Before I leave this chapter, I want to share a few ways that parents who may not be great and voluminous readers themselves can help children get the reading habit.

It's good for your children to see you reading, but this doesn't have to be a diet of masterpieces to do good. It's important to read with your children, but that, too, doesn't have to be *War and Peace*. It can be the kind of reading that an adult has to do every day — a form, an ad, a newspaper article, a recipe, the TV schedule.

One of the best at-home reading exercises for developing comprehension is to read directions that come with a new piece of furniture to be assembled. By the time you get the piece put together, you've also had a lesson in overcoming frustration.

Or try reading a computer manual together. It's not Shakespeare, but it can test your level of understanding in similar ways.

If you have a mortgage, take out the contract and read it together. Find your insurance policy and try to read it. It may be the first time you have actually read it.

If you have credit agreements, look those over. Read bank statements. You may be spending money for service charges at one bank that you could save if you moved your funds to another.

Let children follow along as you go over a tax form. They might see a deduction that you've missed. Everyone gets junk mail. Before throwing those mailings away, read them. Some of it provides good laughs as well as reading experience.

The point I am trying to make is that to get children reading, they have to read. There is a lot of reading besides Shakespeare and textbooks. I devoured comic books and movie magazines as a child. Maybe it wasn't "good" reading, but it kept me reading, and that was the important thing.

So read those menus, read the ads, read maps, read medicine labels, read the big print, read the fine print — but READ.

Chapter 16.
Writing: The Revolution
Can Start at Home

Every class I have ever known has so much to say until the teacher announces it's writing time. Then students get very quiet. They're scared. Writing is scary if you don't get practice at it. Like learning to ride a bike or drive a car, writing takes practice.

There is a great deal that every parent can do at home to help children both want to write and learn to write. It's not necessary to know a participle from a gerund. The point is to help children write more and feel more comfortable writing. Even essays can be easily taught, as you'll see in this chapter.

Most of the activities that follow are really good at any age. Look them all over and pick the ones that you think will work for you.

In doing these activities at home, worry more about doing lots of writing and less about spelling and grammar. I want our children to use correct spelling and grammar as much as anyone else. But you can't teach everything at once. In these activities, you're teaching the pleasure of writing.

I looked into the shoe box where I have kept young children's writing — samples from those I have taught and those others have taught. As I describe the activities for young children, I'll include some of these writings so you can see what delights are in store for you when you try these early writing activities at home.

GETTING STARTED

Getting started is tough. The piece of white paper without a scratch on it can be daunting. It looks as though everything you write has to be perfect. So put a few scratches on it.

Sometimes young children don't need these scratches as much as older ones who have gotten scared of the empty page. The scratches I'm talking about are scribbles. They loosen up the muscles and lower the inhibitions.

THE JOY OF SCRIBBLING any age

Stretch out a large piece of brown wrapping paper or ordinary shelf paper and let the kids "go to it," writing any words or drawings they want to. A name over and over is fine. New studies call this "emergent literacy." It's great fun and can result in a bright mural for decorating the house.

SENSE AND SAY ages 4–6, or younger

To write, to gather impressions, you need to use your senses. Fill old shoe boxes with the objects (or similar ones) listed below. Use them in a game of "Sense and Say."

In this game, blindfolded youngsters are offered an object from a "mystery box." They feel or hear or smell it and then talk about what they find.

Touch Box: Cotton fabric, stone, a piece of glass with smooth edges, sandpaper — any items that give children a chance to experience softness, hardness, smoothness, roughness.

Shape Box: wooden block, marble, ball, book, spoon, a triangular shape, a paper cone.

Smell Box: an assortment from the kitchen, including mustard, cinnamon, vinegar.

Sound Box: whistle, bell, key chain, a piece of crumpled paper.

Here's how it works. Children have a sense to use and an object to use it on. Smelling mustard is an example. Ask them what it reminds them of. The mustard may recall a picnic on a beach where sea gulls landed. Encourage children to open up and to talk descriptively. Then trade places and let your children blindfold you.

All of us have special smells or tastes or sounds that remind us of home, of certain people, of pets. A picture, a touch, a piece of music, a taste; even in fragments these evoke memories deep within us — sometimes happy, sometimes sad, but always vivid. These are the experiences from which writing grows.

PICTURES AND WORDS ages 4–8

Use magazines and newspaper pictures worth ten thousand words. Any popular magazine is a gold mine of good pictures. Start keeping a file of appealing pictures from advertisements you come across. In this activity, everyone selects a colorful photograph. The idea is to look at it, observe the details, and figure out what's happening in the picture.

Ask the following: What's happening here? What do you think happened just before this picture was taken? What do you think happened afterward?

Everybody jots down ideas. Read these aloud and compare answers. If there are preschoolers looking on, let them dictate their versions.

Here's one, just as it came from the writer:

GOING PLACES

Once upon a time, there a little girl. She Lived in a pretty house
I am at the park   the park is nice
I sit down on a bench
now I go home to the house
A nice warm fire
I go to bed dreaming

It doesn't have to make complete sense to be completely helpful.

STORY AND SEQUENCE ages 4–8

Sequence can also be learned with those trusty pictures (see "Pictures and Words"). Everyone selects three or four or five pictures (depending on your child's level) that together tell a story. Paste these on cardboard pieces. Then number the pictures.

Using the pictures in numerical order, your child then tells a story. Even preschoolers can take part without very much extra help. Then shuffle the pictures and try again. It's fascinating for kids and grown-ups alike to see how the stories change.

Here's an example:

THE STORY OF THE WORLD'S FAIR

There was a fine lumberJack. one day
They are very smart I hope you like them
I went on a ferris wheel. Do you like ferris wheels?
I was on a rollercoaster one day.
The dinosaurs are nice but not so nice

Children can write down or scribble their tales. Very young children, it's been shown, remember what their scribbles say. Prewriters might dictate their stories, perhaps to an older sibling. This provides writing practice for the older child.

ROUND-ROBIN STORY BUILDING ages 4–8

This is another sure way to get ideas rolling. Start a first sentence, "Once upon a time," and everyone adds a sentence to keep the story moving. Some of these will be silly, but the point is made about how to build a story.

Get kids talking — and from this talking comes writing.

SUMMARIZING ages 4–8

Children need to develop the ability to tell stories that have beginnings, middles, and ends. I don't really enjoy those long, rambling stories that children delight in going on and on with. I know I am supposed to say I enjoy every word. But after about five minutes, I take refuge in asking, "How does it end?" It's good for children to know that even a good story has to have an ending.

FINISHING UNFINISHED STORIES ages 4—8

Start out with one person, probably an adult, telling a story. But stop before coming to the end. Let children finish the story, at first perhaps working together, then alone.

Before finishing a story that you're reading aloud, stop and ask your children how they think it will end and why they think this. (See also "Story Telling" in Chapter 15.)

LOGICAL ORDER PUZZLES ages 7—9

Clip paragraphs from the newspaper. Or ask children to write their own about any subject that comes to mind. Paragraphs written by professional writers in large advertising print work well for this exercise.

Cut and separate the sentences and mix up the pieces. The challenge is for the youngster to work these sentences back into a logical order. Elementary graders enjoy this game and particularly enjoy having parents participate. The cut-up sentences are hard to keep together, so it's a good idea to put them in a little envelope. The activity is enjoyable on its own, but what's being taught is the important understanding that sentences need to follow one another logically.

WRITING MEMORIES any age

Among the most prized mementos of my children's growing-up years are the scraps of paper containing their early writings.

There's the invitation to the fifth birthday party: "Be a Smarty — Come to My Party." There's the excuse note to the teacher: "Dear Mrs. Field, Please let me stay in today is that OK. By the way, I get too wet outside. Sincerely yours, the Riches." It didn't get sent, but it provided good writing practice.

And there are poems and stories about the little mouse, the snow, the cuckoo clock, our flute. We didn't have a flute, but that didn't matter. What matters is that they got a chance to write, and the pleasure was both in the writing and in the reading of it decades later.

PULLING THOUGHTS TOGETHER

In many ways, writing is like making the pieces of a jigsaw puzzle fit together. The puzzle pieces are thoughts. They need to connect. These activities provide practice in making these connections.

LOOKING AT ADVERTISEMENTS ages 8–12

Use those glamorous, colorful advertisements to illustrate the idea of a main point, or "thesis." Ask the following: What's the main idea in this ad? What's it trying to persuade us to do? A strong, handsome man drinking a certain soft drink in a fancy car with a beautiful girl at his side is telling us something about that soft drink. Even young children get the message. All of the details are organized to back up the ad's message, main point, or thesis. For now, look at and discuss these pictures. The time to write will come.

TYING UP IDEAS ages 8–12

Good writing needs not only ideas but ideas that are united, combined, and tied together to make a logical whole. Try the following activity. It can become a bit silly, but it helps teach the pulling-together formula. You need a blackboard or a large piece of paper.

Everyone jots down an idea or name of a thing. The goal is to combine these items into a logical sentence. Let's say you get the words "toys," "trip," "sunny," "teachers." You might come up with this: "On sunny days, teachers often let their classes take toys with them on school trips." Even when your ideas defeat logic, putting them together is good mental exercise and gives everyone lots of laughs.

SUBJECT BOUNCE ages 8–12

In this activity you toss subjects and statements from youngster to parent and back to youngster. *Example:* Jan names the subject, "Cats," and turns to Jim to come up with a statement about cats. His might be, "Cats are mean," or "Cats are pretty," or any other statement he can think of. The statement giver then gets to come up with a subject for someone else to make a statement about.

The game pulls together listening and writing skills. It's best to encourage children to make "big" statements about a subject. Take, for example, the subject "mother." The statement, "My mother likes cereal for breakfast," is a relatively narrow idea. It is easier for essay development, later, to make a broader statement, such as, "My mother is busy all day."

The younger the children, the more help they may need at first. But the game itself, once under way, has never failed to involve everyone and, more important, to teach these two basic skills in writing: (1) Having a subject, and (2) Having something to say about it.

BRAINSTORMING FOR SUBJECTS ages 8–12

Working together, even if it's just a group of two, jot down all the things you can write about. It can be anything at all, from parents to ice skating to cooking to homework to baseball.

Pick one of these to be a subject that you and your child will work on. Let's say, for example, you've picked "family." Keep on brainstorming. Think of all the possible things you both can say about the family. Don't try for any particular order. Jot them down as they come to mind.

Now you have a list of what you might write about the family. Decide what you would say first, second, and so on. You may find some items on the list, as you examine it, that shouldn't really be there, or you may think of others that you should have included. As you go down the list, decide what should come when, and eliminate those items you can no longer use. Add the important new ideas. After all, you may have forgotten to include Aunt Lily!

At this point, you have a list of what you hope to include in your writing, and you have them identified in numerical order. You're almost ready to write (and most of your work has already been done) — but not quite.

There's one more important step that will help. I call this "The Umbrella."

A RECIPE FOR WRITING ESSAYS: THE UMBRELLA

Even as an English teacher, I had been assigning essays for years before I ever really thought about how to teach them.

The day I had to think about how to teach them was the day my own daughter came home with her first essay assignment and asked, "What's an essay, Mom?"

The usual definition from Webster's — "a short piece of writing on a single subject" — would not do. She'd already heard that at school.

So I thought a bit. My eyes came upon an umbrella in the hall that, luckily for me, was not in its right place. There it was in the middle of the floor — just waiting to be discovered.

The open umbrella (if you're superstitious, open it outside) provides a visual form for the structure of an essay — really, for any direct, informational piece of writing.

The umbrella provides a structure to help young writers organize their thoughts. I have used it in both the early elementary grades and graduate school, and it works in both places. It will delight you to see how easily it works and how much it helps.

The Subject

First you have to have something to write about. This is called the "subject." Let's say, for our first example, that the subject is "ice cream." On the umbrella, it fits in here:

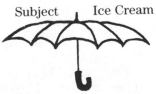

Subject · Ice Cream

We all like that subject. Now, having a subject is nice, *but it isn't enough* for writing. You need to say something *about* your subject. That's called "making a statement."

The Statement

Here are some statements children might make about ice cream:

I love ice cream.

Ice cream comes in many flavors.

Ice cream is better than spinach.

We'll pick one to show how the statement fits in the umbrella:

The Proof

Having a statement is nice, but it isn't enough. You have to explain your statement to the reader. That's called "proving the statement."

Everything you tell about loving ice cream must fit under the umbrella statement.

The proof can be something like this:

Proof   It is sweet and cold. Ice cream comes in many flavors. There are chocolate, vanilla, strawberry, chocolate chip, vanilla ripple, and many more. Ice cream in any flavor cools me on hot days.

Everything goes together — like the parts of an umbrella. First comes the subject. The statement is about the subject. The proof explains the statement. It would be pretty silly to write, "I love ice cream," and then go on in the same paragraph to explain the love of roast beef. But that is the kind of silly thing that happens to writers who forget to stay under the umbrella.

A BROKEN UMBRELLA

Here is another example to help illustrate, one by one, the three parts of the umbrella and how they need to match.

Part One: Start with the subject or the topic of the umbrella. The subject in this case is "dreams."

Part Two: This is the statement — what is being said about the subject. This is the part that fits in the umbrella itself. The statement in this umbrella is, "My dreams are silly."

Part Three: This is the proof. It has to tell about the subject "dreams" and it has to explain how your dreams are "silly." It has to stay under the umbrella. It can't go off to tell us about something different from silly dreams.

Ask your child to read the following paragraph aloud.

DREAMS

My dreams are silly. Two nights ago I saw a gorilla flying south. Last night I saw a flag waving at me. Tomorrow I will probably see shoes running down the street.

Ask the following: "Is this a good umbrella?" "If not, why not?" We don't see umbrellas in the paragraphs in the books we read, but the umbrella parts are there — even when we don't see them.

Soon children will be able to write paragraphs without the umbrella to help. But in the meantime, try the umbrella to make thinking and writing easier.

SIMPLE AND COMPLEX UMBRELLAS

You might have an umbrella like this: "My family is wonderful." This is a big, broad, simple umbrella. A more complex umbrella would be, "Having a big family has its advantages," or "Our family home is the place to be at holiday time."

These more complex umbrellas narrow the topic and ask that the writer prove a very definite point. This is what good umbrellas do: They actually make essay writing easier by limiting the subject, making it possible for even an inexperienced writer to write well.

A WRITING FORMULA

So you see, it's really pretty easy to teach and to write a formula umbrella paragraph. It gives every child the recipe to write a paragraph. Once that has been learned, a child can go on to bigger and better writing projects. As students go through school, they will be able to move beyond formulas to writing with a developing mastery of usage, form, and style in order to put across ever more effectively what they have to say.

DIALOGUE: WHO SAYS WHAT? ages 8–12

Try writing some parent-child conversations about typical household problems. *Examples:* tracking mud into the kitchen, making time for homework, children refusing to do chores. These dialogues are tremendously revealing for both parents and children, and they're great writing practice.

COMBINE HISTORY WITH WRITING ages 8–12

Use famous persons. Everybody writes a pretend page from the diary of a famous person. You can all choose the same person, or everyone can choose someone different. The choice is fun in itself: Clara Barton or Helen Keller, Buffalo Bill or Reggie Jackson, Mick Jagger or John F. Kennedy.

A variation of the activity is the interview. One person poses as a famous person, and everyone else interviews him or her. Usually the person picked is in the news. This exercise is fine incentive for current events class as well.

DETAILS MAKE A POINT OF VIEW ages 8–12

What we write is governed by our point of view, as is illustrated by this exercise. You and the children write two contrasting paragraphs about the same subject. *Example:* Jim describes the living room as though he's feeling sad and gloomy about everything. In his second paragraph, he describes the same room, but this time he's feeling joyous, on top of the world. The details he picks and his choice of words should make clear the point of view. In the happy paragraph, for example, the blue wall may be "the color of the sun-filled sky."

A similar selection of particular details and their wording can be done with people. Writers are always doing this to make us like or dislike a character. If Spencer Jones has a "long, funny nose," we tend to like him. If his nose is described as "long and bony," we distrust him.

This is a sophisticated exercise that illustrates the many choices that writers make.

HOMEMADE POETRY any age

Probably almost every poem in print was written outside of school. Yet seeing poems in bold, black type in big, thick anthologies makes many people hesitate to write poetry, as if it were something produced by superhumans in some out-of-this-world place.

There's poetry in everyone, just waiting for a chance to show itself. One of the nicest things about poetry is that it takes many forms: long, short, happy, sad, rhyming, free form, unrhymed. It's Lewis Carroll and haiku and Emily Dickinson.

Parents who have some favorite poems are in a good position to work with poetry at home. That old-fashioned image of those quiet minutes with children seated around their parents is worth preserving. And when you share your favorite poems, fill the children in on your experiences with them — how your father read that poem to you, or how a certain poem was your third-grade teacher's favorite.

Even if poetry is unfamiliar territory to you, your children are not strangers to it. They've been playing delightedly with words and rhythms since they first started to babble.

Here's an example from an elementary grader:

Under the cherry tree
I sat and watched a dream that I
could see wonderfully
A dream of elves, fairies, and dwarfs

A dream with dew all
over the trees.
All was on new years day
A wonderful day in the forest was
to have this bright holiday.
And the wind was blowing
all through the trees.

Poetry is word play and word feeling. Delight in words and in the pictures they evoke is the key to poetry at home. If both you and the children are exploring poetry for the first time, get hold of a children's anthology of verse from your library. Read some of these poems aloud. Take turns reading to each other. Make a game of picking the poems by closing your eyes and letting your fingers land at random on the table of contents.

Music sparks imagination. Especially good are those selections that tell a story, like *The Sorcerer's Apprentice* or *Coppélia*. Compare your children's interpretations of the music with the original story versions available in most libraries.

YOU HAVE A POEM! any age

Practice a game of associations. Ask questions: What does yellow remind you of? A big yellow sun? A sweet, spring flower? An infected sore? How about love? Mother? Sister? Your bed? The morning alarm?

Take one of these as your subject: spring, insects, trees, flowers. Anything from nature is a fine takeoff point. Jot down all the descriptive phrases about them that come to mind. Encourage children to use words that "paint" pictures.

After you have about ten phrases, stop. You have a poem! It may not be terribly artistic. But it has the basics of poetry — words that paint pictures and convey feelings.

A parent's aim in helping children with poetry writing is not necessarily to turn children into poets but to increase their overall ability to use expressive language freely.

Here is an example of homemade poetry written on paper grown yellow on my kitchen wall. Our daughter Rebecca composed it while on a Sunday walk in the country:

Whenever the woods I walk among —
Are very green and very young —
The trees in the woods
They wave so nice —
With a little
Path that
I follow.

All right, I know it isn't Shakespeare. But I treasure it, as would any parent, as a masterpiece.

GAMES HELP, EVEN WITH GRAMMAR

In grammar teaching, from the middle elementary grades through the senior grades, the student is taught and retaught the making of a sentence. There may be a few additional refinements in each year's curriculum, but by and large it's a program taught in a similar way, usually from one text series.

Some students learn their grammar rules first time out. Others continue to have trouble, no matter how many English classes they sit through.

GETTING THE "FEEL" OF THE SENTENCE ages 7–12

The important point in grammar is to help children get the "feel" of a sentence and to help them enjoy experimenting with different kinds of sentences. You can teach the feel of a sentence without going into subject-verb technicalities. But if you know them and your child is receptive, it won't hurt to point out that every complete sentence has a subject and a verb. This subject-and-verb combination is sometimes called a "kernel" sentence. Here's one: "Boy runs."

The fun is in elaborating and building on this kernel: A boy runs; A small boy runs; A small boy runs quickly; A small boy runs quickly to the swimming pool; and so on. Children enjoy doing this. You can do it both orally and on paper.

WHERE IS JOE'S COW? ages 7–12

Imitating sentence patterns is good grammar practice. Start with the simple statement, "Joe has a cow." Children, depending on age and ability, can either repeat what you say or come up with the same structure by using their own words, such as "Sally has a horse," then "Joe and Ted have a cow," and so on.

Now change to the question form: "Where is Joe's cow?" Move to the command: "Joe, bring me that cow!" And, of course, the exclamation: "Wow, what a cow Joe has!"

Fill-in exercises can be helpful in teaching grammar. They work best when read aloud, so that the "feel" of the sentence sinks in. Parents can make up paragraphs, being sure to leave some spaces blank. Children enjoy filling in the blanks, perhaps with humorous words. This makes it more of a game.

Older children with some knowledge of grammar will enjoy the "string of letters" game. This consists of giving children a group of letters — for example, *a, d, f, m, p, r, w* — and then asking them to make up a sentence using words that start with these letters. These strings are then exchanged. This provides lots of laughs. Who says writing has to be grim?

WRITING, WRITING EVERYWHERE any age

Encourage writing practice around the house wherever and whenever you can.

Let children write your notes to the postman, to anyone who needs reminders or greetings. Keep paper and pencils all around the house.

On trips, provide each child with a notebook in which to keep a travel log or diary. Children can take notes on what they've seen, things they've liked, foods they've eaten. At home, you can frame some of these remembrances along with a marked map of where you went and some pictures of what you saw.

Start a library of homemade storybooks. The books themselves can be made by stapling colored paper as a cover over several sheets of folded lined or unlined paper. Pre-writers can dictate their stories, with the parent putting down a sentence or two at the bottom of each page. Children can fill in their own drawings. Don't forget the all-important bold print for the author's name.

KEEP THE PRAISE COMING

Try not to overcriticize a child's initial writing work. The aim of these exercises is to build writing confidence in an atmosphere of shared experiences.

The need for children to learn to communicate through writing has never been greater. In the past, there was more dependence on oral communication. Today, you have to be able to put words on paper.

Standard English is still standard English — it is the English that is rewarded with a job, with a place on the payroll. This is English that all children can learn.

This chapter on writing is designed as a start. It is a takeoff point for your family's ideas. And do remember that the best medicine for writers, young and old, is steady encouragement and honest praise.

Chapter 17.
Math: Getting Comfortable with Numbers

I would rather read a story than a column of numbers. I would rather try to write a poem than fill in a ledger sheet. I am number-averse, and it is a definite handicap. I remember my high school math with deep feelings of failure, even though I passed. In college I skipped math altogether. I feel for people like me, and I suspect there may be a lot of us.

I was in a drugstore the other day buying a pair of pantyhose on sale — "20 percent off" said the sign. The reduced price was not marked on the package, nor was it stored in the cash register computer. So the young man (he told me he was a college student) who was collecting the money had to do his own figuring. The hose were originally $2.50. He struggled and struggled. At one point, he said I had to pay $2.75.

Finally I showed him how to do it. I had made it through percentages before my number problem took over in algebra and geometry. I think I could have told him I owed him a dollar, and he would have taken it. Here was a fellow sufferer.

Over the years I have become friendlier with numbers. Actually this came about through "number sense" activities I did with my children. Many of these activities are in this chapter. (See "Money Common Sense" in Chapter 11 for activities using money.)

The idea is to help children feel comfortable with numbers. Even with calculators and computers to help, we still have to cope with numbers. And we have to be able to face them as fearlessly as possible.

Here is what I mean by number sense. This example may seem

far-fetched, but it is a real one, and it's duplicated many times in homes and classrooms across our nation. A fourth grader was asked to estimate how much his parents would pay for three nights in three different hotels. The first night would cost $32.00. The second night would cost $28.00, and the third night would cost $30.00. This youngster immediately jumped to the answer: $9,000.00!

His parents asked, "Don't you think that's a high price for three nights' lodging?" It was not until his parents added up the bill with him that the youngster understood the difference between $90.00 and $9,000.00. It's just a matter of decimal points — but oh, those decimals!

To succeed in math, I'm told by those who know, a child really needs not a storehouse of math tricks but rather a storehouse of math experiences to call on. These are all around us.

A MATH WALK THROUGH THE HOUSE

The plan for this chapter is for families to take a math walk. This is literally a hunt for numbers in our everyday environment. Keep a pencil, small pad, and tape measure with you. There will be many occasions to use them.

The Kitchen

AROUND-THE-STOVE MATH any age

Math is good in the kitchen at any age. For the pre-reader: Set the table and count the settings. For the early reader, measure ingredients and read recipes. For the older elementary grader, divide and double recipes.

EGG CARTON COUNTER any age

Save those old egg cartons. In the bottom of each egg section, write in a number. Make some of these negative, or minus, numbers to get the excitement going. This is great for matching or pitching games with two or more people. Give each person an equal number of pennies or stones. Try to land in the sections that have the highest scores. When the pennies or stones are used up, total your scores.

PLAY STORE ages 4–6

Save milk cartons and other boxes. Use play or real money. (Real is more fun!) Have youngsters price items. How much for a quart of milk? For a can of corn? Young readers can check prices using newspaper ads.

NAPKIN FRACTIONS ages 7–9

Make fractions fun to learn and get the table set differently every night. Paper towels or napkins can be folded into all kinds of big and little fractions. Start with easy halves and move to eighths or sixteenths. Use markers to label the parts.

UNEVEN EATERS ages 7–9

This old standby is still effective. Let's say you have three for dinner and only two hamburgers. How will you divide them? What about five eaters and only four baked potatoes? Everyone can still eat — but they'll be digesting fractions, too.

THE LONG RECEIPT ages 7–9

Check grocery receipts against your purchases. Have your child match prices on items coming out of the bags with the numbers on the receipts. Did you get everything you bought? Sometimes you paid more for an item at the store than you realized.

WHAT'S IN THE HOUSE? ages 8–12

Before going to the store, ask children to help you figure out what's needed by looking at the fractions of items you still have.

What's left of the sugar? All gone? Two pounds? How much bread is on hand? A quarter of a loaf? How much milk? Half a gallon? How many eggs? A third of a dozen? You don't have to actually measure. You're estimating and "talking fractions."

FOOD LABEL NUMBERS ages 8–12

There's a lot of math on food labels, mandated by law. What's the expiration date? How heavy is the can? What percentages of different foods are contained? It comes as a surprise to many to learn that the first ingredient listed is the predominant one in the container. If water is listed first, that's what you get most of.

Ask older students to read for natural versus additive ingredients. The long, hard-to-pronounce words are usually the additives. How many and how much of them are included in your product? They are not necessarily bad. Your children just have to know what they are buying.

MATH CONCEPTS IN THE KITCHEN ages 8–12

Who Ate the Cake?

Do this with foods that can be cut up, such as cupcakes, apples, or oranges. Cut them into pieces that can be reassembled. The concept is that the whole can be divided into parts and reassembled to form the whole — unless someone eats a piece or two.

Is Taller Bigger Than Shorter?

Find two containers of different shapes that hold the same amount of water. These might be two measuring cups or coffee cups with the same capacity.

Illustrate this by filling one of the containers with water and then pouring the water into the other container. Chances are, your young child will guess that the taller container holds more water than the shorter one. Up to a certain age (about age eight or so) children tend to say that the taller container holds more water than the shorter one — even when they see you put the same amount into each cup. The eminent Swiss psychologist Jean Piaget identified this as a lack of operational understanding, which children tend not to acquire until the middle elementary school years.

Can an Orange Be an Apple?

Illustrate this by cutting up two different items, such as an orange and an apple. The parts of that orange put together again will combine to make a whole orange. The parts of the apple can be reassembled into a whole apple. But try putting parts of an orange together with parts of an apple. They do not combine, at least not readily.

Living Room / Dining Room

GAMES = LEARNING any age

Math is basic to indoor games, from simple bingo to complicated bridge. Even while children are playing, they are putting to real-life test their math workbook exercises.

For young children, make dot-to-dot puzzles using different number sequences: 1, 2, 3 . . . for young children; 3, 6, 9 . . . for more sophisticated players.

A storehouse of games — lotto, bingo, dominoes, hopscotch, crazy eights, Parcheesi, jackstraws, fish, beanbag throws, war, Cootie, tenpins, I Win, darts, Uncle Wiggily, casino, Monopoly, rummy, canasta, cribbage, bridge, pinochle — all build number comfort and skills.

MEASURE FOR PLEASURE ages 4–8

The world is filled with things and spaces to measure. How tall is the lamp? How wide is the room? Use yardsticks, tape measures, string — anything that can measure. Jot down the results to share with the family.

Look around. Count the windows and doors in any one room. Then count the number of rooms and make a projection about how many windows and doors are in the entire building.

NEWSPAPER NUMBERS ages 7–9

Open almost any page of the paper, and you'll find numbers galore. As a starting point with young children, ask them to circle every number they see. Start with one column at a time to keep the task from seeming endless.

Move on to more sophisticated assignments: Find all numbers over fifty or over one hundred or over one thousand.

Ask children to look at ads for all those specials that end in ninety-eight or ninety-nine cents. Let them get practice in rounding off those numbers by estimating, for example, what four shirts that sell for $7.99 each will cost, or what five pounds of potatoes that sell for eighty-nine cents a pound will cost.

MATH BOUNCE ages 7–9

Bounce the ball (if indoors, not too vigorously) to show your math answers. What's twelve minus nine, divided by one, or six plus eleven? Children get exercise and give their answers by bouncing the ball the right number of times.

FAMILY FRACTIONS ages 8–12

Think about different people you know and their ages. By what fraction are little brothers and sisters younger than you, and by what fraction are your parents older? If you are twelve and your mother is forty-eight, what fraction are you of your mother's age? (*Answer:* one fourth.) Make up these fractions for other people in the family and for friends.

PRACTICE PERCENTAGES ages 8–12

Look around the room. Figure the percentage of people in the room who are wearing sneakers. Look outside. Count the cars on the block. Figure the percentage of black or white cars of all the cars on the block. Figure the percentage of time (number of minutes) that commercials take during radio or TV programs.

MATH WORDS ages 8–12

There are three M's and an R that students will hear about whenever a lot of numbers come together.

It can be hard to keep these apart. It was for me. So I make up sentences to help.

Mode: The number that appears often. As in: "That jacket this year is really the mode, just the style you want."

Median: The middle number in the list. As in: "The median line divides the highway."

Mean: This really measures the average. As in: "The mean temperature for July was eighty-five degrees."

Range: The limits; how far the numbers extend. As in: "Our family ranges in age from four to forty."

A good way for children to get comfortable with these words is to use them and to hear them used.

Try out this activity at a restaurant as you're waiting for a meal to be served. Ask to hold on to the menus after you've made your choices. Look at all the prices for the appetizers or entrées — keep to one category — and ask these questions: What's the range? What's the median? The mode? Some can be eyeballed; that is, the answer can be arrived at without calculations on paper. The mean usually takes pencil figuring.

FAMILY AGE, WEIGHT, HEIGHT ages 8–12

Another activity for the three M's and the R is to figure family ages or weights or heights. In a young family, you will find a mean age in the teens. In an older family, you will get up into the forties.

DIRECTION WORDS ages 8–12

When you tell a person how to go from your house to the school and you talk about walking "parallel" to this street, "perpendicular" to another, and crossing at a certain "intersection," you are using words important in math. Help children become comfortable with these words and encourage them to use them as they give directions.

SPORTS, STOCKS, AND NUMBERS ages 8–12

Children who balk at math in class are often youngsters who figure out batting averages in their spare time. Some even understand the financial pages.

Capitalize on these interests to help a child overcome math resistance in class. Try questions such as these: Which team has won the most games this season? Who are the high scorers? How much higher are they than the others? Use the newspaper to get the answers.

HOW LONG AM I WAITING? ages 8–12

There's little we can do, once we're waiting, to make a person show up on time for an appointment. But we can spend some of that time figuring out just how late "late" is. Check your watch. How many minutes or hours? What fraction or percentage is that of an hour, a day, a week, a year?

This is a solid math exercise, and it passes the time productively. Of course, when that person shows up, there will be some other words to deal with.

MATH IN HOBBIES ages 8–12

Photography

Shopping for a camera is an experience in mathematics, and it's not just in the initial cost. Compare film prices: How many pennies per exposure? Is it cheaper to buy a roll of twenty exposures than to buy twelve exposures? How much do you lose when a picture doesn't turn out?

Gardening

Figure out what you need: How many rows will fit in a four-by-four-foot garden plot if they are six inches apart? Eight inches?

Twelve inches? If seeds are to be placed two inches apart, how many can you fit in one row? How much fertilizer is needed for a lawn of one hundred square feet? It's mind boggling how many numbers are involved.

ASK THE CALCULATOR ages 10–12

Certain questions are made for the calculator, and they build the love of numbers and the excitement of estimates and projections. I know there is concern that once kids start using the calculator, they will stop using their heads. But that can't happen if they are asked to use their heads to ask the questions and to know the steps they're taking to get to the answers.

For example, take this question: How many miles do you think we will drive this year in our car? To get the answer, you first have to figure out how many miles you drive in a week or in a month and then multiply appropriately to arrive at your answer. The key is to keep kids talking about what they are doing as they try to figure out the answer.

Try other questions like these: How many dozen eggs do you think this family will eat in a year? How many quarts (or gallons) of milk will we drink in a year? How many steps do you take in a week? In a month? In a year? How many hours or minutes in a month? How many hours until Christmas? Making up the questions is almost as much fun as coming up with the answers.

As long as your children know how they get to the answer, the calculator is more to be loved than feared.

Bathroom

MATH IN THE BATHTUB ages 4–6, or younger

Water play for a young child can provide fun, cleanliness, and solid math instruction. Equip the tub or sink with plastic containers of various sizes: cup, pint, quart, liter, gallon.

Then in go the children to experiment. Ask questions: How many of the small-size cups fit into the larger one? How many quarts are in a gallon? It's not necessary that children memorize the names of the measures. What is important at this point is that they experiment and enjoy the experience with numbers.

WEIGH ME ages 4–8

Bring out that bathroom scale and start weighing — anything and everything. First let your children make guesses about how much different things weigh, including themselves. Weigh the wastebasket, the clothing just taken off, a full glass of water.

WEIGHT WATCHING ages 8–12

This is a national pastime that provides useful math practice. Every day for a week, have children read the scales for a family member. Can your youngster find the heaviest and lightest family member (or any two willing participants)?

Does someone in the family weigh double another person's weight? If you weigh 130 pounds and in the next two months gain 5 percent of your weight, how much will you weigh? These are intriguing questions that are fun and provide math practice.

TILE-A-WHILE any age

Often there are tiles in a bathroom. How many and how wide and long are they? Start counting and come up with some hard data. You can even find out how much area the tiles cover by multiplying the size of one tile by how many there are. This can be lively information at the dinner table if you first ask for guesses from the family. Who comes closest to the correct answer?

MATCHING AND PILING ages 4–7

Laundry contains numbers. Match the socks and count them. Count the sheets and fold them into fractional parts, down to half, down to one quarter. You'll find all the socks and have a neat linen closet!

INGREDIENTS IN CLOTHES ages 8–12

What are our clothes made of? These days labels rarely read "100 percent" of anything. Check them to figure out what percentage of ingredients are in the garments you see before you.

WATCH THE CLOCK ages 7–9

Practice estimating times: How long before Mom or Dad gets home? How long will it take us to get ready for this trip? How long will it take to get to school?

MY OWN CALENDAR ages 4–7

There can be one in every child's room. Use the promotional ones given away at the end of the year; they often have big numbers. Check off the days until different events happen. How many days and hours until that special day?

WHAT'S YOUR SIZE? ages 4–9

Equip children with rulers, yardsticks, or string to check the length and width of their hands and feet. Talk about the family's sizes: shoes, dresses, and suits. Who has the biggest hands? The shortest feet? The longest legs?

There are memories, often about numbers, that bless and burn. They provide revealing topics for family conversations — discussions that even adolescents find interesting.

Can you tell about a time when knowing fractions (or not knowing them) made a difference to you? Was there a recipe you ruined or a deal you botched when you thought that four eighths was more than one half?

Have you been to a restaurant and had the problem of trying to figure out who owed what and how much the tip ought to be? When you paid the bill, did you sometimes pay less than your share or come up with a tip that was too big?

Do you agree that ability with math helps in coping with the demands of everyday life? Talk about this. Tell about a time when someone in the family used math to solve a problem. This does not have to be a "big" deal. It can be an overdue traffic ticket or a refund from a department store.

Keep the talk about numbers flowing. It builds the comfort level for work with math, in school and out.

REASSURING MATH

Numbers can relieve anxiety, not just make it. In a recent film, a basketball coach from a very small town brings his team into a huge fieldhouse for the big championship game. It's clear from the boys' faces that the massive fieldhouse awes them and that they feel there is no way they can play and win there.

The coach takes out his tape measure, holds it to the basket, and lets it drop to the floor. He asks the team to look at the number. Then he measures the distance from the free-throw line to the basket. He asks the team to look at the result. They are the very same measurements as in their little gym back home. The boys' faces register their reassurance, and sure enough, they go on to win the game.

DON'T WAIT FOR THE ROBOT

The increasing use of computers by government, industry, and business demands an awareness of computer uses and limitations. An expert in artificial intelligence (the subject of programming knowledge into computers) recently confided that it was much easier for a computer to "learn" calculus than for the computer to stack blocks — a task most people consider children's play.

Involved in stacking blocks are hundreds of steps that children understand and learn by watching adults. The computer's universe is far more limited. Within those limitations, programmed by a person, the computer may work more efficiently than a person. But in the world of almost unlimited and unprogrammed daily choices, the computer can't cope.

Managing a household, for example, is far more difficult to program than managing a factory job with a limited number of tasks. A household robot will take longer to develop than a factory robot. There's just so much going on in a home all at once.

Math may look cold and calculating, but it is full of feelings and sometimes anxiety. No robot can take the place of a teacher or parent. What robot can tell a funny story about how that "bargain" really proved to be a "lemon"? Even in math, the human factor plays a critical role. That's why friendly feelings for numbers are so important.

Chapter 18.
Special Education:
Different Teaching for
Different Learners

In education, unlike pantyhose, one size does not fit all. While we know that our left foot is usually larger than our right, both shoes, except for those sold in the fanciest stores, are the same size, and the left foot always pinches. The same is true for bathing suits. Many women need one size top and another size bottom, but because they come in the same size, one part will fit, and the other won't.

Special education is like those different-size shoes. It gives children a special fit for their special learning styles.

We know children who can't see — even though they have perfectly good eyes. They are not stupid. These children have visual learning problems.

We know children who have trouble hearing — yet they have ears that work. These children have auditory learning problems.

And there are children who have eyes and ears and yet can't seem to get these two senses working together so that their hands know what to do. They have eye-hand coordination problems.

These children have specific learning disabilities. With extra help, these disabilities can be managed and even overcome.

More than likely what special learners need at home is not more of the same drill and practice that they are already having trouble with in school. They need and want activities that offer opportunities for success through alternative or different kinds of learning.

This chapter focuses on the extra and different help these children need. In school, Individualized Education Plans (known as

IEP's) are developed for special education students. In this chapter are what I call Home Education Plans (HEP's); they provide specialized help for children at home, to extend and reinforce but not duplicate what children work on in school.

Each activity is divided into **Look, Listen,** and **Do** sections. They separate out from the home learning recipe single activity strands that focus directly on visual, auditory, and coordination skill development.

- **Look** sections provide practice in:
    Visual Discrimination — the ability to see differences between similar objects.
    Visual Memory — the ability to remember what was seen.
- **Listen** sections provide practice in:
    Auditory Discrimination — the ability to hear differences between similar sounds.
    Auditory Memory — the ability to remember what was heard.
- **Do** sections provide practice in:
    Visual and Auditory Integration — the ability to combine the skills worked on in the visual and auditory areas. Emphasis is on creativity and on eye-hand coordination.

PING-PONG TEACHING AND LEARNING

It is particularly important in special education for children to have the opportunity to be active learners and for adults to have a sense that what is being taught is indeed being learned.

That's why in the LOOK and LISTEN sections of each activity, you will find reciprocal, or "Ping-Pong," learning. This is what happens when adults and children work together and send ideas to each other. These activities have been carefully designed to help adults elicit active responses from children.

Before doing these activities, read them all the way through. Read the introduction before going on to the LOOK, LISTEN, and DO sections. You might decide to do only one section, such as LOOK, to build your child's visual skills, or LISTEN, to build auditory skills. But you need the information from the first part for the sections that follow. Use the activities in any order you wish.

SORT AND SACK ages 4–7

This activity helps children develop reading and organizational skills by matching similar items on kitchen shelves. You need at least six cans or boxes of food products, paper, measuring tape or ruler, and markers.

Select one or two easy-to-reach kitchen shelves. You might want to do this activity after you return from the grocery store and have bags full of groceries. Arrange a working space on a table or on the floor near the shelves.

Look

Visual Discrimination. Ask your child to choose at least six cans or food containers and to watch you put the cans in order according to size. Start on the left with the shortest and move to the right with the tallest. Then mix them up.

Now your child, who has watched you, puts the cans back in the left-to-right order that you established.

Now trade places; you choose six other food containers. This time your child puts the cans in order from left to right. You watch carefully. Your child then mixes them up. It's up to you to reconstruct your child's order. Your child judges whether you did it right.

Visual Memory. Together with your child, look carefully at a can and its label. Then hide it. Ask your child to tell from memory what is in the can. What color is it? What shape is it? How big is it?

Trade places. Let your child hide a can and test your memory with similar questions.

Listen

Auditory Discrimination. Name three foods that have the same beginning sound and one with a different beginning sound. *Example:* raspberries, raisins, rutabaga, asparagus.

Ask your child these questions: Do these start with the same sound? Which one is different?

Continue using a variety of cereals, meats, and vegetables to illustrate other beginning sounds. Trade places. Let your child give you a list of words with similar beginning sounds, except for one.

This activity is great because it can be used anywhere. Try it far from the kitchen — in the car or while waiting for appointments.

Auditory Memory. Choose six cans. With your child, look at the labels carefully. Say the first word of the contents of each can aloud. Ask your child to listen carefully and then, with eyes closed, to recall what is in at least four of the cans.

Do

Eye-Hand Coordination. Check out your grocery cupboard. If it's like cupboards in most homes, it's disorganized. You and your child together will "organize" the cupboard.

One way to do this is to label cupboard shelves by types of items. You can put similar products together, or you can use another category, such as size or type of container.

Now you're ready to organize the products according to the plan. The big challenge will be to make sure it stays this well organized.

BODY AND BRAIN ages 4–6

You need a ball, some music, old magazines with sports pictures, a watch or clock with a second hand, and a tape measure. Put on comfortable clothes for this activity. Choose a place indoors that's safe for jumping. Turn on the music. If the weather is good, choose a place outdoors.

Look

Visual Discrimination. Look through magazines to find pictures of people standing up, sitting down, kneeling, or crouching. Find two pictures of people standing up and at least one with someone sitting down.

Ask your child to try to imitate the postures in two of these pictures.

Visual Memory. Do three exercises in a row. *Example:* jump, reach high, touch toes. Ask your child to watch and then to do the exercises you did.

Now do only two of these exercises. Leave one out. Your child watches carefully and does the exercise that was left out. Trade places. Your child does three exercises for you to follow.

Listen

Auditory Discrimination. Ask children to close their eyes while you bounce a ball on three different surfaces. Say the name of the surface as you bounce. *Examples:* rug, wood, linoleum.

Now bounce the ball on one surface. Your child, listening with eyes closed, names the surface.

Then bounce the ball in a rhythmic pattern while your child listens carefully. Your youngster's task is to bounce the ball, duplicating your rhythm. Trade places and keep the rhythm going.

Auditory Memory. Ask your child to bring you an object from another room, but do not use its name. *Example:* "Go to the garage and find something that is round and red and rolls." Your child listens, repeats your directions, finds the object, and brings it back.

Do

Eye-Hand Coordination. Have a contest! Get all members of the family to take turns doing several exercises to music. Use a clock or watch to time each other. Increase the number of exercises and the length of time you do them.

Lay a tape measure in a straight line on the floor. Walk along the tape, one foot before the other, heel to toe. Check the number on the tape when someone steps off the line. The person who keeps to the straight and narrow the farthest wins!

FAMILY VIEW ages 4—8

This reading activity helps families recognize the good things they are doing. You need magazines with pictures, family snapshots, scissors, paste, and a piece of cardboard. (You'll be making a poster of family "likes.")

Look

Visual Discrimination. Cut out pictures of people doing different activities. Point to those done *indoors* and those done *outdoors*. *Examples:* Vacuuming is indoors. Running is outdoors.

Mix up the pictures. Your child's task is to put the pictures of outdoor activities in one pile and the pictures of indoor activities in another pile.

Visual Memory. Let your child choose a picture of an appealing activity. Both of you look at it carefully, and then turn it over.

Now ask questions about the picture and what your child can recall. *Examples:* What is the person wearing? Is the person outdoors or indoors?

Talk about your family's activities that are like those in the pictures.

Listen

Auditory Discrimination. Name three activities that you enjoy. Examples might be biking, reading, playing basketball. Ask your child to repeat these activities.

Now your child names three activities enjoyed at school. Examples might be lunch, art, math.

Ask your child to listen as you repeat these three activities. But say them in a different order, and add one or two different ones. *Example:* science, gym, lunch, math, and art.

Your child's task is to listen and signal upon hearing activities different from the ones he or she named.

Auditory Memory. You say a sentence or two that your child hears and then recalls. Here is a classic example: "Peter Piper picked a peck of pickled peppers." Your child listens and repeats this and then says a sentence for you to repeat.

Keep listening and repeating and adding to the sentences you say. You can use any topic — clothes, pets, people. Depending on your child's ability and your memory, you can keep trying to remember and repeat all of the sentences, or you can repeat just the last sentence.

Do

Eye-Hand Coordination. Find and cut out magazine pictures of families doing activities together. Arrange and paste them on cardboard or large sheets of poster paper. Use words, too.

Choose a title for each poster. *Examples:* "What I Will Be When I Grow Up"; "If I Were an Only Child"; "If I Had More Sisters and Brothers." Hang the posters where the family can see them.

MAPPING IT OUT ages 4–8

This activity helps children learn to read maps and give directions.

You need a city or state map. Spread it out on a flat surface so that when you look at it, north (N) is at the top and south (S) is at the bottom.

Look

Visual Discrimination. Point out different colors on the map, one at a time. Ask your child to locate colors that are the same.

Point out the symbol for railroad tracks. Do the same for other symbols, such as those for rivers and highways. Ask your child to locate other tracks and rivers.

Visual Memory. Point to the four directions on the map. Ask your child to watch you and then to say and point to those directions.

Cover the map. Let your child remember and point to north, south, east, west. If possible, place the map on your table so that the directions on the map correspond to actual directions. In this way, the north and south on the map will match the north and south in your home. Find a place on the map your family would like to visit. Ask your child to find other places your family would like to visit.

Listen

Auditory Discrimination. Say aloud the names of three streets near your home. Ask your child to listen and to repeat these names.

Name a river and a park in your community. Let your child repeat these names.

Now say, "I'm going to say the names of a park, a river, and a street. Raise your hand when you hear the street name." Then repeat the street name with the names of the park and the river.

Auditory Memory. Together look for the streets where your friends live. Tell your child the names of friends and the streets they live on. *Example:* "Our friend Chris lives on Elm Street, and Anne lives on Newport Street." Ask your child to listen and to repeat what you said.

Together find three towns that are nearby. Name them. Turn the map over and ask your child to remember and name these towns.

Do

Eye-Hand Coordination. Put the map on a wall where everyone in the family can see it. Together make dotted lines (. . . .) showing your child's route from home to school and yours from home to work. Make each route a different color.

THINKING OF YOU ages 7–9

This activity helps children develop writing skills while learning to be thoughtful. Children who don't yet write can dictate their ideas. You need paper and pencil.

Look

Visual Discrimination. Write two good things about your child, each on a separate slip of paper. *Examples:* "Bill smiles a lot"; "Bill minds his manners." Ask your child to write two good things about you on two other pieces of paper.

Exchange these slips of paper, read them, and return them. Write a new compliment about your child on another piece of paper. Include this one with the others and give them to your child. Your child's task is to read and find the new compliment.

Visual Memory. Jot down three names, each on a separate piece of paper. Write a compliment to go with each name on three other pieces of paper. Read these to your child and then match the compliments to the names.

Mix up these slips of paper. Taking turns with your child, draw out a slip of paper from the pile and read it aloud. Your child's task is to guess who is being described or to provide the compliment for the person named.

Listen

Auditory Discrimination. Use the compliment slips you wrote for your child. Add one more word to each. *Example:* If a word on the slip is "happy," put the word "very" in front of it. Read these new compliments aloud.

Ask your child to listen carefully to the words and to name the new word.

Auditory Memory. Make a list of four friends, neighbors, or relatives that you would like to compliment. Read the list aloud. Ask your child to listen and to repeat this list.

Tell one thing you like about each of these people. *Examples:* John is a good driver; Tina tells good jokes. Ask your child to listen and to repeat these compliments.

Do

Eye-Hand Coordination. Send written compliments to friends or relatives. Some can be hidden to surprise them. Leave Mom's under a pillow. Put Brother's in his dresser drawer.

Let your child choose stationery and write notes or even scribbles to friends and family members. Handwritten notes are always a delight to receive. Talk about how it feels to get a compliment or to give one.

TV OR NO TV? ages 7–9

This activity helps the family make choices about TV programs to watch. You need a TV set, a weekly TV schedule, scissors, paste, and paper.

At the beginning of the week, post the TV schedule. Read it aloud. Talk about why one program might be better to watch than another.

Look

Visual Discrimination. Look at the TV schedule. Point out one channel's number. Ask your child to find two other channels with different numbers.

Point to a television show that begins with the letter *T.* Is it a good show? Ask your child to try to find one or two other shows that begin with the same letter. Are they good shows? Why? Why not?

Visual Memory. With your child, look at shows listed at the same time on two different channels.

Ask your child to name the shows at seven P.M. on channels four and nine. Which one might the family watch, and why was it chosen?

Listen

Auditory Discrimination. Tell your child the name of a television show you watch regularly and why you watch it. Ask your child to name this show.

Now name this show again, this time in a list with three other shows. Ask your child to listen and signal when the show you first mentioned is named again.

Trade places. Ask your child to name a favorite TV star. You listen. Then your child names other TV stars, including the first one. Now it's your turn to listen and raise your hand when you hear the first star's name.

Auditory Memory. Pretend you are a TV announcer. Your job is to announce the names of three shows. Your child listens and repeats the names of these shows in the same order. Which is a favorite show?

Watch a television commercial together. Ask your child to listen and recall. Was music used in the commercial? What product was advertised? How many people appeared in it?

Do

Eye-Hand Coordination. Save a few TV schedules so that they can be cut apart . . . and put back together. The task is to construct your very own guide of favorite TV shows for at least one day.

Talk about and compare the choices of different family members. What shows would you run if you managed a TV station?

SAVING UP ages 7–9

This activity can help children save money and increase their knowledge about banks. You need the usual papers that accompany bank transactions. Even if banks do not use the old bankbook, they all have brochures, deposit slips, and statements.

First you may want to call or visit banks to get information about services. Check which bank is most convenient and which welcome small depositors. Ask about fees and interest on savings accounts.

Look

Visual Discrimination. Point out and read the name of the bank on the bank materials. Ask your child to find the name of the bank on the deposit slip.

Using the deposit slip, point out the account number and the space for writing the depositor's name. Your child then looks at the deposit slip and finds these sections.

Visual Memory. Show your child the account number on the deposit slip. Ask your child to look at it carefully, turn over the slip, and then try to recall the account number.

Write down the account number and two other numbers. Put each on a separate piece of paper. Point out the account number. Mix up the papers. Now your child's task is to pick out the correct account number.

Listen

Auditory Discrimination. Say the name of the bank where the account has been opened. Your child listens and repeats the bank's name.

Give your bank's name and the names of banks with similar names. *Examples:* First Federal, First American, First National. Your child listens and signals upon hearing your bank's name.

Auditory Memory. Look at the bankbook and name the date that the account was opened. Ask your child to listen and to repeat the date.

Give three dates on which deposits were made. Your child tries to repeat these in the order given.

Name the amount of the deposit and the date of the last deposit. Again your child's task is to listen and to repeat the deposit amount and date.

Do

Eye-Hand Coordination. To save up for deposits, children can keep money in a special place or container — such as a piggy bank. They can count the coins and put them in the paper coin wrappers provided by the bank. Then these coin rolls go to the bank.

This activity combines organizational and social skills important in helping children work with others. You'll need note cards, sandwich makings, cans of soup, milk, fruit, and the usual eating utensils.

Organize an informal meal to share with friends. Decide on the menu. Talk about the amount of food needed. Sandwiches, fruit, soup, and milk make a nutritious lunch. Keep the menu simple so that the lunch can be prepared entirely by children.

Decide together how many people to invite and about how much to spend on the food. Make phone calls or send notes to the guests giving day, time, and place.

Look

Visual Discrimination. Together prepare a grocery list for your menu. Print each item on a separate card. When you get to the store, your child uses the cards to find all the items.

At home, show a sample place setting with napkins, spoons, plates, bowls, glasses. Remind your child how many are coming. Your child's task is to set the table by following this sample model.

Visual Memory. After the places have been set properly, take a second to scramble one. It's all in fun. The challenge for your child is to put the place setting back the way it should be.

Put the foods to be used on a counter. Ask your child to look carefully at what is there.

Take away one item. Now your child tells what is missing.

Trade places and let your child play this on you, if you have time before the guests arrive.

Listen

Auditory Discrimination. Name the first and last names of all of the guests. Now name the guests again, but mix first and last names. Your child's task is to tell you which names were mixed up.

Name all of the guests plus one person who was not invited. Ask your child to signal upon hearing the name of a person who was not invited.

Auditory Memory. Name the foods on the lunch menu in the order they will be served. Ask your child to repeat this order. List the steps taken in preparing the lunch. *Example:* planning, shopping, preparing, serving.

Ask your child to listen and to repeat these in the same order.

Do

Eye-Hand Coordination. If you're planning an adult party, try to include children in the meal preparation activities. Children can pour beverages into the glasses, put spread on bread or crackers, cut sandwiches or appetizers into parts, put out the place settings. (If needed, provide one place setting to serve as an example.)

UNIQUE REWARDS

We've found that the specialness of these activities rests not only in the success they provide for children but, perhaps just as important, in the feelings of success they provide for parents. The usual word used for special learners is "challenging." That's true, but special education can also be "discouraging" for children and for those who work with them, especially when what is being done at home is exactly like what is being done at school. A mother in one of our programs had followed for years the drill-and-practice workbook route at home with her child. To her delight and her youngster's, she found that it was possible to teach math without the pain and discouragement that both of them had been feeling. For her and for her child, these activities were liberating. They became an enjoyable time that she and her child spent together. Tears were replaced with smiles.

Chapter 19.
Special Times:
Vacation / Holiday Learning

Just because children are on holiday from school doesn't mean that they're taking a vacation from education. I am not talking about remedial exercises or catch-up homework. I'm talking about the time for discovery and the joy of learning that take no holidays — and may, in fact, be enhanced during holiday periods.

Vacations are a great time for families to reinforce and extend children's learning — without it looking or feeling like school. For example, when you say, "Let's make greeting cards," it won't seem like "language arts," but it gives that class a big boost at home. These activities feel special because they provide fun and learning at the very best times of the year.

WHAT CAN I DO NOW?

That's the often-asked vacation question. Answer it with a **Vacation Bulletin Board** (any age), a way to stimulate your child's ability to plan and be responsible for having things to do.

Ask the family to post ideas about what they'd like to do during the holidays. Children can cut out articles from the newspaper and write notes suggesting their ideas.

A list of household responsibilities can be posted on the board so that children can sign their names to the jobs they will do. Be sure to list "glamorous" jobs, like menu planning, as well as the everyday jobs, like sweeping floors and making beds.

Post a **Vacation Family Calendar** (any age) on the board. Use large sheets of paper, leaving plenty of blank space for each day.

Talk about what everyone wants to do. Make plans not just for outings but for home projects, too. As children get ideas, they pencil them in. This gives children practice in doing independent research and in working out compromises with family members who have different ideas.

Parents should write in their own schedules so that children come to understand and sympathize with parental obligations and responsibilities, even during holidays.

Not all time needs to be scheduled, nor should all family members have to do everything together. Children need time during vacation to relax, to be free of the usual fast pace of school. It's a good idea to encourage youngsters to get their homework done early in their vacation to avoid having it hanging over them every day.

Suggest that youngsters choose new activities to try for the first time or that they develop old ones further. Perhaps it's ice skating or cookie baking. Seek out active experiences, especially those that offer opportunities for success.

Make an effort to be alone with each child for some time during the holidays. This might be going to a movie or taking a walk in a shopping center. Use this opportunity to talk, and try to listen more than talk.

Set up a **Home Interest Center** (any age). On a table top or bookcase, put out books, articles, or pictures on a particular subject. Spark breakfast conversation and encourage newspaper reading with "My Picks in the News." Get these by asking everyone to clip pictures or articles for discussion.

PREPARING FOR THE WINTER HOLIDAYS

With the holiday preparation ideas below, beware of taking too many of the active roles, leaving children only passive appreciation. There is MegaSkills practice in almost every step, so parents need to make sure kids get their share.

Greetings, Gifts, and Decorations   any age

Encourage children to create their own greeting cards and the thank you notes that follow the gift giving. Don't grade them on this home writing. If they miss a capital letter or a comma, so be it. Then youngsters can stamp and mail the notes. It may take a little longer, but it's worth it.

Children learn to give as well as receive. They can save for and select their own purchases at the store or make gifts at home. Homemade presents that can be produced by the very young include jewelry made from shells or colored macaroni, cookies, paintings, and collages. Older children can embroider, design games, and write poems and stories for gifts. With colored paper, scissors, crayons, and paste, even the youngest child can make decorations that will add to the festiveness of the day. Try paper placemats and door and window paste-ups. Older children can make place cards and homemade favors for the guests.

In any case, even preschoolers can help in the wrapping of the gifts. Youngsters enjoy wrapping presents in imaginative, mysterious ways, such as putting a small thing in an enormous box.

The Pleasure of Involvement ages 7–12

Let the children share the work and accomplishment of planning and cooking holiday dinners. Together make up a list of all that has to be done, from the shopping trip to the cleanup. When your children realize what needs to be done and pick their own jobs, gripes are minimized and the necessity for compromise is clear.

Make out the dinner menu together, discussing time and cost, which govern the choices. Have children who read well enough look up the recipes and list the ingredients. Let them check the grocery inventory to see what's already at home. Then they can refer to newspapers to find the stores with the best prices.

Children can have their own grocery lists. Choose an uncrowded time in the stores. Right after dinner is usually good. Stay close to your young shoppers to help them compare prices and quality.

Involve children in the dinner preparations with easy cooking jobs, table setting, and serving duties. After dinner, you might try an informal talent show or family skit.

Not all of this will work, but parts of the plan will — and that's about what you can hope for. Children who are self-starters will be delighted with the opportunity to do projects on their own. Others who've had less practice with independent projects may need encouragement and help in gathering necessary materials. But once they get going, it's time for parents to get going — out of their way.

The cookies may come out a little burned and the pencil holders may be a bit crooked, but a child's personal satisfaction will be first rate. You're providing your child with a thrilling sense of personal accomplishment unobtainable from any toy.

A Summer Trip Around the World — Without Leaving Home   ages 7–12

The long summer vacation can be hard on everyone. Even kids get bored after the first flush of freedom wears off.

Here's a solution: Take the youngsters on a trip without leaving home. With imagination, your living room trip can smack of the grand tour, especially in the social studies education it will provide.

Tack up a large (the bigger, the better) map of the world. With the family working together, chart a travel course. Lightly pencil it in at first, until all controversies (such as whether to visit Rome or Naples) are resolved. Once these are settled, apply the trusty felt-tip pen. Use a contrasting color to mark your progress as the trip goes on.

On the wall next to the map, post your itinerary of dates and places. Here's an example:

July 15	Depart by air to London
July 16 A.M.	Arrive in London
July 20	Boat train to Paris

Be sure to talk about time changes, and plan the trip as realistically as you can so that children understand concepts of distance and time.

This trip can last all summer. Spend some time on it each day or refer to it once a week, depending on the time you can spare and how much it interests the children.

Try to plan the trip so that a few countries of special interest and contrasting appeal are highlighted; perhaps visit France, Japan, and Russia. For these countries, your trip details can be in depth: weather, food, music, history, geography, daily life.

Avoid a textbook approach to the study. Try special nights: "An Evening in Paris," with the children planning a French meal and singing French songs; "An Evening in Beijing," with Chinese food and chopsticks. These evenings need not be elaborate. The important point is that the children themselves do the preparing.

Try some of these activities in connection with your trip:

Have your children make replicas of the different national flags. String these up for decorations.

Start collections, such as dolls, stamps, and coins, to stimulate interest in different countries.

Visit local foreign restaurants (good eating and education as well) and stores in ethnic sections of your city.

Gather material — and much of it is free — on what it's like to live in other lands. Check with travel agencies, embassies, and tourism offices.

The library is a great resource, with everything from geography books to fairy tales of other countries.

While this trip is not the real thing to be sure, preparing for it may be at least half the fun.

Meeting Famous People — Without Leaving Home   ages 7–12

For another unique way of traveling around the world without leaving home, collect famous people.

I know a man in his forties whose hobby is writing to ask for pictures and signatures of famous men and women. He's been doing this since his early teens. He's not just an autograph hound. Each of the letters he sends is individual, and he receives individual answers from presidents, from famous people in prison, from religious leaders. His is an astonishing collection — file drawer after file drawer. You can see young Richard Nixon and a young Pope Paul. It's more than a collection. It's a trip through history, and it's a hobby available to all.

Going Places   ages 7–12

Outings are more than fun. They put into practice the educational theory that people learn best from actual experience — by going and doing.

The best outings for children are neither extensive nor expensive. For a young child it can be a walk to the library or a browse and a small purchase at the drug store. For an older youngster it can be a trip to a bowling alley or a visit to a factory. The trick lies in exploiting the potential of even an everyday type of event.

Do some planning. Take the calendar off the wall and discuss dates and budget. Together with your children, decide where to go. Seek out some less-traveled places, especially when you're on trips. Parents can get tired of the same old places, and so do kids. Industrial sites often have special tours for visitors. I recall going with my children through a beer factory in Milwaukee and through a car assembly line in River Rouge, Michigan. They were as fascinating to me as they were to the kids.

All trips need not be planned in detail. Spontaneity and flexibility are important. For a touch of excitement, try a mystery-trip journey to a nearby location with the children blindfolded in the car, not knowing where they're going.

For new ideas on what to see, give each child a map of your area (often available at gas stations) so they can find places they'd like to visit.

PLANNING THAT'S NOT BURDENSOME

Planning can enhance even the most modest outing, and it doesn't take a lot of time.

Before. Preparing children for what they're going to see helps them see more when they get there. For example, if you're going on a picnic and you'll be scouting birds, tell children what they might expect. They like to anticipate what's coming and to recognize it when it appears.

During. Encourage children to collect souvenirs as you go: pictures, menus, postcards, for a scrapbook later on. Children may enjoy keeping a trip diary that they write themselves or dictate to you.

After. Build on the particular interest the outing inspired. After a tour through a cookie factory, for example, your children may come away eager to bake new kinds of cookies on their own. Whenever possible, tie up new interests with trips to the library for books.

Don't be discouraged if an outing, even though planned, doesn't live up to your expectations. The idea is to go on so many that even when one is disappointing, others will make up for it.

THE POWER OF SPECIAL TIMES

Going places together creates the stuff of which memories are made. My mother died when I was young. I cannot hear her voice any longer, but I remember very vividly where we went together. She never drove a car, but we went many places on the Greyhound bus that stopped across the street from our house. She liked to shop, and even when we didn't buy, we went at least once a week from our home in Monroe to the big city of Toledo. I remember those trips with a special joy not because they were exotic or expensive. We were alone together, exploring streets and places. Oh, the power of these special times, and how long they live within us!

Chapter 20.
Transitions: Keeping Up
with Children's Learning

Beyond the confines of the elementary school years is an emerging adult world that is at the same time both exhilarating and discouraging for children. Fortunately our youngsters, with even a few developing MegaSkills, bring enormous strengths to these challenging years. But like plants, which need water to grow, children need ongoing support from their environment, their family, and their teachers in order to continue their healthy growth.

In these activities, which cover a range of topics from shyness to job applications, children look at themselves, and they look to others and to their community for assistance and information. They get help in being themselves and in resisting peer pressure. Each is another step in their evolving maturity.

SPEAKING UP ages 10–12

Shyness is a painful condition that affects many youngsters. It may cause them to miss out on important times with their friends. This activity will help youngsters learn ways to accept their shyness and to develop strategies to overcome it. All that's needed are thinking minds.

Together make a list of three or four situations that cause your youngster to feel shy. This could be speaking up in class or talking to classmates of the opposite sex. Pick one to work on.

Make up a pretend situation with a believable set of events. *Example:* A group decides to go for pizza after school. Your youngster wants to go but doesn't know the kids very well. He doesn't go. He feels unhappy.

Discuss some ways to deal with this kind of situation. *Examples:* Walk along with the group. Start a conversation with another person, and say, "I'd like to join you, OK?" Taking this risk of possible rejection is no worse than thinking you've already been rejected.

Make up a list of "overcoming shyness" exercises that your youngster can do without running great risks. *Examples:* Ask a policeman for directions; ask a teacher a question after class; praise someone's new clothes.

Rather than having your youngster be overwhelmed by shyness, suggest taking small steps such as these. The small successes will add up and will give your youngster confidence to try again.

UNDER CONTROL ages 10–12

Everyone gets angry at times. Our children need to know that it's OK to show feelings but that starting a fight rarely solves a problem.

This activity helps youngsters face up to and control their anger. You need thinking minds.

Talk with your youngster about what to do when, for example, a friend calls at the last minute to cancel an appointment, or you find that your baby sister has broken your favorite record.

Choose a TV program to watch together. Look for situations that make people angry. Most of the responses include the use of guns and knives. Because there is so much of this, children might get the idea that these are realistic responses. That's why it is so important to talk together about what to do in real life. Ask children to think about their behavior when they are angry. Do they try to cool off before speaking? Do they talk things over with someone? Do they start a fight or scream? Would you like to change any of this? If so, what would you change? Encourage children to watch people's faces, hands, and legs when they are angry. This is called body language. Sometimes you learn more through body language than from the words people say.

YOU BE THE JUDGE ages 10–12

This activity gives children an understanding of how we sometimes let others make decisions for us. This might be how drinking alcohol or taking drugs starts. Sometimes we try to please other people so much that we don't please ourselves. For example, children might buy clothes and records because friends have them, not because they like them. This activity gives youngsters practice in thinking for themselves. It starts by talking about clothes. It can move to a conversation about pressures to drink or try drugs.

Ask your child to choose a favorite piece of clothing. It might be something for school or an outfit for special events.

Start with questions like these: Why is this piece of clothing your favorite? Is it the color? Is it because someone special bought it for you? Do your friends own clothes like yours? Would you wear these clothes if you knew your friends didn't like them? Would you wear them if they weren't popular?

Now you might talk about the judgment your child needs to face peer pressure about alcohol or drug use. Does your child know anyone who has been hurt? Is there anything you can do to help? Share a mistake of your own. Tell about a time that you bought something or drank something you didn't really want to just because it was popular. Was it a good or bad decision? Why?

TODAY IN THE NEWS ages 10–12

Young people need to realize that what happens anywhere in the world today can affect their own lives.

This activity provides practice in following news events and talking about them. It helps children become aware that half a world away is not so far away after all. You need a current newspaper.

Find at least two articles that tell of events in a foreign country. *Examples:* Winners announced in European bicycle race. Drugs seized at the border.

Talk about these. Could any of these things happen here?

Find in the paper or think of a situation that affects your area. *Examples:* Proposed shopping center adds to traffic problems; neighborhood school to close.

Talk about these happenings. How do you feel about them, and what, if anything, can you do about them? What's interesting about the news? Is it relevant to your lives? Can children tell others about it? In this way, they show they understand what's happening.

VOLUNTEER AND LEARN ages 10–12

Volunteering in the community is a fine way to help children gain work experience and to learn about the needs of others. Many nursing homes and hospitals recognize the value of having young people around to mix and mingle with the elderly.

Check also with neighborhood recreation centers. And there are local fairs, church groups, and community functions that need help.

When you find an organization to work for, call to set up a meeting with the volunteer coordinator. Because of your child's age and transportation needs, you will probably be involved in making the volunteer connection. But it will be worth it.

In advance, work out with your child some questions to ask: How long will tasks take? How many hours a week will training be offered?

Volunteering is not without pitfalls. Sometimes an institution is delighted to welcome a volunteer but does not provide support and supervision. After one or two visits, a youngster can become discouraged with just sitting around and doing nothing or not enough. Before signing up, make sure that there will be sufficient direction for volunteers to enable your child to work and to learn.

REACHING OUT TO OTHERS ages 10–12

It is important for children to get the sense of themselves as helpers, able to reach out to others to do something to make them happy. This activity combines reading with volunteering.

Select an elderly person in a nursing home or hospital to whom your child can read. A local social service agency will have names of shut-ins in your area. If you belong to a religious group, ask your pastor, priest, or rabbi for names.

Find out the older person's special reading interests. Your child should be able to read the material well. Before beginning, discuss how long your child should stay. Ten to fifteen minutes a session may be a good length of time. Decide on this before your child reads so that no one will be disappointed.

Contact the person to whom your child will be reading and make a date for a first visit. Let your child tell a little about your family and then ask about the other person's childhood. Suggest that your child read only a short time the first day. Later at home, practice the reading selected for the second visit. You will probably have to accompany your youngster at least for the first trip.

In between visits, your child can write notes or cards. Everyone loves to be remembered, and this gives your child practice in letter writing. This activity could count as a service project for scout groups.

By helping others, children help themselves. They realize that not all happiness is tied to things like toys or clothes. Some of the best things in life really are free.

HELP AVAILABLE HERE ages 10–12

This activity helps preteens get experience in securing jobs right around home — jobs that fit into student schedules. One of these is the age-old profession of baby sitter. Really, a better name is child care helper.

Together make a list of friends or neighbors who may need child care. Help your child write a flyer that includes the following information:

- Name, address, phone number
- Activities you do with children (play games, teach songs, practice good safety habits)
- What you charge and when you are available

Distribute this flyer to the people on your list. Post it in supermarkets and community centers.

There are other jobs near home besides child care. Among them are raking leaves, washing windows, shoveling snow, walking dogs, addressing envelopes, and so forth.

Ask youngsters to keep track of the calls they get and to write down when they are expected on a job and what supplies they may have to bring along, such as a rake or shovel. Remind them to ask about how long the job will take and what pay, if any, is being agreed upon. This is really valuable experience, and it can be put on a résumé as a first "real" job.

THE NEED TO KNOW

Kids learn a lot from their peers. Everybody says so. They give each other needed support. The problem is that they also give each other a lot of immature ideas, too. This immaturity needs to be seasoned with some adult thinking in order for kids to start having adult ideas.

The possibilities for ten- to twelve-year-olds to learn from adults — even from those who are not their parents — is enormous, but first the adult world has to let them in.

One of the entry points is to talk about jobs and to help kids get a taste of what the "real world" is like. Here are a few activities that help.

JOBS AHEAD ages 10–12

The job world is changing. Driving a truck used to be a man's job; being a nurse was always woman's work.

This activity helps youngsters start thinking and talking about what they might like to do when they are older. It helps them understand that men and women today have more job choices.

Together make a list of as many family members, friends, and neighbors as you can. Next to each name write that person's job. Are any of these jobs unusual for men to be doing? For women?

Suggest that your youngster cut out articles and pictures of people doing different jobs that might be interesting as a career. *Examples:* flying a plane, farming, working with children. Ask your youngster to talk about these choices. And share your views, too.

For a change of pace, have each member in the family do a job at home that is usually done by someone else. Boys might try doing the things the girls (or Mom) have been doing. Girls could do the boys' (or Dad's) jobs.

WHAT DO YOU DO? ages 10–12

In this activity, children talk to adults to gain an understanding about jobs. They also get a "handle" on how to get conversations going with adults by asking questions and getting information. You need willing friends, neighbors, parents, other family members. This is a "talk about" activity.

Ask your child to prepare some questions in advance. *Examples:* "How did you choose your job?" "What are the advantages and disadvantages?" "Did you need special training?" "Did you have to pass a test?"

Do they have any advice for young people who are thinking about jobs? Nobody has all the answers in a crystal ball, but talking with others helps youngsters sense what questions they need to think about for the future.

LETTING GO

All parents would like to be able to protect children so that no one pushes them around; so that they make good judgments, avoid costly and hurtful mistakes, sort out the phony and false from the right and true. But we can't.

As children start their trip into adulthood, most of us parents will do a lot more watching and talking together rather than telling and yelling. It can be very hard to pull back. But having helped our children pack their suitcases with MegaSkills, we can be more confident that they'll have a good trip.

Section D.
The MegaSkills Support Network: People Helping People

Introduction.
Beacons in the Fog

My father and mother came to the New World, America, from Europe in the late 1920s. They were part of a great wave of immigration. From their small community in Poland came about a hundred others. Some were relatives, but most were not. They called each other "landsmen," people from the same land.

They came from the same old place to many different, new places. They did not all stay together. They scattered across this new land to earn their way. But they acted to help one another, even if they were miles apart.

My parents came to a small town in southern Michigan. The closest place any landsman had settled was Detroit. When I was a child, every Sunday we packed into the car and traveled what seemed like a very long journey — about forty miles — to Detroit to be with landsmen. There my parents talked Yiddish, and I heard stories exchanged about what had happened to whom during the week. It was pleasant talk — but it was more. I heard people arranging ways to help one another. They were making connections. It was about money — but it was more. It was support. It gave these landsmen the strength and courage to face another week in a strange place. I did not understand this then. I thought it was a terrible thing to have to go to Detroit every week, and I got carsick to prove it.

But the feelings of the connections must have seeped into my imagination. I remember that as we made our way back home in the dark, especially on the foggy nights that scared me, I envisioned the taillights of the cars in front of us and the headlights of the cars in back of us as part of a great chain winding along the highway. I recall this vision still. It gave me comfort then, and it continues to do so today.

In a sense, all of us now raising families are in new territory. We are explorers and innovators. We have to be.

Just as businesses are learning that the rules for success are changing, so, too, is family life changing. We are involved today in new patterns of family life, new relationships, different responsibilities and opportunities. Like a dark, foggy night, it is scary.

One of the brightest beacons in this fog is the chain of connections, like lights in the dark, that we form with the people — parents, teachers, child care helpers — with whom we come in contact every day. This is a coalition, the support network, that helps us and our children build and keep MegaSkills.

In this section are specific ways we can help each other get through each day a little more easily and happily —

How parents help other parents.

What teachers and parents need to know and understand.

How single parents and schools can help each other.

How parents can form a real team with child care helpers.

What children need to know about school.

We are pioneers and discoverers in a new landscape. It may not be the moon, but it can feel like it. We need friends and allies in this major effort to help ourselves and our children.

Chapter 21.
Parent to Parent: Looking to Each Other for Help

Having grown up in a small town, I find myself not quite at home in a big city, even when I live in one. It feels lonely to walk down a crowded street where you don't know anyone. The tall buildings seem impenetrable and uncaring. When I go into a large school building or a gigantic supermarket, I feel the same way.

Maybe that's why I try to turn almost every place where I am into a small town. I try to bring things down to a scale I can understand and manage.

I need to know my neighbors, whether they live in the house across the street or work down the hall. I need to share and give tips: Have you a doctor to recommend? Do you know a good, cheap restaurant that welcomes children? Who's in charge at the playground? When do we register for school? It's a parent-to-parent support network that many of us depend on and more of us could use.

The activities in this chapter focus on how to help create and structure this network. The core of the plan is the school. I use the school for three very good reasons: (1) There's a school in almost every neighborhood, and it might be free after three P.M. and on weekends; (2) It's the place where children come together; (3) It's a natural place for parents to come together to assist each other and to learn ways to help their children.

Almost the first place — maybe it *is* the first place — families go when they come to a new town is the school. If you have children, the decision of choosing a place to live is often based on what schools your children will attend.

School is central in the lives of families, and not just between the hours of nine and three, half the days of the year. We need to capitalize more on that centrality to provide parent-to-parent support for dealing with the larger, colder world.

WHO'S GOING TO DO IT?

If you think I'm talking about teachers taking on this work, you're wrong. This is parents helping themselves and each other. Join your PTA / parent-teacher organizations. They are doing important work, and they deserve and need more hands. Activities in this chapter illustrate how it can be done. They do take some time and effort. Good things just don't happen by themselves — someone has to take the lead. And it can't always be the same people.

We are an educated, democratic society, and we need more people to say, "I'll start. Let's check with the school. I'll call five people. We'll get the ball rolling."

We're all busy, and there will always be excuses. But if we want better lives for ourselves and our kids, these efforts have to be made — and not just by others, but by ourselves.

The activities that follow are carried out by parents, but they require the cooperation of the school. Administrators are responsible for what goes on in the school building. Invite them early in the planning, and expect questions. They need to authorize the activities. It's helpful to meet first with the parent group, whether it's the full PTA or a committee, to discuss what activities to propose, how they will be conducted, who's responsible for what, and what costs, if any, are involved. Administrators want to open the school doors, but they can't do so until details have been worked out.

INFORMATION CENTRAL

The school is an ideal source of information, for parents as well as children. Here are three information-sharing activities that respond to parents' need to know. They move from very easy to more complex, in step-by-step stages.

Q-and-A Brown Paper

The easiest parent information exchange consists of a long sheet of brown paper. Ask the principal where it can be displayed.

It can have these headings: *Date, Question, Answer, Contact.* Parents don't even have to know or see each other to make this activity work. In the *Question* section you might ask, "Where can we buy furniture?" "How do we find reliable child care?" A few days later, check to see who has filled in an answer. It might be a student, a teacher, a school visitor, or another parent. *Contact* tells whom to call for more details beyond what can be written directly on the brown paper.

Attach next to the paper a marker that just cannot be removed. Put up a new sheet every two weeks. But be sure to save the old ones. You may want to refer to the old answers. There may be enough good answers for the school principal to want to produce a compilation of "Brown Paper Answers" as a booklet for all parents.

Café Parent

Every parent needs someone to brag to as well as a shoulder to cry on. Parents need a place to get together to talk, share experiences, have a cup of coffee, put their feet up.

Some schools have empty classrooms. One of these can be set aside for Café Parent. (Grandparents are welcome, too.) Volunteers — perhaps senior citizens — can open the door and set up the coffee pot. Request donations of easy chairs, a table, a bulletin board, lamps, a rug, and other amenities. Special programs can be arranged, or the room can be open for parent use. It's an ideal place for a parent reading shelf with books and materials that can be checked out for home use. Teachers may want to display class materials so that parents can learn what's going on in different subjects. The Café needs to be kept open at least one evening a week and perhaps on Saturday mornings. This is a low-key operation, but it may be what's needed to identify a corps of parents who want to continue to work together in more intensive ways.

The Family Learning Center

This is a parent center in the school with a multifaceted approach serving a variety of parental needs. Like Café Parent, it uses donated furniture, books, and materials, but without option, it requires at least a part-time staff person. It may evolve from Café Parent or spring full-blown in response to community interest. All of the services listed below may not be needed in every community, but they provide a sense of the range of activities that a Learning Center can offer.

Book/Toy Lending Library. This is a collection of toys for children and materials and books on parenting, schooling, and family issues that parents can check out for use at home. The collection is made up of toys and books that families no longer want. These are brought to the library to be exchanged for toys and books that other families have finished with. (An adaptation of this is the "Toy Market" in this chapter.)

Parent Workshops. Parents get together to learn together. Parenting is a subject none of us knows very much about — especially before problems arise. You don't always need an expert to run these sessions; we all have good ideas to share. Talk about discipline; talk about balancing work and family responsibilities; talk about how to keep kids off drugs, away from sex, and into their books.

Child Care. This service can be offered while parents use the center. Ask administrators about involving upper elementary or teenage students. In this way child care is available and the older youngsters gain job experience.

Sewing Materials. Parents may use these for repairing or making children's clothes. A sewing machine can be borrowed or donated for use in the room.

Typing/Office Equipment. A typewriter, computer, or copier might be made available for parental use in the Family Learning Center.

This list of equipment and services may seem extensive at first glance. However, community businesses are often willing to donate useful items as charitable contributions.

Teachers can be invited to use the center so that parents and teachers meet informally in this informal place.

DOING TOGETHER — PARENT TO PARENT

It feels so good to join together with people to do something. The sense of team effort and accomplishment can almost be touched and felt.

Here are three easy-to-do activities that generate these feelings.

These are not major school fairs or extravaganzas. These are ways in which neighbors help neighbors.

In each of these activities, people are in "business," selling and buying toys or books or homemade crafts. Tables to hold these goods are set up in the school gym, cafeteria, or auditorium. Every family is responsible for its own business. There are two ground rules: (1) The items for sale must be from one's own house (used but not abused), or they must be gifts or crafts made by family members; (2) the tables are to be manned by the family — parents, grandparents, family friends, and children.

Because each family is responsible for setting up and taking away the tables, pricing the goods, and selling them, no one else is burdened. Unsold items, such as toys no longer wanted and books that did not sell, can be donated to the school or to a charity.

To raise money to cover flyers, postage, refreshments, and a small honorarium for the event coordinator, each family could contribute two dollars or so.

Toy Market

This is a way for families to sell toys their children have outgrown. Children and parents together find the toys, clean them up, price them, and bring them to the sale.

With children handling the sales, they gain communication as well as money management skills. They can lower their prices as needed to make sales and then figure out how much has been made after the sale is over. This is an ideal event to precede the winter holidays. One family's trash is another family's treasure.

Book Fair

This provides adults and children with good low-cost reading material, and it can also increase the library collection. With each family handling its own table, these books don't need to be collected or priced in advance. On the day of the fair, families come in with their boxes and begin to display the books. If possible, books should be priced from a nickel to fifty cents so that every child can buy some. The school librarian can be given the choice of the books left over for additions to the school's library. Once again, children handle the sales themselves, negotiating with buyers on the spot and also sharing opinions — "That book was good," or "That one is not so great!"

We Made It Ourselves

This activity provides incentives for children and parents to produce handmade items and to pursue hobbies for pleasure and profit.

If children can bear to part with their treasures, from model airplanes to candles to soap sculptures to jewelry, here is an opportunity to share, show them off, and perhaps sell them. Remember to bring along children's paintings and any place mats and paperweights they've made.

This is a time for children to garner praise. At an adult art show recently, I admired a potter's wares and saw her young son at the side of the table with his hand-lettered sign: MAGNETS — 50¢. He had painted designs on her leftover pieces of clay and had attached small magnets. The paint was still wet. I asked if I could buy two. He seemed very pleased and very shy. As I left, his mother came up to me and whispered, "Thanks." I had not bought them from her, but it was as if I had.

TALKING TOGETHER — PARENT TO PARENT

Two major topics I hear parents worry about are (1) teachers and schools (how do we know they're good?), and (2) discipline (how can we help our children grow up and avoid trouble?).

About Schools

To judge whether a teacher is good, bad, or in between, you don't need to be an expert on education. As a teacher, when parents visited the classroom I tried to give them clues on how to look at my work. First I urged parents to give me and the school a fair chance. Then I made the following points:

- Don't be impressed with the bulletin boards, with whether the desks are neat and the room is quiet. Some of the best learning in my classroom goes on in what probably looks like minor bedlam, with students moving about, making noise, even laughing.
- Try to sense the atmosphere of the room. Is there a feeling of security among the students? Are they waiting expectantly for my pronouncements as teacher? Do I encourage divergent

opinions and answers, or am I "answer pulling," looking only for the exact one I have in mind?

- How do I treat "wrong" answers? Do I discard them? Do I try to point out reasons why one answer is better than another?
- How are my assignments? Are my directions specific and clear? Do I ask the whole class to do the same assignment, or do I sometimes try to provide for some individual, independent work?
- How do I treat "difficult" children, and what do I define as "difficult"? Chances are, you won't see many problems since we're all on company behavior. But if you do, it's possible that your children, on their problem days, may get similar treatment.
- Look carefully at me and my personality. It's natural that you'll take more to some teachers than to others. I need not be beautiful, but like all good teachers, regardless of whether I'm bubbling over or reserved and shy, I need to convey to students the qualities of optimism and encouragement. Do I?
- Don't base your opinion of me on just one visit. Try to come back to see me more than once. If you come away pleased with what you've seen, tell me. Teachers need praise, too. If something upsets you, discuss it with me.

For the best evaluation — not just of me, but of the school — I suggested that parents look to their children. Are they interested in learning? Are they eager to go to school each day? When this is happening, the school year is good. When it isn't, there is trouble ... trouble that all of us — students, parents, and teachers — need to look into.

Then I urged the parents of my students to pass along these tips, if they found them useful, to other parents. It helps to know what to look for when visiting a classroom in action.

About Discipline

I wish we'd all share more tips about discipline — what has worked and what hasn't worked in our houses. I want us to give each other advice and stop worrying that no one wants to hear it. We can discard what we don't want or can't use. We might think that what happens in our house is nobody else's business. Well, not everything is, but if others can help us, wouldn't it be grand if we could let them?

Here's an exercise I call "A Piece of My Mind," from our Parent-to-Parent programs. We say what comes to mind when asked the following questions:

What one piece of advice would you give to a new mother? To a new father?

What's one thing that you wish your parents had told you?

What's one thing you are especially glad your parents told you?

What do you wish your parents would have told your teachers?

What's one thing you would do differently in disciplining your children?

What do you think you should tell your child ... that you're hesitant to tell?

What kind of information about your children would you welcome from the parents of your children's friends? From your children's teachers? From your neighbors?

What do you think your children would tell you ... if they had the nerve?

In short, what can we tell each other that we need to know? What do our friends know about our children? Do we have to wait until someone says, "I knew that all along, but I didn't say anything"?

This exercise works when you're thinking to yourself, when you are with one or two friends, or when you're in a larger group. Even if you never talk with someone else about these questions, think about and "listen" to your own responses.

A number of years ago as I was driving down the street, I saw a neighbor's young teenage daughter. I knew her only to say hello, but I saw that she was lighting up what looked to be a marijuana cigarette. She was alone. I was tempted to stop the car, get out, and yank the cigarette out of her mouth. I didn't, but maybe I should have. That night I picked up the phone to call her mother. I put it back down, thinking, "I don't really know this woman. What will she say? Will she say it's not my business? Will she be upset?"

I backed away, and yet I have not forgotten that day and have often wondered what I should have done. Knocking the cigarette out of the girl's mouth probably would have been too dramatic. But I think I should have called, no matter what the mother said to me.

That teenager got into some scrapes not long afterward. In a little while, the mother and daughter moved away. No one on the block has heard from them since. I wonder if what I could have done that day might have made a difference.

Helping Each Other

As parents, we need each other; we need to learn from one another. There's a lot we can do to help each other. We need to be part of a neighbor-to-neighbor exchange. In some ways, it can be constricting and oppressive. But it's also comforting. It's good to feel that you know people who care about you and what you and your children are doing.

Chapter 22.
Parents and Teachers: Superpowers, Not Superhuman

The trouble with schools today is not that teachers and parents don't care anymore. That's the usual complaint, but it's not true. Caring is as intense, perhaps more intense, than ever. The trouble is that there may be so much focus on the school as an institution that there is not enough focus on the needs of the adults, within and beyond the school walls, who must work together in order for schooling to succeed.

I did not say the needs of *children*. I said the needs of *adults*. We know that we have to meet children's needs. What we sometimes don't realize is that in order to meet the needs of our children, we have to meet the needs of the adults who make schools work.

Education is a very human partnership. It depends for its strength, to a great degree, on how teachers and parents feel about one another and what they do to meet each others' adult needs.

In this complex world, it takes more than a good school to educate children. And it takes more than a good home. It takes these two major educational institutions working together. To bring this about demands, I believe, a restructuring of how teachers and parents relate and connect to one another.

This is a new era for families. It is a new era for teachers, too, and not necessarily a worse one for either. But it is a time that presents some new problems for us to solve. Some involve institutional changes, such as how long schools stay open. Much of the change, however, is at the personal level of parents and teachers as people, as partners.

This chapter focuses on what parents and teachers can do now to provide stronger adult-to-adult support for each other, on how we hurt each other, and on the obstacles we have to overcome so that we can work as a team to help our children achieve.

I've long worn two hats — as a parent and as a teacher. I know there are a lot of smiles at Back-to-School nights, and I know that parents and teachers are supposed to get along. But it doesn't take a Geiger counter to detect the fears and frustrations beneath the smiles when parents and teachers meet — and perhaps, especially, when they don't meet.

With my parent hat on, I want to tell you about the meanest and the nicest things a teacher has said to me.

I think the meanest thing a teacher ever said to me happened when I brought my first child to school to register her for kindergarten. I was nervous and wanted to make a good impression. Being a teacher, I was concerned about not being a bragging parent. But I was also concerned that this teacher know about my child.

So I told the teacher that this youngster entering kindergarten could already read, and I asked what provision would be made for this. The teacher put her arm around my shoulder and proceeded to reassure me in this way: "Oh, don't worry, Mrs. Rich, they all *even out* by third grade." Evening out wasn't what I was concerned about. It was not what I or any parent would want to hear.

The nicest thing a teacher ever said to me came in a telephone call when my younger daughter was in fourth grade. She had been absent from school for three days. Her teacher called to ask about her. "How is she? When is she coming back? We miss her." This teacher knew how to make students and their families feel important. The other did the opposite.

The meanest thing I ever said about a teacher — that she didn't like her students — is something I probably should have said to her face. Parents of students were talking behind her back, and so was I. Something about this teacher made every child in her third-grade class feel unloved. It's an unfortunate attribute for any personality and a devastating one for a teacher. Maybe if I had said something, she might have made some changes.

Probably the most important thing teachers can do for parents is to make them feel important and needed, and the most important thing, as parents, that we can do for teachers is to let them know how important they are to our families.

This is *the* MegaSkill for the home-school relationship, and this point is reinforced again and again as I ask teachers and parents about each other. A grandmother who was a PTA president in 1937 has never forgotten this fifth-grade teacher's remark: "You are as essential to this school as the bricks in the walls." But she also remembers the principal, who said, "Why don't you let the school educate your child, and you stick to your business?"

We do hurt each other. And it's not just teachers ganging up on parents. As a teacher, I have seen a wide variety of parental anti-school behaviors. Among them:

- Hard-to-please parents who march into the school office with a daily complaint. At the other extreme are the scared, "helpless" parents who somehow can't bring themselves even to visit the school.

- Parents who use the school in a way that destroys any good feelings children may have about schooling. Is it any wonder a child would balk at going to school after hearing, "Just you wait till you get to school — they'll know what to do with you!"

- Parents who hope, even expect, the school to do for their child what it never did for them, or who expect it to do all the things their home is unsuccessful at. They grow increasingly bitter against the school with each passing day. When the miracles do not occur, they tend to infect their children with this attitude: "That school's no good — what's the use of trying?"

- Parents for whom any change from what they knew as schoolchildren is threatening, whether or not they liked what they had. Some parents get upset when they see children actually having fun in the classroom. I think of this as the "iodine theory" of education —it has to hurt if it's to do any good.

- Parents who identify so closely with their children that they see themselves, not their children, walk into that school. These parents react to every teacher's comment and every award won or lost as if reliving their own schooldays.

All this isn't to imply that parents should not criticize teachers or schools. Constructive criticism is essential. But stale attitudes from a parent's own school days are worth recognizing as such and then discarding.

If you like your child's teachers, you won't be tempted to put them down. In fact, you'll probably say nice things about them at home and thus encourage your child to have a good relationship with them, too.

The real test for how well you can handle yourself vis-à-vis school comes when you don't like a certain teacher. What can you do, what should you do, in a ticklish situation like this? First of all, try to examine your attitudes to figure out if you are suffering from an old case of school phobia. Without knowing or wanting it, parents can infect children with certain immature and self-defeating attitudes about school. School is a place where a lot of adults start acting like kids again, perhaps because of their own schoolday memories.

One way to find out if you're suffering from a form of school phobia is to check your physical responses to school.

Does your stomach tighten when you walk through the school door?

Do you sleep well the night before a parent-teacher conference?

Do you find yourself trembling when you talk casually to your child's teacher?

Do you sit brooding for days, biting your nails, pondering the deeper significance of a teacher's offhand comment about your child?

Many parents remember school days with burning resentment for what school did to them. It's time to say, "This is a new day!"

Try not to tear down teachers in front of your children. This doesn't mean you need to whitewash the school and blame children when they come home complaining about something. But agreeing with the child that the teacher is "stupid" or "dull" defeats any good purposes. Watch out especially for your phone conversations, when children can overhear you complain about the "boring" homework they have been assigned. Instead talk to someone at the school, where it can do some good.

GETTING ALONG WITH THE SCHOOL

We need to find a middle ground between too much griping about schools and not enough. Schools need to hear from parents but not be besieged. Schools have an unwritten hierarchy of appeal. Always start with the classroom teacher. Classroom teachers have legitimate cause for anger if you bypass them and go straight to the principal without giving them a chance to brief you and work out the situation. Principals have a right to be angry if you come to them before trying to straighten things out at the classroom level. If both the teacher and the principal are unable to work things out or balk at your concern, you may then proceed with clear conscience to the director of elementary education or district superintendent.

These examples illustrate when a complaint is called for:

• You have a right to assume the school cares about your child. If you ask for a conference with the teacher, it's legitimate for you to expect the conference to offer specific details about your child and not generalizations about how wonderful or difficult all seventh graders are. Keeping parents informed is a function of the school. You should raise the roof if you are not told before the end of the year that your child is having trouble.

• You should let the school know when children are at the mercy of erratic homework schedules that may dump four hours of homework due the next day and then give none at all for days.

• You should let teachers know when your youngster feels overlooked or picked on in class. A ripple effect of discouragement can set in. Sometimes teachers are not aware of the effect they are having on students until they hear about it from parents.

Above all, parents have to stop griping behind the school's back — over the back fence or cocktails. It's unfair to complain that the school isn't helping if you haven't asked for help.

FACE TO FACE: THE PARENT-TEACHER CONFERENCE

It looks so benign, but don't be fooled. Among the most challenging and emotional encounters in history is the typical parent-teacher conference, complicated by hope, desire, worry, and defensiveness.

One of the great difficulties of the parent-teacher conference is getting through to each other. Teachers say that parents take everything said about their child as a personal attack. Parents accuse teachers of lecturing instead of listening, accusing instead of understanding.

Too many parents come out of parent-teacher conferences having learned only that their child has a problem and nothing more, with no suggestions from the teacher on how to help the youngster. Too many teachers come out of those conferences gnashing their teeth about parents who refuse to act and who want to be helpless.

Getting along with the school isn't easy. It probably never really was, but it seems harder today. Parents are more involved with their children's education. While parents are critical of schools, many are afraid to utter a critical word. Many's the parent who's said to me, "If I ever said anything was wrong, my child would suffer."

It would be Pollyanna-ish to say such things never happen; they do happen, but far less often than parents think. Schools may not be able to reassure a really fearful parent, but it would help if they repeated at frequent intervals that their doors and ears are open, and that parents have nothing to fear.

Schools are beginning to give teachers help on how to relate better to parents at conferences, but often it's the parent who needs help.

Here are some points used with success in our Institute programs:

1. Start out by saying something positive about the teacher or the classroom. There must be something that's good — artwork displays, books lying around invitingly, science corners. Teachers need good words, just like anybody else.

2. Tell the teachers about any special family situation affecting your child: divorce, death, illness, a new baby, a recent or impending move. It's especially important to tell the new teacher in the fall about any upheaval in your child's life over the summer that might affect school attitudes.

3. Discuss your child's talents, skills, hobbies, study habits, and any special sensitivities, such as weight and speech difficulties.

4. Tell teachers about areas in which you think your child

needs special help and about any undesirable habits you hope will be overcome.

5. If your child has already received some grades, ask what went into these marks and how your youngster is being evaluated. (See Chapter 25, "Parents and Students," for more information on this point.)

6. Ask for a general outline of what will be covered this year. Some teachers, but not enough of them, provide this at the beginning of the school year. Ask about specific ways to help your youngster at home.

7. Don't leave the conference unsure of what teachers have said. If you have questions, ask them. One way to clarify in your mind what a teacher means is to put in your own words what you understood. This gives everyone the chance to clarify issues if any misunderstandings have taken place.

8. At the conference, *really listen*. Some teachers complain that it doesn't matter what they say to parents. Some parents, they believe, have their minds made up before the conference begins, and nothing a teacher says makes any difference.

9. Follow up on the conference. If the teacher indicates some areas in which your youngster needs improvement, don't sit biting your nails waiting for months to find out what's happening in the classroom. Check back — not the next day, but in a few weeks — to see how things are going.

10. Remember that a teacher's evaluation of your child, even though carefully considered, can never be completely right. Teachers once classified Thomas Edison, Charles Darwin, Oliver Goldsmith, and Winston Churchill as "dull" boys. Their parents probably knew all along from the exciting things they did at home that they were bright kids. With early home-school conferences, their parents and teachers could have shared this knowledge.

A conference early in the school year can prevent serious academic and social difficulties. Some elementary schools have started the excellent practice of mandatory conferences at the time of the first report card.

In the secondary grades, parents may have to take the initiative and persevere to schedule a conference. In junior and senior high school, parents wanting to see teachers are often thought of as "babying" their children or "pressuring" the teacher for better grades. This is no reason for any parent to be deterred from asking for a conference. Students should participate in the discussion whenever possible.

WORKING TOGETHER AS A TEAM

Parents may complain about the inflexibility of the schools, but school people trying to initiate change often find that parents are the big obstacles.

Teachers can get mighty discouraged. Parents, for example, talk about being interested in curriculum; but hold a curriculum meeting, and three parents show up.

Schools will attempt open-discussion meetings, but parents often won't open up. I recall moderating a school forum during which we pleaded with parents to raise all their doubts, to ask any question. A few came from the audience, but I overheard more questions — "When will my kids learn to read?" "How will they learn discipline?" — whispered in the hall afterward than I had in the meeting. I asked one father why he hadn't asked his question so he could get the school's answer. He shrugged.

Parents have to be willing to engage in meaningful dialogue with teachers, coming together to talk about such questions as these: What can we realistically expect of one another? What is the role of the school today? What is the role of the family? How are these different from yesterday's roles? What can we do to help each other and the children?

I look to the day when teachers get the help they need to work with parents in an educational partnership. Teachers need training in working with adults so that they don't talk to parents as if they are children. And they need to be given time and extra hands to do this important job of connecting with the home.

Parents and teachers are in the same difficult situation together, besieged by outside experts usually pointing all too clearly to what is wrong. Not enough is said about what is right, both at home and in school. This has to be pointed out and sought just as carefully as the problems are.

Let's praise each other. We need to hear in word and deed how important we are in each other's lives. And we have to trust each other more. In talking with teachers and parents across the country, I hear a message from each that says, "Trust me; respect me." Parents have got to tell teachers what they need to know. Teachers cannot be left in the dark about difficulties at home that affect children's work in school. Teachers need this knowledge to be able to help.

Let's share affection. It's difficult to be a parent, to juggle a lot of conflicting demands. Teachers, too, have similar problems. Let's be gentle, forgiving, and loving.

WHEN THE BLAMING STOPS ...

I look to the day when the blaming between parents and teachers stops, when more parents turn to themselves and to other parents for help, when parents stop looking to the school to solve their problems.

I promise to keep working with teachers to help them understand and treat parents for what they really are — their most important allies. But parents have responsibilities, too, and these have to be met.

Teachers are discouraged by parents who don't want to face up to their responsibilities, who act like kids themselves, who want teachers to do the parenting for them. When one teacher called home about a student's habitual tardiness, the parent said, "I tell him to get up. He just doesn't do it. What am I supposed to do?" And what's a teacher supposed to think?

We teachers and parents are not yet sufficiently tuned in to each other and each other's needs. It's getting better, but in the meantime, let's be good to one another. We don't have to be perfect to be good.

Chapter 23.
Single Parents and the Schools: Making the Connection

The ad shows a woman in an ice cube, and the caption reads, "Feeling isolated?"

I don't know what product is being advertised, but I am struck by this graphic image of isolation and how much it reminds me of experiences recounted by single parents. The difference is that the ad is funny, and isolation isn't.

There is a lot still to learn about families and about what goes on in two-parent homes. But divorce has come under study, and it has been found that the pain of divorce is an isolating experience that has a negative effect on children's work in school — at least for a while.

This chapter is about what single parents can do to lessen the sense of isolation by making connections with the school and building a network of support.

Not too many years ago, it was said that what happens to the family is not the school's business. But the importance of the family in children's education is now known. Schools are in a unique position with single parents, because schools are the continuing, stable institution in their children's lives. The very regularity of the school day can be a comfort.

Up to now, schools have not been known for their support of single parents. At a conference our Institute conducted on single-parent families and schools, the concerns expressed were almost a cry of pain:

- School personnel are insensitive. They stereotype our children and expect less from them.
- Schools do not provide the before- and after-school care that our children need.
- Parent-teacher conferences are scheduled as if parents do not work and there are still fathers/mothers in the home.

It is hard for schools to change. Families change a lot faster. For some years now, schools have been playing catch-up. When it comes to meeting the needs of today's family, schools have not yet caught up.

But I know they want to. Teachers themselves are employed parents; they are single parents. They want to help, but knowing what to do is not easy.

Single parents can help themselves and the schools at the same time by following through on the suggestions in this chapter. The activities combine three elements: they bring single parents together to lessen isolation; they provide support for children's upbringing; and they save money.

INFORM THE SCHOOL

One of the very first things to do if you are going through a divorce or separation is to get in touch with the school and set up a conference. Many teachers say they can spot troubled students even before parents file for divorce. Major signs that show up in school are loss of concentration, daydreaming, and sadness. Boys appear to be more affected than girls. Children of all ages — not just the young ones — need extra support. Adolescents, who may act as though nothing is bothering them, especially need parental love and guidance in this trying period.

During the conference, try to be as honest as you can about what's happening to the family. Don't predict what terrible behavior you expect your child to develop, but let teachers know you will want to be kept informed and will work closely with them to solve any problems.

Request that your child's report cards and records be sent to your child's other parent, too. Let the school know of any change in address, phone number, or job so that they can always reach you. Schools wait for you to volunteer this information. Be sure it's complete.

ASK FOR THE SCHOOL'S ATTENTION

Single and working parents should ask that conferences be set up in the late afternoon and early evenings, rather than during the work day. Suggest that the PTA sometimes hold meetings on the weekends so that employed parents can attend. Encourage programs especially for single and working parents on such topics as how to meet the demands of home and job life.

Find out if child care can be provided during meetings for parents. A high school's family-life class could provide child care while parents attend school functions.

Above all, start thinking about and working with the school as a community resource center. Single parents need special services. I don't mean to exclude two-parent families, but single parents need to meet each other in groups for a chance to develop parent-to-parent support systems. The groups would meet at the school and could include Parents Without Partners (PWP). The idea is to set the action at the place where members' children are involved and to bring families together.

Anyone can start such a group. It does require the cooperation of the school; you don't just charge in and take over. What's needed are the school facilities once or twice a month and a list of the school's single-parent families. Ordinary but important details need to be addressed; find out the fees, if any, for covering insurance and a custodian. These concerns are not insurmountable and should not take forever to clear away. Usually the fees involved are (or should be) modest. If not, and support is needed to cover costs, the matter should be brought up at school-board meetings. Schools cannot be shut tight when their facilities are needed by the community.

A small group of families can band together and set up their own activities at the school. Once a week you could have a pot-luck supper, with everyone bringing a dish. Movies borrowed from the school or library can follow dinner. Other family outings can include roller skating, hiking, and amateur-night shows. On weekend evenings, members can take turns sitting for children in the group.

THE SCHOOL AS A PARENT CENTER

Here are details on school-based activities that parents can run for each other.

Movie Nights

This is a way to provide low-cost family entertainment, expose children to films of good quality, and make money for the PTA or school. You need a movie projector, a film rental catalogue, and someone to sell tickets and snacks.

Order films from the catalogue. Select and publicize the movie series. Schedule the films for suppertime or just after supper on Friday evenings. It's an ideal kickoff for the weekend. Charge a reasonable admission fee. Encourage parents to attend with their children.

Family "High Brow" Outings

This activity gets families together at a cultural event in the community.

Select a play or museum exhibit to see. You'll need one or two organizers to arrange for tickets and transportation. Some funds will be needed for tickets, which can usually be obtained at discount. Tickets might even be donated. A bus or private cars are needed for transportation.

Announce the event with a flyer from school sent home with the kids. Include a response form. When tickets are distributed, provide the play or exhibit program, if possible. The group can meet for a potluck dinner and travel together to the theater.

Fees can be charged to raise additional revenue for the school, the PTA, or as a stipend for the organizer. Money paid by theatergoers above the cost of tickets is tax deductible if proceeds are used for school purposes.

Eat a Lot for Little

This activity is a gala family eating at "a dime a dip." You need food donations and some volunteers to set up tables, serve, and clean up. A few dollars are needed to purchase paper plates, utensils, and cups.

Choose a date, gather volunteers, and announce the event in the local paper and school newspaper. Ask each family to donate one dish to feed four persons — meat, vegetables, salad, or dessert. Provide a response slip at the bottom of the newspaper notices. Request that food be brought to school at least fifteen minutes before the event.

Plan for two serving lines, each with several food choices in every category. Serve a dip of each item as requested. At the end of the line, the cashier, who can be a student, totals the number of "dips" and multiplies by a dime. It's possible to eat a balanced, big meal, including dessert, for seventy cents. A family of four can be fed for under three dollars. This event might precede a Back-to-School night or other special event.

Family "Follies"

This activity gives children a chance to meet and know adults beyond their own family. Plus, it's a showcase for family talent.

Announce the Follies and advertise open-house auditions. The show can be an informal, spur-of-the-moment event or a more elaborate affair. If more elaborate, use a parent/student committee to select acts for the program, and form committees for invitations, programs, publicity, tickets. If possible, video-record the show for later screenings.

Come to My House

This activity gives parents an opportunity to get together in an informal atmosphere to share mutual concerns about their children. Even though this event is held on "home ground," it's about school and education-related issues.

Parents are asked to "sponsor" a meeting by inviting neighbors into their homes for an informal get-together. This builds personal ties between neighbors. At the meeting, one member might tell about good, inexpensive places to go with children, while another might share tips on getting chores and homework done.

The value of such meetings is that they are help, not gripe, sessions. One family's good idea helps another family. What works in one house might work for someone else. This is truly self-help based on mutual support.

Raincoat and Boot Exchange

This activity is a real money saver, good for all families but especially for single parents who may have tighter budgets.

When have you had a raincoat or boots that have worn out? They don't — they just get outgrown. Here's a way to keep them in circulation.

Early in the school year, ask parents to bring outgrown rainwear to school. Designate certain days for the exchange. To save administrative work, ask all parents to put their own prices on the items. What isn't sold can be returned or donated to local organizations. To keep costs low, ask that no item be priced over two dollars. In this way, the exchange becomes a real bargain.

All parents — not just single parents — should be encouraged to participate. A single-parents club may want to conduct this exchange and other activities in this chapter to demonstrate its commitment to the school and to the community.

A New Kind of Saturday

Who says weekends are fun? Many single parents, especially noncustodial parents, report that weekend outings are often repetitive and costly. One father on his way to pick up his children said, "Here we go to the zoo again, followed by a movie and an expensive supper. My kids are getting bored, and I'm exhausted. On some days we freeze to death. On others we melt."

Here's a "recipe" for a new kind of Saturday at the school. It's not just for single parents, but it will be appreciated by single parents, especially by that dad who can come inside.

The goal is to provide a way for children and parents to come together in groups to do enjoyable activities in an atmosphere of shared fun and learning. It can be as simple as one program and one class or as complex as a multiclassroom Saturday School.

Start with a small group of interested parents, perhaps a specially constituted Saturday Committee. It need not be large, but help is needed to do certain tasks.

Find out what the students themselves want in the program. Give them a blank sheet for any and all ideas, or give them a list of activities that you know you have the teachers and equipment for. Asking children to choose what they want to do is an important difference between Saturday and regular school.

Use as group leaders parents who are actually mathematicians or cooks, carpenters or writers, during their work week. In this way, every parent can contribute and have something to teach.

There might be a Working World Club, where parents with different occupations come to talk about what they do, and an

Around the World Club, in which children and parents who have lived in different parts of the world tell about life abroad.

You need a school building, or even a few rooms, and parents and children who want activities they don't get enough of during the week. These might be drama, art, science, music, cooking, sports, sewing, carpentry ... The teachers are parents who have expertise in these subjects that they are ready to share. It's a people-to-people program with parents reaching out to help other parents.

Work out a schedule. *Example:* Dance in the auditorium from 9:15 to 10:05; Science in room 23 from 10:15 to 11:05. Children might sign up for two or three groups a morning. Run short terms, three to five weeks long, so that if you want to do it again, you'll be able to vary course offerings frequently.

Keep groups small, no more than ten to twelve in each, so that children who are in large classes all week long can get more attention. Set up groups in a nongraded way. This is another difference from most regular schools. In this way children can learn from each other and meet new friends.

Use older children as teacher aides with younger groups. And parent leaders can team together, too. The writing group can compose plays for the drama group to perform, and so forth. To make sure that children and parents get to meet with each other, use the breaks between the activities for milk and cookies in the lobby.

Charge a small fee if it's possible to do so without keeping out parents and children who should attend. This money will provide at least honorary payments for that very essential coordinator. This person will handle scheduling, registration, and the many sundry details it takes to get this plan into action.

Look into payments that may be available to leaders under the provisions of funds for school districts from the U.S. Department of Education. More parents could volunteer if they knew that their out-of-pocket expenses would be paid.

A parent-and-child program can run simultaneously with the children's program to provide activities in which parents and children participate together. This program might appeal most to parents of preschoolers, but it would also work with parents of older children who want to learn together a musical instrument or foreign language.

Involving parents as teachers is good for everyone. Parents learn a lot more about children, and youngsters get a sense of pride from seeing their own parents teaching. Plan for some informal "teacher" training. Extra time will be hard to come by with this busy group, so one morning will probably have to do. Invite children to come along to be minded by a corps of teenagers in another classroom.

In this workshop emphasize what it means to be a Saturday Teacher — a teacher who does not grade, who encourages, demonstrates, and then steps back to let children take over. The workshop should cover specific points, from how to plan creative activities to how to keep order.

In-service training is useful, too, if only the time can be found. If your plan calls for children to eat lunch at school, parent leaders could meet during lunch. They can share what they've been doing, how it's working, and what their plans are for the next week. Planning is vitally important, especially in informal programs.

Students need more time in their week when the choice of what they learn is theirs and when they can be with their parents. Parents, especially fathers, need more time to be with their children. And school officials are more ready than ever to have their buildings put to greater use.

"A New Kind of Saturday" by any other name or any other day is an idea bound to please.

HELPING OURSELVES

The message of this chapter is *Don't wait*. Don't wait for institutions to change. Don't wait for others to come by to help you. No activity in this chapter is so difficult or costly that it can't be done in every neighborhood in this country.

Chapter 24.
Parents and At-Home Child Care: Making Sure Sitters Do More Than Sit

"I wish I could clone myself so that my child is not deprived of me when I am away, and I wish my household help would do just what I do."

You don't just sit, and neither should your sitters. The chain of MegaSkills support is only as strong as its weakest link.

In this chapter are common-sense responses to the increasingly common desire for sitters who do more than sit.

To work or not to work — that is *not* the question for the majority of mothers today employed outside the home. The result is often talked about in extremes — it's awful or it's great.

Reality is currently somewhere in between.

"In between" is precisely the difficult place many parents today are in. Families are on the front lines of social change, waiting for reinforcements — changes in institutional policies and attitudes — that have not caught up with their lives. For example, schools still generally open and close regardless of normal work schedules, and jobs start and end regardless of children's school hours.

Parents, especially mothers, are caught in between.

In the short run, things do appear harder (even with Pampers) than they were in the sentimentalized post–World War II period, when mothers were at home, concentrating on child care. But evidence now emerging indicates that for parents and children the present is not as bad as some would have us believe, and the future looks a lot brighter.

The spotlight on the role of the mother in this chapter is in no way meant to exclude the responsibility of the father in the care and education of children. However, there would be little concern about latch-key children and after-school care if mothers were not employed. Therefore this chapter attempts to deal with the different responsibilities for household management that have resulted because of mothers' outside employment. Fathers' help is not only welcome but greatly needed.

NO MORE "CONVENTIONAL WISDOM"

In analyzing current research on the effects of mothers' work on life at home and on children's achievements, I've uncovered a picture that defies conventional wisdom. The information is new and sketchy — until recently there was no data on the working mother — but it points to children doing well academically even though mothers work, and to mothers feeling less — not more — strain when they work outside the home.

Conventional wisdom would have children of working mothers performing less well in school. But a recent two-year review of studies by the National Academy of Sciences says that's not so. In general, the achievement of children of employed mothers differed little from that of nonemployed mothers. There are some studies, including those of the U.S. government, that suggest caution in making quick deductions about these effects. But the common-sense summary of the National Academy review reflects much of what is now known: Don't ask if working mothers are good or bad for kids because the answer is: It depends. It depends on the parents, on the child, on the circumstances, and so forth.

What "it depends" on, to a very great extent, are parent at-home management skills, whether or not additional help is available. Families fortunate enough to have household help are in a strong position to gain MegaSkills support from these people, but, once again, it depends. This chapter discusses what it depends on and provides suggestions on what to do.

MAKE SURE SITTERS DO MORE THAN SIT

There is more to child care than finding someone to do it. Even if your children are in schools or day care centers, they usually spend some time with child care help at home in the evenings or on weekends. This is precious time in the lives of children, and it pays to be concerned about how it is being spent.

When you choose a center, you are not really in the driver's seat. The activity schedules are set by others. But when you hire someone to care for your children at home, you are the employer and manager of the program.

Here are some tips for dealing with this responsibility.

Define the Job

The majority of children today whose mothers work full-time are cared for by a helper other than a relative. Chances are, you do not know as much about this person as you would know about a relative. And this helper does not know you and your family values. That's why you need to spend time talking with applicants about how you want your child's time spent and what you expect of each other.

Decide how much of your helper's time you want used in child care and how much in house cleaning. Your priorities have to be made clear. Your helper cannot be washing windows and walking with your child in the park at the same time. Provide a clear message of what needs to be done and when.

Look for Doers

You really don't want "sitters." You want your child care helpers to come up with activities and projects, to take pride in this educational work with your child.

The kind of helper you want is also determined by the age and interests of your children. Ideally you want a responsive and friendly person who is willing to listen and who enjoys being with children. For infants you may want more warmth and patience than is needed for older children. For children ages six to twelve, for example, you want care givers who can respect a growing child's needs for independence and privacy while still being able to set limits.

Look over applicants and check their references with these goals in mind. In the interview, give applicants sample problems to solve. *Examples:* A child is cranky and bored. What do you do? A child wants to eat dinner, but it's not yet time. What do you do?

Ask your potential employee to try out an activity with your child — while you watch informally. You'll get a sense of your helper's teaching style and know right away whether active care or just sitting is what this person wants and is able to do.

Make a Plan: Stock Up on Activity Ideas

Talk together. Ask for your helper's ideas on what to do with your child. And ask your child, too. How long should all this planning take? Probably no more than thirty minutes each week. And think of the worry that you'll be saving and the constructive activity this planning will make possible.

List activities for different days. Try to vary quiet activities, such as reading, with vigorous activities, such as playground games. Look for shorter and longer activities. If you know, for example, that making a school box (to hold all the child's school supplies at home) is being planned, you'll know what materials to get ready. Let the helper and your child have a hand in gathering the materials — box, the paper, the crayons. If you know that each day they'll be reading together, go to the library with your child to pick out books.

Encourage helpers to compile an informal list of activity ideas as they come to mind. Keep a notepad handy to jot down such ideas as, "Try collages with Sara"; "Help John bake cookies." A list of ideas can be really helpful when it comes to the challenging job of varying activities for several children in one home.

Children themselves are resources for activities. For example, an eight-year-old can read stories to preschoolers; an eleven-year-old can help cook the family dinner.

Even if they are able to, helpers shouldn't do all the work. Some work should be saved for the kids. This capitalizes on their early offers to help and enables children to feel purposeful and to acquire good work habits.

Jobs given children must be real and not make-work. Even a very young child can recognize a phony job. Short jobs (see examples below) that children can finish fairly quickly are very satisfying.

Preschoolers love water play. In the summer they can do water work: sprinkling the lawn, washing bicycles, hosing down the front porch. Older children can help with grocery shopping, cooking, and even polishing shoes (their own and their parents).

Helpers may need tips on how to set up and arrange the work area. Preparing for the after-effects of the work is important. Newspapers, plastic drop cloths, or old shower curtains should be spread down before work starts, so that quick cleanups, not screams, follow a child's efforts.

Prepare a Special Child Care Box

This is an all-purpose box that needs to be kept stocked and ready. For its all-purpose use, it needs the traditional arts and crafts supplies: crayons, pencils, paper (several colors and textures), round-edge scissors, glue, scraps of cloth, washable markers, ruler, string, old magazines with pictures.

Beyond these basics, it can be more imaginative, with even a surprise now and then. For older children, add something to talk about . . . an article, a surprise book, a treat to eat. Leave word of a household chore to be done. Or leave a note about a game to be tried. One that's always good is "What's Missing?" Five or more objects are put on a table. Children look at them and then close their eyes. One is taken away, and the children then try to figure out which one is missing. You can keep taking away more and more objects. Everyone takes turns. This game is fun and builds skills needed for reading.

Schedule After-School Time

Here's a sample schedule for young children. Use it as a takeoff point for your own ideas.

3:15–3:30   **Snacks:** milk, cookies, carrot sticks. Helper and child can make treats the day before.

3:30–4:00   **Activity Time:** Walk around the block. *Example:* Count cars, look for different kinds, colors.

4:00–4:30   **Story Time:** Take turns reading aloud. Ask each other questions about the story. Stop before getting to the end; ask how it will turn out.

4:30–5:00   **TV-Watching Time** (if wanted): Let the child pick show and select time. Helper watches along with youngster and then talks about show when it's over.

or

4:30–5:00   **Arts Time:** Do a quick arts and crafts project. *Example:* Make place mats from ordinary paper to use for setting the supper table. Children do drawings with markers. They can add names of the people who will be eating. These make nice surprise presents for the family. With older children, play board games or do a puzzle together.

5:00–5:30   **Homework Time:** For youngsters with homework to do, set aside time. It may take a longer or shorter period.

5:30–6:00   **Set table and/or help get supper ready:** Prepare for the meal; make snacks for the next day.

Straighten house for parents' arrival.

Use any extra time for activities that got short shrift because of heavier homework obligations or special activity that occurred that day.

TV can play a part in this schedule. But to be effective, TV time should be limited. In a three- to four-hour period after school, it's wise to plan for no more than one hour of TV watching. To make this limit more appealing to your child, let your child choose the shows. (See "Tackling TV" in Chapter 3 for related activities.)

Allow for variations in the plan. The playground may announce a baseball game on a lovely afternoon. The schedule needs to be flexible enough to include such changes.

Check Up. How will you know the schedule was followed? Ask your child, your helper, or use a check-off sheet. Children can put checks next to each completed activity.

Health and Safety Rules. Be sure your helper knows what to do in case of household emergencies. Keep your emergency phone list up to date and a stocked first-aid box handy. The activities found in Chapter 12, on "Problem Solving," in the special section on safety, will also be useful.

Follow Household Rules

Your child care helpers will, generally speaking, be better off if they can stick to a minimum of rules — ones the family needs, ones that are reasonable and enforceable.

Each family's rules will probably be a little different from the neighbors', and those differences may cause friction. Children will say, "Susie gets to stay outside until supper"; "Tommy can go to the supermarket alone." That's why it's good to have reasons to support rules. Share these with your helpers so they can speak in your voice to your children. Children, grudgingly or not, tend to listen to reason.

Assure helpers that it's normal for a child to test, to see whether or not they are really serious about sticking to rules. It may be that this testing will, after discussion, reveal that the rule isn't a good rule. For example, children may legitimately object to an inflexible demand that they have a bath before supper every night. Nobody loses face if the child mounts an argument so persuasive that the rule is changed.

Adults should try not to go back on their word. This includes helpers. If children know they can't go out until the work is done, then it's important to stick to this, unless a really important reason for changing it comes up. Children, even young ones, can assist in setting rules and seeing that they are followed.

What happens when children don't follow the rules? How is your helper going to punish your children? If nothing is to be done other than the issuing of a stern warning, such as, "Wait until your parents come home!" make sure this is clear. If something is to be done, such as withdrawal of TV privileges or sending children to their room for a certain period, make sure this is clear. If corporal punishment is out of the question, be sure your helper knows this. In short, don't leave these decisions up to the tensions and emotions of the moment. Make sure everyone knows what to expect.

Talk About "Talk"

Young children are learning language. It's vital for your helpers to talk as much as possible with young children — even with babies, who may not seem to understand. Helpers can talk as they cook and as they vacuum. They should keep young children near them so that children can watch and listen. Helpers can talk as they push the stroller and as they roll a ball back and forth to a child. Language is the critically important ingredient in early learning, and it starts and continues at home.

There is no denying that a helper who speaks clear and correct English is a strong asset. Increasingly, however, many families have very reliable helpers who do not have strong English skills. Many are immigrants who speak another language. If a helper is bilingual, of course it is possible that a child can pick up two languages. But by and large, fluent bilingual speakers are not in child care work.

Here are tips on what parents can do to assure that young children hear English every day.

- Encourage your helper to take your child to the playground or community center in order to be with others who speak English.

- Tell helpers to take your child out into the wider community. Walk through a shopping center. Go into a store to look at and talk about the merchandise. Explore new blocks. You can probably map out a month's worth of walks.

- Use a tape recorder. Record your own voice and those of others your child knows. Read a story. Send a greeting. The idea is to have your child hear English spoken daily. Show your helpers how to record your child's voice. When you come home, you can hear the message your child has sent to you.

Working as a Team

Introduce your helper, if possible, to other workers on your block or in the neighborhood. Encourage them to share ideas and activities.

Set up a back-up system. When you are depending on one person to show up at your home each day, you run into the difficulty of what to do when that person or that person's child is sick. Look into the possibility of connecting with an elderly person in your neighborhood who can pitch in. Be sure, even on those days, that your substitute help knows what you expect and has the materials to do the job.

One of the pitfalls as well as the strengths of having household employees is that they are indeed a real part of your household. This means — whether they live in or not — that there is a greater likelihood that you will come to know their personal lives — their joys, their sorrows, and their concerns about their own children.

Providing the schedule and support outlined in this chapter offers the possibility of helping your employees in their own lives. Knowing how to organize time with children is a useful skill for their own homes.

And don't worry about losing your children's love to this wonderful helper who knows all these terrific activities. Studies show that children know their own parents and gravitate to them. There's a wonderful and sometimes frightening bond between parent and child. These activities strengthen that bond. They show that you care, even when you are not there.

Keeping mothers at home, even if it were possible, wouldn't

solve all the problems of our children's growing up. It's not known whether intensive mothering is good for children over the long haul.

Today's employed mother may well be providing as much or more care and concern for her child as did the traditional mother of the past, who spent a great deal of time running the house rather than focusing on the child. The answer about which type of mother is better may never be fully known and is not relevant. What is relevant is dropping outdated, conventional wisdom and finding approaches that work for parents and children today.

Chapter 25.
Parents and Students:
Helping Children Feel More
at Home in School

Schools are complex worlds, with rituals, routines, and practices — a way of life that may at first appear frightening, imposing, and difficult for children to figure out.

Some parents tell me that years after they've graduated, they still haven't figured it out and are glad they no longer have to. There's an old joke (is it a joke?) that comedian Henry Morgan used to tell: "I'm forty-four years old and every day when I wake up, I thank my lucky stars I don't have to go to school anymore."

When I talk with groups of teachers, I remind them that we may be the only ones who really liked schools. We went back into them of our own free will.

School buildings are not immediately congenial-looking places. Why they look the way they do I will never know. Many generate a forbidding atmosphere guaranteed to harden the heart of the most eager first grader. Older school buildings can pass for mental asylums, and new ones, though much improved, are large and have an institutional look. To be sure, more and more schoolrooms do exude warmth, using bright colors, but most won't win prizes for their welcoming quality.

Children can be prepared for the look of the school and how a school works — even before they enter one or move on to a new one. In this chapter are a number of ways parents can help children find schools to be more congenial — no matter how they look, no matter who is teaching in them, no matter what grades are on their report card.

ABOUT THE SCHOOL ITSELF — BUILDING, CURRICULUM, ACTIVITIES

I know what it's like to move to a new school, to be an unknown and feel unknown. It's not a good feeling. I spent my early school years in a small school in a small town, where everyone knew me and I knew everyone else. After my mother died suddenly, my father decided to move the family to a large city nearby. I entered a very large school where I knew no one. This was in my high school years. It was a tough time, and one I have not forgotten.

In a way, my experience was not too unlike the move all children must make when they enter school for the first time or move on from a smaller elementary school to a large junior high. Any new entry is hard. It's easier in the early grades, in a small school. But it's still hard. And so I urge parents to help children feel as comfortable as possible as early as possible in a school year, in any new school situation. Help children try to visualize themselves in this school. Get information about the school, talk about it, make choices, and be ready to make this coming school year as terrific as possible.

If this is a new school for your child, whether it's for kindergarten, sixth grade, or tenth grade, visit the school with your child before the term begins, if possible. Walk through the halls, stop into the front office, introduce yourselves.

If classes are in session, ask to stop by. Try to walk along the very corridors your children will be walking along when they are students at this school.

In short, get the feel of the place. Start to feel at home there. Ask about and discuss with your child the curriculum: What will be covered this year? What are the possibilities for extracurricular clubs and activities? When do these have to be chosen? How do bus transportation schedules fit in with before- or after-school programs?

It's important to try to feel as comfortable as possible with the school in advance. Once the hectic pace of the school year begins, it's harder to get a reassuring first impression.

ABOUT TEACHERS

Today's sophisticated children are ready to understand that teachers are human beings and that, like anyone else, they can be right and they can also be wrong. In the past, respect in the classroom and often at home was one-sided; all from the child to the adult, and no back talk. Respect today has become more two-way.

Urge your child, right from the beginning, not to hesitate to question the teacher. This need not be done in a smart-alecky or disrespectful way. Students have to know how to stand up for what they think is right. You may want to do a little role playing at home, acting out a scene in which your children question a teacher politely yet firmly. Most of these questions will probably deal with grades, but students may also question a teacher's point of view.

Here are possible scenarios:

Student: "Mr. Thompson, can I have a few minutes to talk with you about the last test?"

Teacher: "Sure, what's on your mind?"

Student: "I thought I had the right answers to questions four and five, but they were marked wrong. Is there something I need to know that I don't understand?"

Or how about this one:

Student: "Mrs. Smith, I need more information about the grade on my report card. Here are papers from the last marking period. They are all B's, and yet I got a C as my mark. Can you explain what went into that C?"

In trying these out, you'll notice that these are not personal attacks, nor is the tone defensive or hostile. It's like asking for a raise without threatening to quit or being overly humble to the boss. It can be hard to maintain this composure when your feelings run high, but practice can help.

Lest you think that teachers don't alter grades when solid evidence is presented that changes their thinking — you're wrong. Teachers are generally reasonable people who want to be fair. I have changed a number of grades in my time. By the way, I have never known a student to complain about an unearned high grade. And there are always some of those, along with the ones that are too low.

Just as parents aren't always wonderful, neither are teachers. The only reason to make this obvious statement is that children, especially young children, can tend to believe or want to believe that teachers are always right. When they find that teachers are not perfect and can be unfair, they can be terribly disappointed and disillusioned.

Children should not need to have teachers love them every day in order to feel good about themselves. A child's self-confidence should not have to depend on a teacher's constant approval. Sometimes even the best teachers get angry.

It's possible to prepare children for the realities of teachers as people without undermining children's confidence in school. It can be helpful for children to know that teachers can be rejecting, bullying, dull, lazy, uncommunicative, unhelpful, and discouraging. Teachers can also be enthusiastic, supportive, smart, helpful, imaginative, caring, understanding, and sincere.

There are good teachers and bad teachers, but above all, a teacher's personality can make or break a class. No magic wand will alter how teachers conduct classes and the personal characteristics they bring to them. Children need to recognize that there are less than wonderful situations for which they are not to blame. And they need inner strength to live through these.

I really do believe that the good teachers outnumber the bad ones. And since children have so many teachers in their lives, the chances that they will have their share of good ones is strong. (For more details on this subject, see Chapter 22, "Parents and Teachers.")

ABOUT FRIENDS

School can be the place where children make lifelong friends. Or school can be a very lonely place if children have no friends. Children who have trouble making and keeping friends need help.

Teach youngsters that friendship is like a seed. It must be planted and tended. It demands loyalty, affection, and a willingness to go all out, to keep promises, to be considerate. Use specific examples to explain these ideas. You may want to recount some of your own experiences in school. Tell about when you were popular and when you were lonely, too.

Help children sense that friendships have ups and downs — today you're angry, tomorrow you make up — and that the friends will change. At five they may need someone to go on a swing with;

at fifteen, someone to discuss books with. At any age, they may want different kinds of friends at the same time.

Fears often handicap friendship. Some children, like adults, are afraid even of trying to make friends, afraid of being rebuffed. Expecting to be excluded, they set up barriers they don't even see, such as excessive shyness or overaggressiveness. Once contact is made, they may be afraid to get close to a friend, avoiding this by spreading themselves thin over many acquaintances.

When you see these fears and the immaturities of always needing to get rather than give, discuss them with your children. Try to avoid "Nobody likes me" explanations and stick to "How can we work together to help you have the friends you want?"

The friends your children want may not be the ones you'd choose. Try to respect your child's choices, but watch for any unhealthy situations that crop up. These include youngsters exploiting each other: social butterfly Sue using bookworm Ann to write all her book reports; aggressive Tom consistently venting anger on passive Jim.

When you see these patterns, bring them to your children's attention. They may know what's happening, too, but continue the relationship because they don't think they can attract anyone else. Talk about this.

Encourage children to bring friends home from school and to invite some along on family outings. Make youngsters feel welcome in your home. Try to avoid nagging about moderate noise and dirt. Try to set aside a place for children to entertain in, and work out arrangements for their cleaning up after everyone's gone.

Really shy children may need specific help to start friendships. If you hear your children mention a friend at school, help them set a date and make the first difficult phone call. With junior and senior high youngsters, a parent plays a less active role, but you can help direct them to the activities and clubs where they can make new friends.

Older students have trouble when they try to be what they're not, conforming to some popular image of whom they ought to like and what they ought to do. Often they'll tag along with a crowd whose company they don't even enjoy. Adolescents need to be reassured that their judgment is sound and reminded that they needn't worry about what other people think.

ABOUT REPORT CARDS

Except for the few students who bring home all A's (and their parents), nobody really likes report cards, not even teachers. Teachers will admit that no matter how hard they try, they cannot accurately judge what a student has learned. But even while report cards themselves are flunking, they continue to exert a mighty influence. The difference between a C and a B can determine whether a student goes to a certain college or gets a certain job.

Children can be helped to get the best, not the worst, out of report cards, no matter what the grades are. This is important because it appears that report cards are here to stay.

Parents can provide support for children who must receive grades by helping youngsters see the report card in perspective — what it is, how to view it positively, what dangers to avoid, and what changes can be asked for that schools and teachers are in a position to provide.

Anyone who's been to school, and that's almost all of us these days, knows the abuses grades are heir to. One teacher gives a C to a paper; another teacher might give it an A. The same teacher grading the same paper over again may grade it differently. Some teachers use low grades to make students work harder. Others use high grades for the same reasons.

Specific injustices rankle in the memories of anyone who's ever sat in a classroom. More harmful in the long run, however, are the attitudes that can surround grading: grades that become ends in themselves so that nothing is remembered when the exam is over; children labeled early as poor students unable to break the chains of low marks; threats about grades that cripple children with a fear of failure; grades given but unexplained, so that parents and children are left to wonder and guess what they mean and why they were given.

Yet despite all that is known about the errors in grading, grades continue to be regarded as prophetic, all-knowing measures of children's abilities. If the school says so, and says so in black and white, it must be right.

Ironically, parents who question many other things about the school may hold this belief in grades. In practice, most parents don't object to grading systems or even question them. Parents rarely even ask teachers why they grade as they do. Even when a parent knows better, a low grade will tend to make parents think less of their child.

This is dangerous, and efforts need to be made to avoid this trap. Here are some ways:

- Work with your child to see the report card for what it is. It is an attempt by teachers to assess what a student has learned. It is an administrative convenience in school record keeping. It is not an evaluation of the child as a human being — "you're good"; "you're bad." Grades are not all-knowing. The grade itself, whether an A or D, is a mixture of test scores and teacher reactions. All this can be discussed with your youngster so that grades are put in proper perspective without being discredited.

- Try to figure out with your child what's gone into the mark. Refer to school guidelines, check lists, and other comments on the card. On the secondary level, the mark is more mysterious, as it usually arrives without comments. Because these grades are run through computers in large schools, they often can't even have pluses and minuses. If the grade remains a mystery to you, discuss it with the teacher.

- Instill in your children the idea that regardless of the grades they receive, they continue to be accepted and loved. Anxiety about grades can give youngsters the dangerous idea that their value in life and their love from you depend on whether they bring home A's or C's. Since most children will bring home C's, whether they or their parents like it, it's dangerous business to make a C student feel less valuable as a human being because of a little letter that may be wrong.

- Treat failure in a subject not as a total disaster but rather as a sign of a problem that can be helped. Before nonpromotion, parents and teachers should get together for an in-depth discussion. If learning difficulties are revealed, the student's sight and hearing should be checked. An anti-schoolwork, emotional block may call for counseling.

And when your child does finally bring home good grades, bite your tongue before asking that awful question, "Why don't you do this all the time?"

THE SEARCH FOR A BETTER REPORT CARD

Some educators have called for getting rid of marks altogether. Short of that, however (and that does seem remote), report cards can be improved to enable teachers to present a bigger picture of the student.

In a growing number of elementary schools, for each grading period teachers make out forms on which they list various understandings and skills students have attained in each subject. In science, it may be an understanding of gases and liquids. In math it may include use of the protractor. In social studies it may involve knowledge of the economy and geography of Mexico. These check lists are attached to the report card. I've seen teachers use a four-category range from *Excellent* to *Below Average*. Parents are delighted because they feel they know what the child is doing in school and what went into the grade.

Where an elementary school teacher may evaluate a child in many areas, a high school teacher usually gives only one mark, A to F, which must encompass the wide range of the pupil's work. Since this one mark is an average of a student's best and worst, it gives very little information about a pupil's strengths and weaknesses.

Many teachers dislike grades because of this broad categorizing of a student with one symbol; for Johnny may be a C student in some ways and an A student in others. But all that the parent and student see is that one mark, which in Johnny's case may have averaged out to a B. The complexities that make up the grade are usually never known.

We can improve the situation, especially in the high schools. For one thing, I would like to see good-size space on report cards at all grade levels for teacher and parent to exchange comments. Here's the chance for the extra word or two that can make a lot of difference. It might be: "Please call me," or "You're doing a great job."

I'd like to see report cards that allow students to be graded in different ways in each subject. For example, students can be graded on responsiveness to the material, acquisition of facts, use of facts, creativity, precision, and organization. In any one course, a student might be rated "superior" in creativity and "insufficient" in organization. Different subjects demand different abilities and skills.

Teachers need to tell students more (and pupils and parents must ask more) about what goes into the making of the grade. Even when space is provided for teachers' comments, too often what is written is a meaningless: "Johnny needs to do better." Parents need information that is more exact and helpful.

Another step toward better grading would be the junking of the "curve," a ratio that allows just so many A's, B's, and so on in a class. I once had a group of twenty-five students, twelve of whom rated A's. Another group deserved none. If I had used a grading curve, the class that rated all the A's would have received fewer, and the class that rated none would have gotten some. It's just not fair.

Grading as a reward system is not bad in itself. Educational research confirms that rewards, many and frequent, help students learn. The problem with the present grading system is that not many students ever get any of the rewards. Too few of our children receive a real sense of achievement from school.

The answer to this problem is not to give everyone all A's. This would debase grading as a reward altogether.

Forward-thinking schools are experimenting to come up with better report cards. It's up to forward-thinking parents to reassure and encourage teachers to continue this experimentation.

In the meantime, we must come up with more ways, both in school and at home, in which students can excel and feel their worth.

The activities throughout this book provide opportunities for children to excel at home. Through them, children get a sense that they are achievers and succeeders in ways that go well beyond the classroom walls. This sense carries over to the school and makes it possible for children to deal more constructively with the marks on their report cards, even the disappointing ones, and with whatever happens in the classroom.

Section E.
Creativity: The Spark and the Satisfaction

Introduction.
A Sense of Balance

"My kids are learning to read and write. Should I care if they sing, dance, or draw?"

The answer is yes — mostly because of what is being learned about the complexities of our double-hemisphere brains. The left brain gets the workout in school: It handles the language, the numbers, the reading, the writing, the talking. The right brain is the artsy side: It handles music, spatial skills, intuition, and imagery.

Creative activity requires both sides of the brain. When we sing, we read notes (left brain) and produce musical sounds (right brain).

Ideally we want to experience and create as much "wholeness" in our lives as possible. At times when we're sitting in the office or in class, we just know in our bones that we need to get out to use our hands to mold, to use our voice to sing, to use our feet to bike or to dance. This gives us a sense of balance.

We may not be able to determine how in-class time is spent or whether there is enough time in school for both left and right brain activity. Outside of school is another matter. To help our children gain optimal development and use of their brains, they need to give both sides a workout.

In this section you will find:

The "Right Brain" at Home — how to create an arts environment at home.

Inspiration and Perspiration — how to nurture talent in all children; how what works for the gifted is helpful to all of us.

Chapter 26.
The "Right Brain" at Home

Some may think that arts are frills. I don't. Not only do I believe they are important for complete brain functioning, but I feel they are MegaSkills essentials. Perhaps no where else in the entire curriculum do children get to see so clearly that an achievement takes time and that it has a beginning, a middle, and a product. A vase starts with a lump of clay that is rolled, molded, and fired. A poem starts with a single word on a blank page. A dance starts with a first step. A violin starts with a squeak. There is a level of personal satisfaction in the arts that stimulates a child to learn and to want to keep on learning.

The arts are essential also because of the predictions for daily life in the not-too-distant future. By the year 2000, more of us will be living longer and retiring earlier. Some say we will work fewer hours each week and will have longer annual vacations. We will have time for our own interests — and these will grow out of our education and our "inner resources." Fundamental to these inner resources is enjoying and participating in the arts. With the renewed emphasis on what's been termed "the basics," the arts may be in even greater danger in school.

Out of school, however, is another matter. The arts can live in every home, whether a parent is "artsy" or not. This chapter tells how to do it in ways that make it possible for every family to create an arts environment at home.

CREATIVE DRAMATICS

Creative dramatics sounds like an activity almost too imposing for use at home. Actually, home is an ideal place for it.

In creative dramatics, you emphasize the players, not the play. There are no scripts, no awesome, exhausting productions. It's defined well by a ten-year-old boy who said, "In creative dramatics, you can be anything you want to be. If you're fat, you can be thin; if you're short, you can be tall. You don't have to say what the teachers say; you can say what you want to say." A girl adds, "We have feelings in here [pointing to her heart] — they have to come out. In dramatics we can let them come out."

Children already possess what they need for creative drama — lots of imagination coupled with the instinct for make-believe and improvisation.

The Costume Box   ages 4–8

Youngsters love to dress up and imagine they're someone else. To encourage this, provide a costume box of old clothes, including hats and shoes. Small props like the following are especially useful: fans, umbrellas, luggage, toy trucks, masks, dolls for dressing and undressing.

It's wonderful to see the transformation that a flowered straw hat and high heels can do for a little girl in shorts. Suddenly she's a fairy godmother. Put a black scarf on her head, and she's a wicked witch. Let her put on Father's tie and hat, and she's a prince, a spy, a soldier.

You can move this to a next level. To encourage your child to put action to the character, ask, "What are you, John? A cowboy? What does a cowboy do? Show me."

There you have the elements of dramatic characterization. From this, your youngster can develop a play in which a fairy godmother meets a cowboy. What happens after that? That's for you and the children to work out. The shy child who finds it difficult to take part will gain confidence behind a mask and with a prop in hand.

Try to remember to record some of these moments. You don't need a video camera, although these do make for memorable scenes. Use a tape recorder to get the voices, and take some snapshots or slides. These are a delight for the memory scrapbooks and also serve to reinforce children's positive images of themselves.

Our Own Play   any age

Now you may want a plot. Let's say you have Cinderella and a spy. They meet. What happens next? Let the children tell you. Join in the fun as an actor, too. Children love to have parents take parts in impromptu plays.

Act out favorite stories: Your children tell the story first. Divide the parts: Who wants to act what role? It can help to have three or four players. If you don't have that many children at home, call the neighbors.

Children ages three and up will be able to participate if they know the stories and the roles they're to do. Don't fret if everyone, boys included, wants to be Goldilocks. Give them a chance.

Go through the play enough times for all to have the parts they want. Each run-through may last only a few minutes. What the actors say will change each time because they are making up their own lines. Keep your props simple and spontaneous. Cinderella can put on Mother's dress and high heels for the ball. Use chairs that double as beds for the Three Bears. Your children will probably want to perform the plays over and over. As they get the knack, let them take turns as director.

Try pantomimes for fun and dramatic exercise. Eat a dripping ice cream cone, empty smelly garbage, hold a hot coal or an injured bird. Try converging emotions of love, shyness, fear, bravery, anger. Then elaborate on your pantomimes. Cross a street crowded with traffic; do a chore, such as raking leaves, when you'd rather be somewhere else. Build your own family repertoire of pantomimes and games such as show and tell with younger children and charades with older ones. Puppets are especially helpful for shy children. Work up skits for parties and special occasions.

Applause for the Actors

Children grow more self-conscious and conscious of the world about them as they grow older. They may find that dramatizing comes less naturally. It is important to try to help these youngsters to continue using drama as a way to express themselves, to release pent-up feelings, to be anything they want to be.

Drama builds a child's self-confidence and imagination. It also helps youngsters understand others by asking them literally to put themselves in other people's shoes.

ARTS AND CRAFTS

Art activities — both the energetic fury of actual creation and the pleasures of museum going — are too enjoyable and important to be saved for "artistes" alone.

Start an Art for Everyone crusade with art projects for the whole family. The artistically talented are welcome, of course, but open the doors even wider for the "I can't draw" people, who are usually reluctant to try the artsy stuff.

Younger children probably will be less inhibited. Older ones and those who haven't been exposed to what we're talking about in this chapter may need specific ideas to begin. The "I can't think of anything to make" syndrome can be a very real problem.

Art work at home exercises children's inventive abilities (an important component of intelligence) and their eye-hand coordination muscles.

The Work Area   any age

Set up, with children, a work area where they can spread out and be messy. They need a storage shelf for supplies and a display area for finished creations. This can be a corner of a room.

Here are ideas for stocking an arts corner. Almost everything you need can be put together inexpensively, and you don't need everything at once.

Assorted powder tempera and enamel paint

Paste, strong glue

Scissors, crayons, tape, string

Paint palette (muffin tin or egg carton inlaid with foil)

Finger paints (can be home-made with starch, coloring, soap flakes, water)

Glitter

Clay (hard and soft-drying)

Pipe cleaners

Ruler

Scraps of cloth (good for collages)

Wire hangers for mobiles

Bottles, cans, and jars (saved from the kitchen)

Cardboard boxes (different sizes)

Paper (shelf, wrapping, colored, plain white, and plenty of old newspapers for clean up)

Try art materials at home that your children might not usually work with. Paints and crayons are fine, but stretch youngsters' experiences with such materials as toothpicks, wire, burlap, and shells.

A Potpourri of Projects   any age

Depending on children's ability to work on their own with these materials, encourage both free play and specific projects. Generally young children want more free play and prefer short projects that can be finished in one sitting. Older youngsters can do projects in steps over several days.

Here are some art activities that everyone can do:

Flower pots from decorated juice cans

Animals from pipe cleaners, mounted on wood pieces

Paper dolls cut from shirt cardboard

Carved soap sculptures

Decorated bricks for doorstops

Decorated stones for paperweights

Necklaces made from shells

Dollhouses from cardboard boxes

Designs from pasting overlapping colored papers, initials, numbers

Collages from seeds or magazine cutouts

Touch-and-feel scrapbook from magazine pictures, with yarn, cotton, and foil pasted in appropriate places

Try homemade puppets, allowing your children's imaginations to concoct puppets that look any way they want them to. Use an old sock for the head with a toilet paper roll inside to give it body. Stuff the sock with cotton or paper; your child can sew on features (using buttons) or draw them on. Yarn is ideal for hair. Stitch some fabric to the base so that the hand inside can't be seen. Add a puppet stage made from a cardboard box, and you're in show business.

Use arts and crafts for gifts for Christmas and for birthdays. They're wonderful as party favors. Nothing satisfies the receiver or giver as much as a homemade gift. (See Chapter 19, "Special Times," for more ideas.)

Start an art gallery by reserving a wall to exhibit your children's artwork. Trace your child's artistic development by framing and hanging a painting every six months or so. You will have a colorfully decorated wall that draws oohs and aahs from company and a prideful "I did that" from your child. This is a wonderful ego builder. For a rogues' gallery, children can do caricature drawings of their friends, their teachers, and you.

I Made It Myself

Picture Puzzles (ages 4–6). They're practically free, easy to make, and can be designed to be as simple or as complex as children want. Paste a picture on cardboard and then cut puzzle pieces out, with or without drawing lines on the back for guidance. You need magazines that contain large-size color pictures, scissors, shirt cardboard, paste, and large envelopes for holding the pieces.

Dress Me (ages 4–8). This is a variation of pin the tail, with blindfolded players pinning paper cutouts of clothes — shirt, shorts, socks, and shoes — onto paper silhouette figures of children. Children lie down on sheets of wrapping or shelf paper and you draw around their bodies. This combines children's intense interest in themselves with their creative joy in making their very own games. Trade places. Let your child do a silhouette of you. Then stand both silhouettes up against a wall. This is guaranteed to make you laugh or cry!

Master Builder (ages 8–12). With your older children, make a playground, a project that takes both physical and creative effort. In this activity, children create their own outdoor play structures. Household and hardware scraps are welcome: old tires, steering wheels, door knobs, wooden crates. Some tools and a friend or two to help, and this project is on its way.

If your fence needs painting, let the children try it. But improve on Tom Sawyer by letting your youngsters paint flowers or whatever they fancy for a unique job.

MUSIC MAKING

Parents with or without musical "talent" can make music a vital part of children's lives and perhaps start them on an active, lifetime interest in creative music making.

Those little tunes that we almost unconsciously sing to babies while changing their diapers or giving them baths are the beginning of music education. Children soon begin joining in and singing along. "Mary Had a Little Lamb" may seem worlds apart from a Mozart concerto, but in much the same way that children use words before they read them, so children use tunes and musical notes before formal music lessons.

Even if lessons are never given, music can be encouraged at home. For most of us, music may never be more than amateur recreation, similar to baseball or bridge. But for others, it is the start of a lifetime's avocation or possibly even a career. In any event, it is a continuing outlet and release. Brain surgeons have been known for getting together in quartets to play violin chamber music; so have Supreme Court justices. But it's not necessary to have those exalted positions to get the pleasure that music brings all through life.

Musical Instruments   ages 4–6, or younger

Raw materials for musical instruments can come from anywhere. From the kitchen comes the percussion: pots and pie pans. Suspend them on a string, hit them with spoons, and they're gongs and drums. Clang pie pans together and they're cymbals.

Use shoe boxes for strummers. Remove the tops and stretch rubber bands of varying sizes across the boxes. Let children decorate, and in minutes they have homespun guitars.

Small bells are wonderfully versatile for home use. Attach them to children's ankles and wrists. Attach them to pie plates to make tambourines.

Put stones, beans, and sand into cans or closed boxes. Let children decorate them, and you have maracas.

With the rhythm band ready, you're ready to make music.

Children can play individually with their rhythm makers or combine them in a concert. If they hit upon a combination of sounds they want to repeat, jot down what instruments play and for how long. *Example:* bells, two beats; gongs, three beats. If possible, let youngsters hear their music on a tape recorder.

Children can play for each other. One can pound the drum while another dances to the beat. Then the drummer can sing or dance while another child plays the tambourine.

Let children take turns conducting. Show them some motions for loud, soft, fast, slow. Don't expect children's music to be "pretty" or fit standard music-making formulas. Children need the freedom and encouragement to experiment with the sounds of music.

The value of this technique as an early approach is that it encourages children's independent interest in music. Do they want to go on to formal lessons? Once lessons begin, however, youngsters should be mature enough to come to an understanding about the requirements of practice. If music in the home deteriorates into a nagging parent and a defiant child who hates any contact with the instrument, then it's time to assess whether the formal lessons are doing what you hope they will, which is to encourage a love of music.

A practice schedule can become self-regulating. For example, if the requirements are that your child practice half an hour a day, you can say, "Pick the half hour or the two fifteen-minute periods of your choice, up to eight P.M." Children sign up for their choice and then become self-regulators. This may sound too easy to be true, but giving children a choice and expecting them to live up to this choice works remarkably well.

DANCE AND MOVEMENT

All children may not have the makings of a great athlete or dancer, but they need to be able to use their bodies with confidence.

In school, children who need gym class the most often dislike it most — and with reason. Instead of giving the less physically adept youngsters what they need — activity that provides success and a feeling of belonging — in many gym classes, children with "two left feet" are humiliated. They are the first to be eliminated in a game and the last to be chosen for a team.

Parents can do a lot to build physical education and "movement" readiness — just as they can build readiness for academic subjects. This not only helps in gym class but also gives children a better sense of themselves for other activities.

Here are some activities that fall between dance and physical education for ages four through eight, or younger.

Try walking or running at different paces. Beat out a fast or slow rhythm on a drum or pie plate. Encourage children to keep step to the beat, with short, fast steps, or long, slow slides.

When the music stops (you can use a record for this), tell children to drop where they are, falling in a lovely, slow heap, first the legs, then the torso, the arms, the head. Or tell them to pretend they're scrambling in under the ball to second base. Dance, when it's approached in this way, is no "sissy" thing to do.

Play statues. When the music stops, so do the children, exactly as they were when they heard the last beat. Count to ten while the statues hold these positions, no matter how crazy they are. Then start the music again.

Make body shapes. Try a wide shape, a thin shape, a curve backward, a curve forward, a jumping shape, a running shape, a ball shape, a duck shape. There's no end to these as long as your child's imagination holds out.

Play "relax." Tired parents will appreciate this. Lie down on your back and relax. Then concentrate on putting parts of the body to sleep. Start with the toes, move upward to the legs, to the hips, and so on. This teaches concentration and anatomy as well as relaxation.

Encourage movement of all types to help children continue to feel free about using their body: leaping like frogs, twisting like donuts, bouncing like balls, shaking like jelly, stretching like rubber bands, falling like rain.

Keep an assortment of fabrics of different weights, colors, and textures for children to dance with. Use an easy-to-reach box that children can dip into whenever the spirit moves them. Assemble some rhythm instruments — ones children have made or store-bought ones. Put a record player or radio nearby for children to use themselves — with records that make them want to dance. Lively marches and tangos are especially enticing.

Some of my happiest childhood memories are of tap dancing under an archway between our living and dining rooms. I pretended it was a stage and I was the star. I don't think anyone ever saw me, but it didn't matter. I don't tap dance anymore, but I remember those "recitals" with great pleasure.

GOING OUT

Museums   ages 4–9

Go to museums, but do it with children in short doses, about forty-five minutes at a time. Beware not to be done in by "doing" the museum. A museum director told me that he urges parents for their own sake to take their children with them to art galleries. Children like art and respond to it openly.

Look at the artwork, but don't worry about identifying the artist, the period, the style. Children don't have to like or dislike a piece of art for any specific reason — they just have to experience it.

Check the newspaper art listings for news of special exhibitions you'll want to see. Look for children's art exhibits — real favorites — and be sure to check out the children's rooms in museums. They have "Please Touch" exhibits that young children especially enjoy.

While at the museum, let your children choose one or two art postcards.

As children get older, they can rent the lectures on cassettes that increasingly accompany art exhibits. They will want to know about the artists and their lives. While standing across the room, they will want to be able to look at a painting and guess the name of the artist. There are stories in almost every painting, and there are many books about artists who have lived poor but colorful lives. All these facts can follow later, after the initial delights of enjoying the paintings or sculptures.

Plays, Movies, Concerts, Dance Recitals
ages 4–9

There is no magic formula that prescribes when to start taking children "out." The time to start depends on two things: the concentration span of your child and the kinds of entertainment available. Some three-year-olds avidly watch all of *Mary Poppins* or *Snow White*, while older youngsters ask to leave when they are half over.

If you are a theater or concert goer yourself, and if you can afford it, you're more likely to take children at an early age. But even adults who enjoy the magic of theater often need a magic wand to find plays and movies that are suitable for children.

This question of suitability is a problem. Encourage your children to check newspaper reviews and then decide whether certain shows are for them. This is a good way for them to build their critical judgment and to make them more responsible for what they see. They can't blame you for taking or sending them to a bad movie when it's a decision you've all made together.

Don't be surprised if the movie you thought so great doesn't make the grade with the kids. And vice versa; the ones they like may flop with you. Try to be tolerant. Respect their opinions. Hear them out on what they liked or disliked and ask that they hear you out, too.

At-home activities before an outing are useful for young children. Before going to the theater or concert, discuss the plot or what music will be played. If you don't know this, look it up. Young children often feel more comfortable knowing the story in advance. And it's a nerve saver for parents, who then don't have to sit in the movie whispering answers to questions about what's going to happen next.

If you're going to a musical, sing and play some of the songs before you go. Children enjoy recognizing these as they're performed. After the show, help children judge what they've seen. With young children, ask which characters they liked best. What do they remember most about the show? Children's movies need not always be fairy-tale productions peopled only by goody-goodies. It can be very instructive for children to see characters coping with real life, facing temptations, even making mistakes. What's important is that you talk about what you've seen.

The choice of really good movies for children is very limited. So it is reassuring to find that "the experts" believe that, in general, stable children will not turn into delinquents because of what they see in the movie house. Serious delinquency stems from what children bring with them when they come into the theater. It's the memory of conversations with adults and friends about what's real, what's fantasy, what's junk, what's good, that children bring to the movies and TV screens. It's especially talk with parents that enables children to judge the quality of what they are seeing and whether it's to be taken seriously or whether it's just fun.

And children probably aren't ruined for life if they happen to get taken along to an "adult" film. Bedroom scenes often make little or no impression on the very young. It's the preadolescents on a steady diet of sex and violence who can use advice and self-regulatory help on movie going. If you start early and keep up a dialogue with your children, there's far less chance of older youngsters being "infected" by poor movie selections.

ARTS AND THE SENSE OF SUCCESS

The special value of an arts project is that you come up with an idea. You try it. You work. You end up with a finished project —

and all the while build greater self-confidence and control. Plus you get new ideas along the way that you hadn't thought of before.

What's wonderful about the arts is that they can provide children with a sense of success that they might not be getting in other ways. Everyone has to feel this sense of achievement in some way, in some place. It doesn't always happen in the classroom. The arts at home give children this extra chance.

Chapter 27.
Inspiration and Perspiration

Who are those people who sail their own boats across the Atlantic, who invent folding bicycles, who write poems, who hunt microbes? They are the ones who sat next to us in class, but they are not necessarily the ones who got the good grades in school.

There is a lot to be learned from this. It teaches us that no matter what gifts we start with, it takes MegaSkills to use them.

It was Edison who said that genius is 10 percent inspiration and 90 percent perspiration. This has been reconfirmed in the mid-1980s by studies that indicate that no matter what the initial characteristics or gifts of an individual, unless there is a long and sustained process of encouragement and training, that person will not attain high levels of capability in subjects ranging from music to athletics. In short, special, innate gifts are nice, but they are not enough.

Sometimes we can get stuck into thinking that education consists only of school grades and attending the best schools. When we read the honor roll of those who never made the school honor roll, we immediately gain a wider vision about accomplishment.

For example, the top characteristics of productive, creative people include intellectual courage, independent thinking and judgment, courage of convictions, preoccupation with and absorption in tasks, intuitiveness, persistence, willingness to take risks, and unwillingness to accept judgment of authorities.

These do not necessarily lead to the school honor roll.

As a matter of fact, the long lists of school "problems" include men and women who grew up to be distinguished adults. Among them are the authors Thomas Mann, Pearl Buck, and Willa Cather; the inventor Henry Ford; the dancer Isadora Duncan; the scientist Albert Einstein; the composer Edvard Grieg. Disastrous school experiences of creative people are almost commonplace.

At the same time that the author William Saroyan was a terrible school problem, he read every book in the Fresno, California, public library. Sigrid Undset, another well-known author, couldn't stand the school's freedom-curbing discipline.

Youngsters with particular talents resent the school's demand that they scatter their energies, that they become well rounded in all subjects. In those days before compulsory education, many gifted youngsters became school dropouts. They continued their education in specialized apprenticeships and in the informal schooling that went on at home.

Among school dropouts are the Wright brothers, Thomas Edison, Pablo Picasso, Dimitri Shostakovich, Marchese Guglielmo Marconi, Noel Coward, Mark Twain, and Pablo Casals.

Those who stayed in school had similar difficulties. Einstein, who was slow of speech, wanted to learn in his own way. He believed examinations, with their insistence on memorized facts, impeded education, which he felt was based on a "perpetual sense of wonder." It's said that he had a terrible time passing the usual school examinations, as did the composer Giacomo Puccini and the scientist Paul Ehrlich.

Writers who couldn't make the grade in class but who took literary honors afterward include Proust (his teachers said his compositions were disorganized), Stephen Crane, Eugene O'Neill, William Faulkner, and F. Scott Fitzgerald. I'd like to think that as an English teacher I would have recognized their abilities, but I'm not sure I would have or that they would have shown their best in class.

It's encouraging that schools today are showing a greater concern for the individual and are more hospitable to children's differences. Not too long ago, the precocious, exceptionally bright child was popularly pictured as an abnormal, awkward, smarty-pants nuisance. This is far less true now.

Bright children are no longer "bookworms" or "eggheads." Even "nerds" are portrayed sympathetically. We've entered a new era of respect for uniqueness as opposed to the conformity once wished for. "Your child is different" can be a compliment.

Giftedness is a mixture of heredity and environment, and it's not absolutely clear how much of each ingredient goes into the recipe. You can do everything "right" and still not have a gifted child. You can do a lot wrong and have a gifted child.

More is learned about giftedness each year. I am struck by the "invulnerable" gifted resilience shown by children who flourish in the midst of great difficulty — the children of the mentally ill, the children of alcoholics, the children of poverty — children who make it, who go on to lead happy, successful lives despite the odds against them.

Through research, key traits of these resilient children are being identified. They show the ability to bounce back. They can handle frustration. As babies, for example, when their tower of blocks falls over, they go back and try again. They're cheerful and enthusiastic. Perhaps most important, say the researchers, is that as these children grow, they have the ability to seek help from other adults if they cannot get help from their own parents. They may have average academic skills, but they have high social intelligence. Surely this is giftedness, and yet tests don't record it.

There is a lot yet to learn. Now that people are living longer, the genetic seeds set in the womb and the benefits of early nurturing will have a chance to flower over a longer period. Our "late bloomers" could be blooming later than ever.

THE LEARNING ENVIRONMENT AT HOME

Toy and equipment companies today trade on parental concerns about giftedness, advertising "creative" products that "can make children gifted." Buy this or that computer or this or that toy and your child will be gifted. Oh, that it would work that easily!

Even if you give children everything money can buy, you still can't buy an ideal learning environment. The ingredients required to enrich a child's life aren't found in expensive toys and educational hardware. The recipe is made up instead of the inventiveness and the responsiveness of human beings. Much of it is free, but it takes some time and planning.

Special gifts or not, all children need to be able to explore their environment without a constant no, no, no. They need a house that is as safe as it can be and things that they can experiment with. For young children, these can be pots and pans. Older children may be "toying" with ideas.

All children need a home environment that shows a love of

learning and respect for achievement; they need lots of language experience, answers to their questions, serious and intelligent talk, explorations into the world, time with friends, and toys and materials to use freely and imaginatively.

Children need a high frequency of contact with adults. They don't need many adults — only a few who particularly value achievement and who can articulate these hopes for children. Children need adults who respond to them with hugs, words, and emotion. These signs need to be as consistent and clear as possible so that children receive clues on how they behave and how they affect others. When they behave well, they need adults to reinforce and praise them.

Children need time to play in the way that scientists play, looking behind the ordinary to figure out for themselves how things work. The unique contribution of the home, when compared with the school, is the capacity to give these children the playing time they need. In school, children usually have to prove themselves anew each day with prescribed tasks. At home, they can think, dream, contemplate, invent ... in short, do the exercises needed to realize their gifts.

Children need an environment where everything isn't happening all at one time. When the TV is blaring and people are walking in and out, especially in a crowded place, it's hard to focus and concentrate. Children need a sense of stability and mastery over their environment so they can develop reasonable expectations about what is going to happen.

Children need activities suited for their abilities, work that is just a little beyond what they can already do. This isn't easy. It's been called "the problem of the match." The value of having a large repertoire of home activities is that there are more possibilities for making that match.

THE ART OF TEACHING

When we try to teach children anything from how to count to how to take a bath, we can experience the frustrations of having youngsters, occasionally or often, reject these teaching efforts. Children, in turn, are often frustrated by parents who think teaching is a matter of imposing some learning on them. Children may be "born learners," though they certainly won't display this all the time. Many parents are not "born teachers" at any time.

To be a good teacher, patience is essential, but it's not enough. A good teacher needs to be able to work up and down a scale of greater and lesser difficulty. For example, let's say you're reading a book about trucks to your child. With a very young child, first you might ask your child to point to the bigger truck. Then you prompt your child to move to "yes" and "no" responses. The next move is to whole sentence answers and finally to your asking, "Tell me about this truck."

Creativity and intelligence thrive on discussion. Sometimes adults, who need the practice least, do most of the talking, while children sit by passively. This is unfortunate, because it is the interplay of discussion and experience that encourages children to use their minds actively to formulate ideas. Probably the best teaching tip is, "Don't talk too much!"

A good teacher keeps explanations short and backs them up with tangible demonstrations. If you are teaching measurement, actually measure a room. If you are teaching science, let children relive the drama and excitement of discovery.

For example, ask children to stand on a chair, holding a heavy object in one hand and a light one in the other. Now have them drop these objects at the same time. Try different items. In this way, children discover on their own that no matter the weight of the objects, they hit the ground at the same time.

Experiment with Galileo's pendulum discovery. Attach to a tree limb different lengths of string weighted with small stones or bolts. Let children observe and time the swings.

Follow in Archimedes' footsteps with water displacement experiments. Put a cork and an ice cube in water. The cork floats high and the ice cube (like an iceberg) almost sinks out of sight. Show how a ship stays afloat. Place a bottle cap sideways on the water and then lay it flat. What happens?

Challenge children's incentive. Say jokingly, "I'm going to teach you something so hard you'll never catch on." Then when they do catch on, add to their joy with your own excitement. Try to avoid the pitfalls of too-personal involvement. That's the dangerous "do this for me" attitude.

Children can be equipped for their own discoveries easily and inexpensively — a magnet to lure paper clips, a magnifying glass to look deep into pennies to find those almost-hidden letters. Your goal is to keep the love of learning alive.

Be quick in acknowledging your child's correct answers — and be flexible about what is right. If children are wrong, praise them for trying and encourage them to try again. They need to learn to keep going, despite disappointments and setbacks.

THE HOME REPORT CARD

Teachers have tests to record children's growth, but parents have what I call the Home Report Card. The value of this report is that it points to a youngster's developing strengths that teachers are not in the position to see. It gives parents greater faith in their children as accomplishers, as people to be watched and encouraged.

Think about the following for each child in your house and what you've seen over the past year:

New skills learned/Old skills improved. Don't leave out a one, from sewing to swimming, from a preteen learning to baby-sit to a preschooler crossing a street alone.

Accomplishments. Some children torture themselves and you by being dissatisfied with their achievements. They need help in accepting what they can do now. Point these out.

Self-understanding. What do your children know about themselves that they didn't know last year? Interests? Likes? Dislikes? What do they regard as their strengths and weaknesses? Ask children to come up with specific instances in which they showed themselves capable of handling a problem.

Relationships with others. What changes do you see? How do your youngsters get along with you? Are they making friends? Are they keeping them?

The best thing of the year. Answers to this one can be very revealing and surprising. Your quick family visit to a woodworking shop might have had more impact than a week at the beach.

The worst thing. You get to know your children better and they, you, when you compare answers on this one.

Ideas for next year. What would youngsters do differently or the same? If they say they want to go to art classes or take riding lessons, it can mean starting to save now for a future program.

TURNING IDEAS ON, NOT OFF

There's an ad that I keep next to my desk. It shows a light bulb in different panels, from brilliantly lit to completely dark. In the first panel, the words under the bright bulb read, "I have an idea." In the next, with the bulb just a little less light, it says, "A word of caution." Then, as the bulb in each panel shows less and less light, the words read, "A little too radical," "I like myself, but," "It's just not us," "I wish it were that easy." In the final panel, with the bulb completely dark, the words read: "Oh, it was just an idea."

The point is graphically and effectively made; turning off an idea is far easier than keeping it lit.

The world is full of wonder. Keeping that wonder alive is the heart of giftedness and of good teaching. It is the nurturer of talent. It is the bedrock and the strength of emotional and intellectual growth and stability . . . and it's available to everyone.

Section F.
MegaSkills: Powerful and Surprising

Chapter 28.
Secrets of MegaSkills

When I hear myself giving a speech these days, I am usually surprised, surprised and pleased when the words come out quite easily and when I find myself able to use the first words I picked. I used to stutter a lot, and stuttering is not exactly a confidence enhancer. About all I can say for stuttering is that it enlarged my vocabulary. That's because a stutterer has to have a lot of synonyms available for use in case the first or second word that you want to say just won't come out.

It's hard to remember when I began to stutter, but I think it was when I was eleven and my mother became ill. She died when I was thirteen, and there are vestiges of stuttering in my speech even now.

Teachers tried to help me; there was no speech therapist in my school. Teacher help usually consisted of putting me up front on the stage to sink or swim and to get over this thing by reciting a poem or a song before a big audience.

Whether this was right or wrong I am not sure to this day, but it was probably better that teachers expected me to speak, rather than letting me crouch in the corner and shy away from talking.

The benefit of a handicap is that it can force you to call on and build other abilities. In my case, not only did it build my vocabulary, just in case I had to switch words, but, more important, it focused my mind, when I became a teacher, on how problems can be overcome.

For me, this means trying to make opportunities count, especially with children. This takes watchfulness. I am not altogether successful. I try to notice things, but it's not easy. As my own children grew up, I began to see less and less.

Other parents tell me it has happened to them, too. Most of us are very good about noticing babies. We pay a lot of attention to their first word, their first sitting and standing. But pretty soon we're not noticing or seeing very much at all. A lot gets lost.

The cemetery scene in the play *Our Town* illustrates this sense of loss poignantly. Emily, the young mother who grows up and gets married, dies when her second child is born. After she is buried and the mourners have gone home, the cemetery on the hill overlooking the town comes to life. Emily talks to the neighbors, relatives, and friends buried with her on the hill. She tells them she wants to go back for just one more look at life. They warn her against it. But she prevails, and she elects to go back to a happy day, her twelfth birthday. Unseen, she stands in her family kitchen. She sees her mother cooking breakfast and calling to her and her brother to get up for school. She calls out to her family, "Look at me." But they can't hear her. She sees how precious life is and how little we see, even in the most loving of homes. Finally she can't stand it anymore, and she asks to be taken back.

LOOK AT ME

Of course, we will never see it all. A camera won't help. It captures one moment in time. What's happening to us and our children is an ongoing, often mysterious process.

To try to probe into this mystery, I've created a series of thinking questions for parents. They use MegaSkills to start the thoughts flowing. MegaSkills get at very important personal feelings.

The idea is to help us keep seeing our children and ourselves, even as the days go by in a blur of busyness. The questions are not really questions: they are ways of saying, "Look!"

Let's start with the ten MegaSkills in this book. Ask yourself which are the most important to you. Put a check (√) next to the ones you choose.

Confidence	——	Perseverance	——
Motivation	——	Caring	——
Responsibility	——	Teamwork	——

| Effort | —— | Common Sense | —— |
| Initiative | —— | Problem Solving | —— |

You may want to add additional creativity traits, such as:

Curiosity

Independence

Intuition

Courage

Think about why you picked those MegaSkills. Don't worry about whether or not you have them. Not all MegaSkills are equal and equally significant in our lives. Just try to select the ones that, in your judgment, are more important. Then ask, "Why do these matter to me? Do I have an experience or a special memory about any of them?"

Which MegaSkills do you believe you actually have? Using the list above, put an X next to those you claim for yourself. Don't be modest; try to be honest. You aren't expected to have them all.

Which MegaSkills do you believe your child has or is developing? Use the list above to put an O next to those you see in your child. Be at least as charitable with your child as you are to yourself. Acquiring MegaSkills is a lifetime task. Be sure to remember to tell your children about the MegaSkills you believe they have. Ask your older children if they agree, and if not, why not.

If you were a teacher, you would write report cards. What comments might you make about your children on their report cards?

He is motivated because _____ .

She shows initiative when _____ .

He is confident as he _____ .

Her perseverance shows when _____ .

Add more ideas of your own.

Think about what MegaSkills mean for children at different ages. For example, what does responsibility mean at age three, at age six, at age ten, at age fifteen, at age thirty?

Which MegaSkills are now taught in your home? How do you teach them? MegaSkills are all around us, in the texture of daily life and in the small moments that families share together. It's these small moments that can get overlooked. These are the moments that the activities in this book have focused on and that, no matter what has come before, you can focus on today. Nothing is so big that it cannot be taught — in bits and pieces.

JUST THE RIGHT SIZE

MegaSkills are really big things, but they are also small. MegaSkills are part of the responses our children receive from us and from the environment in which they live. You can't sit a child down one day and say, "I am going to teach you responsibility," or "Today you will learn common sense." These come incrementally, and they grow out of everyday life and activity.

ASK YOURSELF: "DO I ..."

If answers to the questions that follow are yes, try to give an example of how you do it. If the answer is no, think about what you could do to change the answer to yes.

- Do I try to set standards and goals for children that are attainable so that children have a good chance for success? Do my children know what these are?
- Do I let my children make as many of their own decisions as possible so that they can learn to live with them and evaluate their own choices?
- Do I encourage my children to learn responsibility by being counted on to do certain jobs?
- Do I give my children many and different opportunities to take leadership roles at home?
- Do I give specific recognition for a job well done and effort put forth?
- Do I allow my children to express their opinions? Do I listen to what they have to say?
- Do I try to focus on my children's strengths rather than on their weaknesses?
- Do I try to hold a realistic vision of my children as individuals?
- Do I recognize that my children, like all of us, will pass through periods in which they achieve more, periods in which they achieve less? Do I accept this in my children ... and in myself?

YOUR CHILD'S FUTURE

In your child's life, which one or two MegaSkills do you think will be the most important? Why? How does the fact that your children will be living their adult lives in the twenty-first century affect your thinking?

- Have you a vision of what your children will be like as grown-ups? What traits do they have now that you think they will retain as adults? What traits do you think or hope they will develop along the way?
- Have your children a vision of what they may be like in the future? If so, do they have a sense of what it will take to bring this about? When children dream of themselves in the future as beautiful, rich, successful, and so forth, they need an idea of what it takes to bring this about. How are you helping them gain these understandings?

When someone says, and it's said often, "Don't worry, it won't matter a hundred years from now," I usually say, "Wait, that might be wrong."

While not absolutely everything we do or think today will matter a hundred years from now or even possibly tomorrow, how we see ourselves and conduct ourselves does matter.

All of us — children, too — need to feel we can accomplish something good and important and necessary, not just for ourselves but for those who came after us. Our children need a vision of their importance — not ego or self-importance, but a strong feeling that they *matter* and that what they do *matters*. Because it does.

PAST AND PRESENT

Lately I have taken to remembering my own childhood, and I have tried to figure out if I have MegaSkills, and if so, which ones, and how I got them.

I remember being on my own a lot to try out things, to choose movies I wanted to see, to bike across the city limits alone into the countryside. I remember being given money to go buy things for dinner, and on one of those shopping trips losing a ten-dollar bill — which compares to losing about sixty dollars today. I was distraught, searching the ground between the store and my house for signs of that money.

But I also remember that my parents, although poor, tried hard not to make me feel any worse. There was no name calling; there were no recriminations. I remember words like, "You tried your best, and these are things that sometimes happen."

What my parents did especially right, I have come to realize, was to provide for me opportunities to acquire a set of MegaSkills. My parents were immigrants. In order to earn a living, they settled in a small town, far away from their friends and relatives. But in this small town, where they were outsiders and so, in many ways, was I, they gave me the freedom to explore, to build courage, interests, and zest for life. They showed confidence in me, they gave me room to roam, to experiment, and to test myself — in those important early school years.

So much has changed in the last quarter century. Today that small town where I grew up, while no doubt safer than a big city, is not a place where little girls go off on their own to the far reaches of the town. It's a place where doors are locked, where schools are bigger, and where not everyone knows your name.

Things are different. But this does not mean that they're necessarily worse. In fact, in schooling things are actually better. There are more choices to be made, more information readily available, and more opportunities to pursue.

This sounds wonderful. But there is danger. Many children, in the midst of this golden age for learning, show signs of not being prepared to take advantage of their opportunities.

Am I saying that it's harder to acquire MegaSkills these days? My answer, and I've thought about it for a long time, is yes, for many of our kids. More children have to watch where they walk or ride and whom they talk to; they're bombarded on all sides by media messages that are often antilearning. Everything seems to scream: "Now! Now! Now! More! More! More!"

Dealing with a society so filled with change, with data, and with hype takes a mind that continues to learn and continues to evaluate. Our children must develop this intelligence. They have more to learn than we did if they are going to keep up. And there are more people out there competing with them than ever before.

In my childhood home, my parents, who knew few English words, knew in their bones and made sure I knew that education was the most important thing in my life. It was from this solid foundation that I went off to school.

Today sometimes even this message from parents to kids about the importance of learning can get lost in the midst of all the other messages. In many ways, the activities in this book, which I did not have in my growing up but which I designed for use with my own children at home, for my students in school, and for teachers everywhere, substitute for the ways in which MegaSkills were taught in the past.

SURPRISES AND SECRETS

Among the most exciting educational research findings of recent years is that human beings have "multiple intelligences," and IQ reflects only part of them. These are secrets just now being uncovered, and they help to explain how "smart" people can be "stupid," and vice versa. The reality is that we are smart in different ways and are smarter in some situations than in others.

It's the same with MegaSkills. You don't need all of them all of the time to do well. A person measuring lower on the MegaSkill scale in confidence, for example, but higher on the initiative scale may have to swallow harder and get sweatier palms but will keep on going nevertheless. MegaSkills are not a matched set. They change with age and even with situations. It's possible to have good judgment (common sense) in one situation and not in another.

MegaSkills are full of surprises. This is one of their secrets that I am still learning. A MegaSkill can lie quiet inside of you for a long time and emerge when you least expect it. I find myself surprised by strengths I didn't even know I had — like standing up spontaneously to speak at a friend's memorial service and saying things that I didn't have to practice, like being able to reach out in friendship to a rival, like finally learning how to listen quietly instead of talking first when my children are trying to explain something to me.

One thing we can expect for sure in life is surprise. As they grow up, our children won't neatly fit the picture we have of them when they're very young. As parents, we need our own MegaSkills to handle some of these unknowns.

I got a call the other day from a friend who read *MegaSkills* in draft. She wanted me to make sure I said that these activities work even when children are adults.

She had just returned from what might have been an uncomfortable visit with her grown daughter. When she got there, she heard her daughter say that someday she would find the time to fix up her study. My friend said, "I'll help. Let's do it together."

It worked. They went to the lumberyard, they put up shelves, and they painted them. They were busy together, and it was satisfying for both of them. Their true, deep feelings of love for each other were expressed in this activity. They were a team. It was, she said, "a MegaSkills weekend."

When parents and children do something constructive together, a special something happens. If there are tensions, especially as children grow older, they seem to evaporate, or at least they don't get in the way. There's a feeling of cooperation, almost like a runner's high. It may not be chemical, but it's real.

One great thing about MegaSkills is that they grow bigger, not smaller. Experience, both good and bad, is the soil in which they grow. There may be no greater excitement in our lives than to see them develop in ourselves and in our children.

MegaSkills are full of secrets, and we will not know all of them. They are the legacy we give our children. They are the report cards our children will give us as parents, even after we are not here to receive them.

Appendix A.
MegaSkills Measure:
A Quiz for Parents

We grade ourselves hard as parents. I've seldom heard a parent say, "I am a darned good parent." Of course, there is no way we can do everything right. But surely there must be some things we *do right*, even me, even you.

In this MegaSkills Measure, the focus is on parent MegaSkills, not in terms of big qualities such as patience, respect, love, and trust, but more in terms of what I call MegaSkills Moments. These are the small, special moments between parent and child. Keep these in mind as you fill in your answers.

The point is to catch ourselves being good parents.

I call this the MegaSkills Parent's Award. We may not be *good* parents all of the time, but we are not *bad* parents all of the time. This "measure" is designed to help us feel more like the good parents we are.

About the scoring: It makes sense that there have to be different scores for parents of different-age children and for parents of children who do or don't go to school. Children under a certain age are probably not going to be doing certain activities, and there's no way for parents to be involved with the school if their child is not yet in attendance. That's why you see different scoring patterns. The idea is to make this "test" as simple to score as possible. So to get your score, you simply count up the number of checks you have made. When you check *More Than Once* also check *Once*. You get two checks for each *More Than Once* answer.

Last Week: Think back over the last week. Ask yourself, "To what extent did I do the following with my child?" It may be that you ate a meal together every day; it may be that you read together at night; it may be that you took walks together. You may have done one of these regularly and another not at all. It's not possible to do everything.

If your child is in the age group **four** through **seven,** respond to and score **a** through **p.** Responding to **q** through **u** is optional. If your child is in the age group **eight** through **twelve,** complete the **entire test.** Remember, if you check *More Than Once,* also check *Once.*

Last week I:	Once	More Than Once
a. Gave my child a hug.	___	___
b. Took a walk with my child.	___	___
c. Laughed with my child.	___	___
d. Read to my child.	___	___
e. Ate at least one meal a day with my child.	___	___
f. Asked my child what happened during the day.	___	___
g. Did not interrupt when my child was independently involved in study, a project, or game.	___	___
h. Let my child hug me.	___	___
i. Told my child about my day.	___	___
j. Watched a TV program with my child.	___	___
k. Told my child I love him/her.	___	___
l. Talked with my child about his/her friends.	___	___

Last week I:	Once	More Than Once
m. Played a quiet game indoors with my child.	___	___
n. Played active sports outdoors with my child.	___	___
o. Checked/regulated the time my child watches TV.	___	___
p. Praised and encouraged my child.	___	___
q. Talked with my child about homework assignments.	___	___
r. Talked about current news and events.	___	___
s. Did some household chores with my child.	___	___
t. Let my child read to me.	___	___
u. Cooked with my child.	___	___

Other: Here you can add an activity or two that is not on the above list but for which you deserve credit.

Last Week Total Number of Checks

ages 4–7 (_a–p_) = _____ + _____ = _____
Other

ages 8–12 (_a–u_) = _____ + _____ = _____
Other

Last Month: Think back over the last month. Ask yourself, "To what extent did I do the following with and on behalf of my child?"

If your child is in the age group **four** through **seven,** respond to and score **a** through **f.** Responding to **g** through **m** is optional. Your score in that section will not count against you. If your child is in the age group **eight** through **twelve,** complete the **entire test.** Remember, if you check _More Than Once,_ also check _Once._

Last month I:	*Once*	*More Than Once*
a. Encouraged my child to have friends visit our house.	____	____
b. Spent time with my child on a hobby or special project over a period of several days.	____	____
c. Listened to my child explain his/her point of view that was different from mine.	____	____
d. Told my child about my own childhood experiences.	____	____
e. Took my child shopping with me . . . and it went well.	____	____
f. Took my child to a church, library, museum, or zoo.	____	____
g. Attended a play, concert, movie, or other entertainment with my child.	____	____
h. Did something my child persuaded me to do that turned out to be a good idea.	____	____
i. Attended a sports event with my child.	____	____
j. Arranged for my child to go independently on a short trip or errand.	____	____
k. Attended a meeting of a club, church, or youth group (such as Scouts) to which my child belongs.	____	____

Last month I:	_Once_	_More Than Once_
l. Talked with my child about the future, possible jobs, and educational plans.	———	———
m. Read and talked with my child about a newspaper or magazine article.	———	———

Other:

Last Month Total Number of Checks

ages 4–7 $(a-f)$ = _____ + $\dfrac{\quad\quad}{\text{Other}}$ = _____

ages 8–12 $(a-m)$ = _____ + $\dfrac{\quad\quad}{\text{Other}}$ = _____

School Year: Think back over this last school year or school term. Ask yourself, "To what extent did I do any of the following with and on behalf of my child?" (If your child does not attend school, do not complete or score this section.)

During the last school year I:	_Once_	_More Than Once_
a. Participated in a conference at school to discuss my child's progress and program.	———	———
b. Attended PTA, Back to School, or a similar meeting at school.	———	———
c. Attended a school play/concert, sports event, or similar function.	———	———
d. Served as a volunteer or chaperone for a school activity.	———	———
e. Talked with a teacher informally and/or socially.	———	———

f.   Contacted other parents   ____   ____
     or a community group on
     behalf of the school and
     educational issues.

Other:

School Year Total Number of Checks = ____

The Count Up: Now you are ready to give yourself your MegaSkills Parent's Award grade. Parents of **eight**- to **twelve**-year-olds have the possibility of **80** + checks. Parents of **four**- to **seven**-year-olds have the possibility of **56** + checks, **44** + checks if the child is not in school. The plus points are dependent on your contributions to the *Other* activity line.

Give yourself a grade of A+ if:
for ages 4–7 but not in school you score 42–44
for ages 4–7 you score 53–56
for ages 8–12 you score 77–80

Congratulations! Congratulations! Are you really this good? If so, you have my admiration and the gratitude (one would hope) of your children.

Give yourself a grade of A if:
for ages 4–7 but not in school you score 39–41
for ages 4–7 you score 50–52
for ages 8–12 you score 72–76

You are terrific. You are doing a lot and doing it well!

Give yourself a grade of B if:
for ages 4–7 but not in school you score 35–38
for ages 4–7 you score 45–49
for ages 8–12 you score 64–71

You sound honest and know you have to keep working.

Give yourself a grade of C if:
for ages 4–7 but not in school you score 31–34
for ages 4–7 you score 39–44
for ages 8–12 you score 52–63

You are probably too hard on yourself, but if what you are saying is true, you would do well to spend some time getting your act together.

Give yourself a grade of I for Incomplete if you score below a C. Come on, go back and try to get a few more points.

KEEP IN MIND ...

The point of this quiz is to recognize and reward yourself for all that you are doing right. Every family has its own way of doing things right. Keep adding to the *Other* line and keep filling in activities as you move through the year. This quiz is suggestive; it points to examples, to directions. This is not a static test, not a fixed score; it's ever changing. The idea is to keep figuring out more things you do right and to reward yourself for them.

You may want to go over this quiz with your children, asking them what they think about your answers. Perhaps they will be harder on you, or perhaps they will think you've shortchanged yourself. It's bound to be a fascinating and useful conversation.

Appendix B.
The Children's
MegaSkills Library

The Association for Library Service to Children/American Library Association (ALSC/ALA),* with assistance from Children's Services, the District of Columbia Library, has compiled the following list of children's books that help to illustrate each of the Mega-Skills in this book, with additional titles about competition.

In this list are age-old classics and books published within the last few years. The variety of books available for children today can be overwhelming. Over two thousand children's books are published annually. This brief list is only a starting point. Recommended ages are approximate. It is fine to read books that appear to be for younger or older readers. Because this compilation is necessarily brief, several adult books are included at the end so that parents can find out more about children's books and ways to share them.

Read books together; listen to your child read; let them listen to you. Talk about the books; enjoy them; let them become part of your lives. Let the power of literature reinforce and extend your children's MegaSkills, building their imagination and their love of reading.

CONFIDENCE

Christopher, Matt. *Jinx Glove.* Boston: Little, Brown & Co., 1974. Ages 8–10.

*Special thanks to Susan Roman, executive director of the ALSC/ALA, and to Maria Salvadore, coordinator, Children's Services, D.C. Public Library.

Cohen, Miriam. *Will I Have a Friend?* Ill. Lillian Hoban. New York: Macmillan, 1967. Ages 4–6.

Freschet, Bernice. *Furlie Cat.* Ill. Betsy Lewin. New York: Lothrop, Lee & Shepard, 1986. Ages 4–6.

Hoban, Russell. *Bedtime for Francis.* Ill. Garth Williams. New York: Harper & Row, 1960. Ages 5–7.

Howe, James. *I Wish I Were a Butterfly.* Ill. Ed Young. San Diego: Harcourt Brace Jovanovich, 1987. Ages 5–8.

Kraus, Robert. *Leo the Late Bloomer.* Ill. Jose Aruego. New York: Thomas Y. Crowell, 1971. Ages 4–7.

Little, Lessie, & Eloise Greenfield. *I Can Do It by Myself.* Ill. Carole Byard. New York: Thomas Y. Crowell, 1978. Ages 5–7.

Seidler, Tor. *The Tar Pit.* New York: Farrar, Straus & Giroux, 1987. Ages 9+.

Snyder, Zilpha K. *Come On, Patsy.* Ill. Margot Zemach. New York: Atheneum, 1982. Ages 5–8.

Taylor, Mildred. *Roll of Thunder, Hear My Cry.* Ill. Jerry Pinkney. New York: Dial Books, 1976. Ages 10+.

Waddell, Martin. *The Tough Princess.* Ill. Patrick Benson. New York: Philomel Books, 1987. Ages 4–7.

MOTIVATION

Andersen, Hans Christian. *The Swineherd.* Ill. Lisbeth Zwerger. New York: William Morrow & Co., 1982. Ages 6–9.

Carrick, Carol. *The Foundling.* Ill. Donald Carrick. New York: Clarion Books, 1977. Ages 6–8.

Cohen, Miriam. *When Will I Read?* Ill. Lillian Hoban. New York: Greenwillow Books, 1977. Ages 4–6.

DePaola, Tomie. *Charlie Needs a Cloak.* New York: Prentice Hall, 1974. Ages 7–10.

DePaola, Tomie. *Now One Foot, Now the Other.* New York: Putnam Publishing Group, 1981. Ages 5–7.

Holman, Felice. *Slake's Limbo.* New York: Macmillan, 1974. Ages 9–11.

Hurwitz, Johanna. *Aldo Applesauce.* Ill. John Wallner. New York: William Morrow & Co., 1979. Ages 8–11.

Hutchins, Pat. *The Tale of Thomas Mead.* New York: Greenwillow Books, 1980. Ages 6–9.

Leaf, Munro. *Story of Ferdinand.* Ill. Robert Lawson. New York: Viking, 1936. Ages 6–8.

COMPETITION

Carlson, Nancy. *Loudmouth George and the Big Race.* Minneapolis: Carolrhoda Books, 1983. Ages 4–6.

Cresswell, Helen. *Ordinary Jack.* New York: Macmillan, 1977. Ages 9–12.

Dygard, Thomas J. *Soccer Duel.* New York: William Morrow & Co., 1981. Ages 11+.

Gilson, Jamie. *Can't Catch Me, I'm the Gingerbread Man.* New York: Lothrop Lee & Shepard, 1981. Ages 8+.

Ginsburg, Mirra. *Two Greedy Bears.* Ill. Jose Aruego and Ariane Dewey. New York: Macmillan, 1976. Ages 5–7.

Heine, Helme. *The Most Wonderful Egg in the World.* New York: Macmillan, 1983. Ages 4–7.

Jones, Diana W. *Charmed Life.* New York: Greenwillow Books, 1978. Ages 9–12.

Lindgren, Astrid. *Ronia, the Robber's Daughter.* New York: Viking, 1983. Ages 8–11.

Lipsyte, Robert. *The Contender.* New York: Harper & Row, 1967. Ages 12+.

Ure, Jean. *Supermouse.* Ill. Ellen Eagle. New York: William Morrow & Co., 1984. Ages 8–11.

Weiss, Nicki. *Battle Day at Camp Belmont.* New York: Greenwillow Books, 1985. Ages 4–7.

Weiss, Nicki. *Princess Pearl.* New York: Greenwillow Books, 1986. Ages 4–7.

EFFORT

Brenner, Barbara. *On the Frontier with Mr. Audubon.* New York: Putnam Publishing Group, 1977. Ages 9–12.

Friedman, Ina R. *How My Parents Learned to Eat.* Ill. Allen Say. Boston: Houghton Mifflin Co., 1984. Ages 4–7.

Speare, Elizabeth. *The Sign of the Beaver.* Boston: Houghton Mifflin Co., 1983. Ages 8–11.

Sperry, Armstrong. *Call It Courage*. New York: Macmillan, 1940. Ages 8–11.

Winthrop, Elizabeth. *Maggie and the Monster*. Ill. Tomie DePaola. New York: Holiday House, 1987. Ages 4–7.

Yashima, Taro. *Crow Boy*. New York: Viking, 1955. Ages 5–7.

Yep, Laurence. *Dragonwings*. New York: Harper & Row, 1975. Ages 9–11.

RESPONSIBILITY

Aardema, Verna. *Why Mosquitoes Buzz in People's Ears: A West African Tale*. Ill. Leo and Diane Dillon. New York: Dial Books, 1975. Ages 6–8.

Bauer, Marion D. *On My Honor*. New York: Clarion Books, 1986. Ages 9–12.

Byars, Betsy. *The Summer of the Swans*. New York: Viking, 1970. Ages 9–11.

Dalgliesh, Alice. *The Courage of Sarah Noble*. Ill. Leonard Weisgard. New York: Charles Scribner's Sons, 1954. Ages 8–10.

George, Jean. *The Cry of the Crow*. New York: Harper & Row, 1980. Ages 9–11.

Green, Norma. *The Hole in the Dike*. Ill. Eric Carle. New York: Harper & Row, 1975. Ages 5–10.

Hurwitz, Johanna. *Aldo Ice Cream*. Ill. John Wallner. New York: William Morrow & Co., 1981. Ages 8–11.

King-Smith, Dick. *Pigs Might Fly*. Ill. Mary Rayner. New York: Viking, 1982. Ages 8–11.

Munjo, F. N. *The Drinking Gourd*. Ill. Fred Brenner. New York: Harper & Row, 1969. Ages 6–9.

Tolan, Stephanie. *The Great Skinner Strike*. New York: Macmillan, 1983. Ages 9–11.

Williams, Barbara. *Jeremy Isn't Hungry*. Ill. Martha Alexander. New York: E. P. Dutton, 1978. Ages 5–7.

Zion, Gene. *The Plant Sitter*. Ill. Margaret Bloy Graham. New York: Harper & Row, 1959. Ages 4–7.

INITIATIVE

Brenner, Barbara. *Wagon Wheels*. Ill. Don Bolognese. New York: Harper & Row, 1978. Ages 6–8.

Brink, Carol R. *Caddie Woodlawn.* New York: Macmillan, 1935. Ages 9+.

Dalgliesh, Alice. *Bears on Hemlock Mountain.* Ill. Helen Sewell. New York: Charles Scribner's Sons, 1952. Ages 8–11.

Hamilton, Virginia. *Planet of Junior Brown.* New York: Macmillan, 1971. Ages 9–11.

McKissack, Patricia. *Flossie and the Fox.* Ill. Rachel Isadora. New York: Dial Books, 1986. Ages 4–7.

Merrill, Jean. *The Toothpaste Millionaire.* Ill. Jan Palmer. Boston: Houghton Mifflin Co., 1974. Ages 8–11.

Myers, Walter Dean. *The Young Landlords.* New York: Viking, 1979. Ages 9–12.

Robertson, Keith. *Henry Reed's Baby-Sitting Service.* Ill. Robert McCloskey. New York: Viking, 1966. Ages 9–12.

Steig, William. *Doctor De Soto.* New York: Farrar, Straus & Giroux, 1982. Ages 5–9.

PERSEVERANCE

Boutis, Victoria. *Katy Did It.* Ill. Gail Owens. New York: Greenwillow Books, 1982. Ages 4–6.

Burton, Virginia Lee. *Mike Mulligan and His Steam Shovel.* Boston: Houghton Mifflin Co., 1939. Ages 5–7.

Cleary, Beverly. *Ramona and Her Father.* Ill. Alan Tiegreen. New York: William Morrow & Co., 1977. Ages 8–11.

Cleaver, Vera, and Bill Cleaver. *Where the Lilies Bloom.* Philadelphia: J. B. Lippincott, 1969. Ages 10–12.

George, Jean Craighead. *Julie of the Wolves.* New York: Harper & Row, 1972. Ages 9–11.

Graham, Thomas. *Mr. Bear's Chair.* New York: E. P. Dutton, 1987. Ages 4–7.

Hoff, Syd. *Siegfried, Dog of the Alps.* New York: Grossett & Dunlap, 1970. Ages 5–9.

Keats, Ezra Jack. *John Henry: An American Legend.* Ed. Anne Schwartz. New York: Alfred A. Knopf, 1965. Ages 6–8.

O'Dell, Scott. *Island of the Blue Dolphins.* Boston: Houghton Mifflin Co., 1960. Ages 9–12.

Piper, Watty. *The Little Engine That Could.* Ill. Ruth Sanderson. New York: Platt & Munk, 1976. Ages 4–6.

Steig, William. *Brave Irene.* New York: Farrar, Straus & Giroux, 1986. Ages 4–6.

Van de Wetering, Janwillem. *Hugh Pine.* Ill. Lynn Munsinger. Boston: Houghton Mifflin Co., 1980. Ages 8–10.

Wilder, Laura Ingalls. *Little House in the Big Woods.* Ill. Garth Williams. New York: Harper & Row, 1953. Ages 8–12. (Also recommended are the other volumes in the Little House series.)

CARING

Aliki. *The Two of Them.* New York: Greenwillow Books, 1979. Ages 6–8.

Aliki. *We Are Best Friends.* New York: Greenwillow Books, 1982. Ages 4–6.

Asch, Frank. *Moon Bear.* New York: Charles Scribner's Sons, 1978. Ages 4–6.

Greenfield, Eloise. *First Pink Light.* New York: Thomas Y. Crowell, 1976. Ages 5–7.

MacLachlan, Patricia. *Sarah, Plain and Tall.* New York: Harper & Row, 1985. Ages 9+.

Mathis, Sharon Bell. *The Hundred Penny Box.* New York: Viking, 1975. Ages 5–7.

Paterson, Katherine. *Bridge to Terabithia.* New York: Thomas Y. Crowell, 1977. Ages 8–11.

Wells, Rosemary. *Hazel's Amazing Mother.* New York: Dial Books, 1985. Ages 5–7.

White, E. B. *Charlotte's Web.* Ill. Garth Williams. New York: Harper & Row, 1952. Ages 7+.

Williams, Vera B. *A Chair for My Mother.* New York: Greenwillow Books, 1982. Ages 4–6.

Yarbro, Chelsea Quinn. *Floating Illusions.* New York: Harper & Row, 1986. Ages 10–12.

TEAMWORK

Burningham, John. *Mr. Gumpy's Motor Car.* New York: Thomas Y. Crowell, 1976. Ages 4–6.

Byars, Betsy. *The Not-Just-Anybody Family.* Ill. Jacqueline Rogers. New York: Delacorte Press, 1986. Ages 8–11.

DeJong, Meindert. *Wheel on the School.* Ill. Maurice Sendak. New York: Harper & Row, 1954. Ages 9–12.

Domanska, Janina. *The Turnip.* New York: Macmillan, 1969. Ages 4–7.

Ginsburg, Mirra. *Mushrooms in the Rain.* New York: Macmillan, 1974. Ages 4–6.

Grimm, Jacob. *The Bremen Town Musicians.* Ill. Janina Domanska. New York: Greenwillow Books, 1980. Ages 5–8.

Hoban, Lillian. *Arthur's Funny Money.* New York: Harper & Row, 1981. Ages 5–7.

Lionni, Leo. *Swimmy.* New York: Pantheon Books, 1963. Ages 4–7.

Roy, Ronald. *A Thousand Pails of Water.* Ill. Vo-Dinh Mai. New York: Alfred A. Knopf, 1978. Ages 5–7.

COMMON SENSE

Andersen, Hans Christian. *The Woman with the Eggs.* Ill. Ray Cruz. New York: Crown Publishers, 1974. Ages 5–7.

Asch, Frank. *Turtle Tale.* New York: Dial Books, 1980. Ages 4–6.

Byars, Betsy. *The Eighteenth Emergency.* New York: Viking, 1973. Ages 8–11.

Cresswell, Helen. *Absolute Zero.* New York: Macmillan, 1978. Ages 9–11.

Duvoisin, Roger. *Petunia.* New York: Alfred A. Knopf, 1950. Ages 5–7.

Enright, Elizabeth. *The Saturdays.* New York: Dell Books, 1987. Ages 8–11.

Gag, Wanda. *Gone Is Gone.* New York: Putnam Publishing Group, 1960. Ages 6–8.

Hale, Lucretia. *The Peterkin Papers.* Boston: Houghton Mifflin Co., 1966. Ages 9 + .

Parish, Peggy. *Amelia Bedelia.* Ill. Fritz Siebel. New York: Harper & Row, 1963. Ages 6–9.

Smith, Robert Kimmel. *Jelly Belly.* New York: Delacorte Press, 1981. Ages 9–12.

Zemach, Margot. *It Could Always Be Worse.* New York: Farrar, Straus & Giroux, 1977. Ages 5–7.

PROBLEM SOLVING

Atwater, Richard T. *Mr. Popper's Penguins.* Ill. Robert Lawson. Boston: Little, Brown & Co., 1938. Ages 8–11.

Blegvad, Lenore Hochman, and Erik Blegvad. *The Great Hamster Hunt.* San Diego: Harcourt Brace Jovanovich, 1969. Ages 5–7.

Brown, Margaret Wise. *Once Upon a Time in a Pigpen.* Ill. Ann Strugnell. New York: Harper & Row, 1980. Ages 4–6.

Clark, Margaret Goff. *The Latchkey Mystery.* New York: Dodd Mead & Co., 1985. Ages 10 + .

DePaola, Tomie. *Fin m'Coul: The Giant of Knockmany Hill.* New York: Holiday House, 1981. Ages 5–7.

Hoban, Russell. *A Bargain for Frances.* Ill. Lillian Hoban. New York: Harper & Row, 1970. Ages 5–7.

Lionni, Leo. *Inch by Inch.* New York: Astor-Honor, 1962. Ages 4–7.

Naidoo, Beverly. *Journey to Jo'burg: A South African Story.* Ill. Eric Velasquez. New York: J. B. Lippincott, 1985. Ages 9–11.

O'Brien, Robert. *Mrs. Frisby and the Rats of NIMH.* Ill. Zena Bernstein. New York: Atheneum, 1971. Ages 9–12.

Steig, William. *Abel's Island.* Farrer, Straus & Giroux, 1976. Ages 9–11.

RECOMMENDED BOOKS FOR ADULTS

Butler, Dorothy, and Mary Clay. *Reading Begins at Home.* Portsmouth, N.H.: Heinemann Educational Books, 1982.

Dreyer, Sharon. *The Bookfinder.* 3 vols. Circle Pines, Minn.: American Guidance Service, 1977, 1981, 1985.

Graves, Ruth. *The RIF Guide to Encouraging Young Readers.* New York: Doubleday & Co., 1987.

Hearne, Betsy. *Choosing Books for Children.* New York: Delacorte Press, 1981.

Kimmel, Margaret Mary, and Elizabeth Segal. *For Reading Out Loud.* New York: Delacorte Press, 1983.

Larrick, Nancy. *A Parent's Guide to Children's Reading.* New York: Bantam Books, 1982.

Lima, Carolyn. *A to Zoo: Subject Access to Children's Picture Books.* New York: R. R. Bowker, 1986.

Trelease, Richard. *The Read-Aloud Handbook.* New York: Viking Penguin, 1982.

Visit your library or bookstore for additional materials relating to these areas. Lists of Notable Children's Books, Newbery Medal Books, and Caldecott Medal Books are available from the American Library Association.

Appendix C.
Organizations to Know About

I work with many organizations that I think parents ought to know about in the fields of education, child care, social service, and self-help. To be effective, parents today have to know many things. That's why I have assembled this cross-disciplinary list of organizations. I know these groups send information to people who contact them, because I wrote to each one of them, asking for samples of their materials.

Provided that these organizations stay at the addresses listed on the following pages, you will be able to reach them, and I believe you will find their work and material useful.

Action for Children's Television
20 University Road
Cambridge, MA 02138

American Camping Association
Bradford Woods
5000 State Road 67 N
Martinsville, IN 46151-7902

American Federation of Teachers
555 New Jersey Avenue, NW
Washington, DC 20001

Appalachia Educational
  Laboratory, Inc.
1031 Quarrier Street
P.O. Box 1348
Charleston, WV 25325

Association for Childhood
  Education International
11141 Georgia Avenue, Suite 200
Wheaton, MD 20902

Association for Children and
  Adults with Learning Disabilities
4156 Library Road
Pittsburgh, PA 15234

Association for Library Service to
  Children/American Library
  Association
50 E Huron Street
Chicago, IL 60611

Boys Clubs of America
771 First Avenue
New York, NY 10017

Boy Scouts of America
1325 Walnut Hill Lane
Irving, TX 75038

Camp Fire, Inc.
4601 Madison Avenue
Kansas City, MO 64112-1278

Center for Early Adolescence
University of North Carolina at
 Chapel Hill
Carr Mill Mall, Suite 223
Carrboro, NC 27510

Center for Research on Women
School-Age Child Care Project
Wellesley College
Wellesley, MA 02181

Center for Social Organization of
 Schools, Johns Hopkins
 University
3505 N Charles Street
Baltimore, MD 21218

Child Care Action Campaign
99 Hudson Street, Suite 1233
New York, NY 10013

The Children's Book Council
67 Irving Place
New York, NY 10003

Children's Defense Fund
122 C Street, NW
Washington, DC 20001

Cornell University
Cooperative Extension
7–8 Research Park
Ithaca, NY 14850

Council for Basic Education
725 Fifteenth Street, NW
Washington, DC 20005

Family Education Center
5238 Bon Vivant Drive
Tampa, FL 33603

Girls Clubs of America
30 E 33 Street
New York, NY 10016

Girl Scouts of the U.S.A.
830 Third Avenue
New York, NY 10022

Institute for Responsive Education
605 Commonwealth Avenue
Boston, MA 02215

International Reading Association
800 Barksdale Road
P.O. Box 8139
Newark, DE 19714-8139

League of Women Voters Education
 Fund
1730 M Street, NW
Washington, DC 20036

National Association for the
 Education of Young Children
1834 Connecticut Avenue, NW
Washington, DC 20009

National Association of Elementary
 School Principals
1615 Duke Street
Alexandria, VA 22314-3483

National Association of Secondary
 School Principals
1904 Association Drive
Reston, VA 22091

National Black Child Development
 Institute, Inc.
1463 Rhode Island Avenue, NW
Washington, DC 20005

National Catholic Educational
 Association
1077 30th Street, NW, Suite 100
Washington, DC 20007-3852

National Coalition for Parent
 Involvement in Education and
 National Community Education
 Association
119 N Payne Street
Alexandria, VA 22314

National Coalition of Title I
 Chapter I Parents
1314 14th Street, NW, Suite 6
Washington, DC 20005

National Committee for Citizens in
    Education
10840 Little Patuxent Parkway,
    Suite 301
Columbia, MD 21044-3199

National Council of Jewish Women
15 E 26th Street
New York, NY 10010

National Council of La Raza
Twenty F Street, NW
Second Floor
Washington, DC 20001

National PTA
700 North Rush Street
Chicago, IL 60611-2571

National School Boards
    Association
1680 Duke Street
Alexandria, VA 22314

National Science Teachers
    Association
1742 Connecticut Avenue, NW
Washington, DC 20009

Orton Dyslexia Society
724 York Road
Baltimore, MD 21204

Parents' Music Resource Center
1500 Arlington Boulevard
Suite 300
Arlington, VA 22209

Parents Without Partners
8807 Colesville Road
Silver Spring, MD 20910

Reading Is Fundamental, Inc.
600 Maryland Avenue, SW
Suite 500
Smithsonian Institution
Washington, DC 20560

Southwest Educational
    Development Laboratory
211 E Seventh Street
Austin, TX 78701

Stepfamily Association of America,
    Inc.
602 E Joppa Road
Baltimore, MD 21204

Appendix D.
The Handwriting on the School Wall

This is not a traditional bibliography. Yes, you will find "Research Notes" at the end of this appendix; they provide additional sources of data supporting the family's role in education. But there is more.

Research on parent involvement represents milestones in my own thinking. Because of this, I want to tell you a bit about the educational journey that has formed my belief about the roles of the home and the school today.

It's hard to believe now, but in the 1960s, when I started thinking about the work of parents as educators, the subject was considered almost radical, dangerous. Those were the days when people really believed that the school could do it all in education.

We know better today, not because schools are worse but because research and experience have shown that while schools are important, they are limited in what they can accomplish alone.

When I first began teaching as a senior high English teacher in 1957, I saw students who, it seemed to me, had no good reason for having trouble in school. So I asked my colleagues about them. The answer I got was that their junior high teachers hadn't done their job. The junior high teachers pointed to the elementary school.

When I went to elementary school teachers, I heard for the first time the word "family." It was the family's fault, I was told, for sending their children unprepared, unreceptive, unable to take advantage of what the school could do.

The light was beginning to dawn. Something really was happening before children came through the school doors in the morning and after the doors closed behind them in the afternoon.

In the mid-1960s, research started to appear that pointed inescapably to the educational impact of the family. These studies, combined with my own experience, began to shape my thinking and have provided the base for the MegaSkills program.

Every time a new study appeared, my pulse quickened. As a teacher, my first thoughts were about how to take advantage of what was being learned, how to empower families to put the research into action.

In 1964, Professor Benjamin Bloom of the University of Chicago demonstrated in his book *Stability and Change in Human Characteristics* that many differences in children's academic development can be traced to the value placed on education at home and specifically to parental reinforcement at home of children's activities in school.

In 1966 came another significant study, *Equality of Educational Opportunity* (U.S. Office of Education), often called *The Coleman Report*. This study again underscored the importance of the family and the home in determining children's academic achievement.

A small but significant group of early childhood projects were begun around 1968 with youngsters in their preschool years in order to prevent school problems later on. In general, it was found that the earliest projects, which tutored children only and did not involve parents, produced immediate test score gains, but these gains were lost in subsequent schooling years. Children in later projects, which involved parents actively, held their gains after the tutoring programs themselves were over. (Professor Urie Bronfenbrenner of Cornell summarized these in *Is Early Intervention Effective? A Report on Longitudinal Evaluation of Preschool Programs*, Vol. 2 [Washington, D.C.: U.S. Office of Health, Education, and Welfare, 1974].)

As a result of these and other studies, confidence in the school's ability to do it all alone diminished. Emphasis began to shift to identifying the out-of-school factors that were influential in education.

I officially launched the Home and School Institute in 1972. I was building on the parent programs I started in the 1960s called "Success for Children Begins at Home." These were evening sessions for parents. We covered such subjects as how to reinforce the three R's at home, how to build children's creativity, and how to do it all with limited time and resources. I brought to these sessions the first home learning recipes, which parents tried out at home each week.

Major studies from Stanford in the mid-1970s helped confirm my faith in the strategic role of parents as teachers. (See, for example, Barbara Goodson and Robert Hess, *Parents as Teachers of Young Children: An Evaluative Review of Some Contemporary Concepts and Programs* [Palo Alto: Stanford University, 1975].) The studies looked at the key models of parent involvement in compensatory education programs that evolved in the 1960s. The evidence supported the model in which parents worked with their children at home, sustaining the work of the school.

The evidence continued to mount, but attention was still not being paid. In my doctoral dissertation I decided to put my home-learning recipe approach to a test. (*The Relationship of the Home Learning Lab Technique to First Grade Student Achievement* [Washington, D.C.: Catholic University of America, 1976].) A group of teachers working with me designed eight home learning recipes for use in first grades in the Washington, D.C., area. After using them over an eight-week period, the first graders in the treatment group scored significantly higher on standardized reading tests than the control group children. Hurrah!

I was very encouraged, but I knew that I had to learn more and do more. This was the very beginning of my national effort to persuade school administrators to use these programs and to train teachers to work with parents as educational partners.

Year after year, from the early seventies to the present day, the Institute has provided School and Family/Community Involvement training (now called "The Contemporary Family and the School") to what now totals thousands of teachers. When you think of the national need for the training, this is a drop in the proverbial bucket, but it has launched special demonstration projects that have put Institute home-teaching methods to the test. A number of school districts across the nation have initiated the use of Institute home-school learning systems that provide families with weekly teaching activities.

Over the years, HSI has addressed special needs using adaptations of the home-learning-activities programs. For bilingual families, HSI programs have been translated into four languages. To involve senior citizens in work with families, HSI designed the "Senior Corps" program. For students who need extra learning help, HSI created "Special Solutions." (These are summarized in the analysis *The Forgotten Factor in School Success: The Family* [Washington, D.C.: Home and School Institute, 1985].)

Results prove that parents want this help, that they participate in these programs, and that children not only show higher test scores but improve their learning attitudes and skills through the use of the activities.

In 1984 a major national development occurred. The National Education Association asked the Institute to design the NEA Teacher-Parent Partnership Project. Associations in twenty-two states have provided this program to families of third graders. The response from families and teachers has been enthusiastic. (National Education Association, *Report on the Teacher-Parent Partnership Project* [Instruction and Professional Development, 1986].)

Third grade was chosen since it is a pivotal learning year. Unlike kindergarten and first grade, where it is assumed that every parent is "involved," in third grade it's considered more of a challenge to reach parents.

The heart of this program model is the series of learning activities that children take home once a week from school. A feedback sheet for parents' reaction is attached to each of the activities. The feedback sheets — and there have been thousands — show the following: 97 percent of the parents said the project activities helped them spend enjoyable time with their child, and 98 percent of the parents felt their children learned something useful. When children were asked how they felt, they were equally enthusiastic; they especially valued the time with their parents.

In 1987, the Institute launched "New Partnerships for Student Achievement," a three-year national program that, for the first time, calls upon community organizations — churches, unions, social clubs — to help families help their children learn. This is a new dimension of community support for children's learning.

Across the country, other organizations and schools are now saying, "Tell us how we can do it."

We at the Institute are ready to help. I see what I call "Learning Cities": communities across our nation taking practical steps to build on and to mobilize the strengths of all families. I see structured programs, MegaSkills workshops that help parents learn more about how to help their children learn. These workshops will take place in schools, in libraries, in health centers, at work places. These are programs to bring families together to share experiences about teaching MegaSkills at home. For more information about how to become a MegaSkills trainer and for workshop materials, write to the Home and School Institute, Special Projects Office, 1201 16th St., NW, Washington, D.C. 20036.

This is my dream, which at last is showing signs of starting to come true — in legislation, in research, in programs.

RESEARCH NOTES

Up-to-date research on the family's role in education is not easy to find in one place. That's why I have compiled the following list of studies. These augment studies referred to in my "educational journey."

Although this list is confined to more readily accessible, recent materials, they may not be available in bookstores and public libraries. Check university libraries and professional libraries connected with school systems. In "Organizations to Know About," I have provided addresses of groups that have data to provide. The Home and School Institute has these documents and can provide further information about how to find them and background on the other research references in this book.

Bloom, Benjamin. *All Our Children Learning: A Primer for Parents, Teachers, and Other Educators.* New York: McGraw Hill, 1981.

———. *Developing Talent in Young People.* New York: Ballantine Books, 1985.

Bradley, Bill. *The Family-School Partnership Act.* 100th Cong., 1st sess., 1987. S.1157.

Clark, Reginald. *Family Life and School Achievement: Why Poor Black Children Succeed or Fail.* Chicago: University of Chicago Press, 1983.

Coleman, James S., and Thomas Hoffer. *Public and Private High Schools: The Impact of Communities.* New York: Basic Books, 1987.

Comer, James P. *School Power.* New York: Free Press, 1980.

Committee for Economic Development. *Children in Need — Investment Strategies for the Educationally Disadvantaged.* New York: Committee for Economic Development, 1987.

Dornbusch, Sanford, et al. "The Relation of Parenting Style to Adolescent School Performance." *Child Development* 58 (1987): 1244–57.

Epstein, Joyce, ed. "Parents and Schools." *Educational Horizons* 66 (No. 2).

Gardner, Howard. *Frames of Mind.* New York: Basic Books, 1983.

Harvard Education Letter. "Why Can't Susie and Johnny Do Better?" *Harvard Education Letter* (July 1987). (Ask also for their issue on homework.)

Hayes, Cheryl D., and Sheila Kamerman, eds. *Children of Working Parents: Experiences and Outcomes.* Washington, D.C.: National Academy Press, 1983.

Henderson, Ann, ed. *The Evidence Continues to Grow: Parent Involvement Improves Student Achievement.* Columbia, Md.: National Committee for Citizens in Education, 1987.

Metropolitan Life Survey of the American Teacher 1987. *Strengthening Links Between Home and School.* New York: Louis Harris and Associates, 1987.

Moles, Oliver. "Who Wants Parent Involvement?" *Education and Urban Society* (February 1987).

National Education Association and Home and School Institute. *Schools and Parents United: A Practical Approach to Student Success.* Washington, D.C.: National Education Association Professional Library, 1987.

Schlossman, Steven. "Family as Educator, Parent Education and the Perennial Family Crisis." In *Child Rearing in the Home and School,* Robert I. Griffore and Robert P. Boger. New York: Plenum, 1987.

Sizer, Theodore. *Horace's Compromise.* Boston: Houghton Mifflin Co., 1984.

Stevenson, Harold. "Classroom Behavior and Achievement of Japanese, Chinese and American Children." In *Child Development and Education in Japan,* ed. Azum, Stevenson, and Hakuta. New York: Freeman, 1986.

U.S. Department of Education. *What Works.* Washington, D.C.: U.S. Government Printing Office, 1986.

Walberg, Herbert J. "Families as Partners in Educational Productivity," *KAPPAN* 65 (1984): 397–400.

Zigler, Edward F., and Sharon L. Kagan. *Early Schooling: The National Debate.* New Haven: Yale University Press, 1987.

It would be remiss not to add that HSI itself has published numerous reports, articles, and handbooks since its founding in 1972. Among the titles available directly from HSI are the *Home and Job Calendar* and the *Golden MegaSkills Game.*

THE NEXT STEP

All of this is terrifically encouraging. But it all depends, and it depends on action — action that starts in every home.

Use the activities in this book to help your children learn. Use this research as you work with legislators, with teachers, and with school boards. Let them know that you care and that you support training, materials, and personnel, in schools and in communities, reaching out to work with parents as partners.

Everyone reading this book is a messenger — carrying the still-too-secret message about the importance of educational partnership.

Appendix E.
MegaSkills "Recipes,"
Chapter by Chapter

To help make this book easier to use, here is a list of home learning recipes by chapter. The age ranges provide some guidance in selecting the activities. They are not all-knowing. Many a four-year-old will enjoy an eight-year-old's activity, and vice versa. The activities have been tested. They work. And they work a little differently with different children. My hope is that all of them in whole or in part will be useful to everyone.

Chapter 26 The "Right Brain" at Home

Acknowledgments

This book draws upon more than half a century of living and almost a quarter century of experience with the Home and School Institute. This means I owe a lot to a lot of people, people who shared their MegaSkills with me. No list can contain them all, but I especially want to thank:

- Spencer Rich, my husband, for making it possible for me to continue this work and for believing in it, even when I sometimes lost heart.

- Rebecca Rich and Jessica Rich, our daughters, who as children valiantly tried activity after activity and who as adults are using their differing MegaSkills as physician and lawyer and who continue to teach me what it is to be a parent.

- Lili Bermant and Harriett Stonehill, coworkers at the Home and School Institute, who get top grades on the Never-Ending Report Card.

- Don Cameron, executive director of the National Education Association (NEA), for telling me I am the "Dr. Spock of education" and for pushing me to write this book.

- Gordon Felton of the NEA and Ruth Hapgood of Houghton Mifflin, who read this book in draft and said, "Tell us more about yourself, give us your personal experience." Without their encouragement, I would have lost this opportunity to think about my own life and to talk with my children about what they remembered about their childhood.

- Teachers, parents, and children in HSI projects across the country for their enthusiasm, their encouragement, and for how much they have taught me.

- Monroe, Michigan, and its public schools, and the family of my childhood, my parents, Hyman and Rose Kovitz, to whom this book is dedicated, and to my older brother, Arthur, who even as a child always tried to figure out how everything worked.

- The John D. and Catherine T. MacArthur Foundation, for supporting the "New Partnerships for Student Achievement" project, in which MegaSkills parent/teacher workshops are being designed and piloted.

- The initial New Partnerships organizations, their staff and volunteers, who pioneered this national and community effort: American Postal Workers Union; American Red Cross; Association for Library Service to Children/American Library Association; National Association of Colored Women's Clubs; and Parents Without Partners.

- Senator Bill Bradley, for his legislative initiative and commitment to this work.

- Miriam (Mickey) Bazelon, for her very special friendship and support.

- Friends and colleagues who shared experiences that help to illustrate the message of this book and who have lent a special hand to put across the message of the family as educator: Among them are John Almacy, Ken Apfel, Deborah Both, John Bottum, Denise Buchanan, Alice T. Day, Arnold Fege, Bill Foster, Alan Ginsburg, Jim Havel, Misbah Khan, Fern Lapidus, Mary Jean LeTendre, Stan McFarland, Ann Milne, Catherine O'Neill, Becky Saikia-Wilson, Elliot Stonehill, Traer Sunley, Jim and Pieter Van Dien, Trudy Vincent, Wanda Wachter, Joan and George Worden, Ed Zigler, and Paul Zywusko.

- Deirdre Miller, for taking illegible scratches and turning them into manuscript without once complaining, and Toni Smith, for her office assistance.

- The people-to-people support network of the Home and School Institute, its Board and Advisory Council, to whom I am greatly indebted, and to the organizations I have reached out to and which have reached out to me, among them: American Association of Colleges of Teacher Education, American Association of School Administrators, Association for Supervision and Curriculum Development, Council for Basic Education, Council for the Advancement of Private Education, Council of the Great City Schools, Education Commission of the States, National Association of Federal Education Program Administrators, National Association of Elementary School Principals, National Committee for Parent Involvement in Education, National Education Association, National Governors Association, and National PTA.

In education, we are all family. This is my larger family. Many thanks!

Dorothy Rich

Index